New Directions in Cultural Policy Research

Series Editor
Eleonora Belfiore
Department of Social Sciences
Loughborough University
Loughborough, UK

New Directions in Cultural Policy Research encourages theoretical and empirical contributions which enrich and develop the field of cultural policy studies. Since its emergence in the 1990s in Australia and the United Kingdom and its eventual diffusion in Europe, the academic field of cultural policy studies has expanded globally as the arts and popular culture have been re-positioned by city, regional, and national governments, and international bodies, from the margins to the centre of social and economic development in both rhetoric and practice. The series invites contributions in all of the following: arts policies, the politics of culture, cultural industries policies (the 'traditional' arts such as performing and visual arts, crafts), creative industries policies (digital, social media, broadcasting and film, and advertising), urban regeneration and urban cultural policies, regional cultural policies, the politics of cultural and creative labour, the production and consumption of popular culture, arts education policies, cultural heritage and tourism policies, and the history and politics of media and communications policies. The series will reflect current and emerging concerns of the field such as, for example, cultural value, community cultural development, cultural diversity, cultural sustainability, lifestyle culture and eco-culture, planning for the intercultural city, cultural planning, and cultural citizenship.

More information about this series at
http://www.palgrave.com/gp/series/14748

Nicola Sim

Youth Work, Galleries and the Politics of Partnership

Nicola Sim
University of Nottingham
Nottingham, UK

New Directions in Cultural Policy Research
ISBN 978-3-030-25196-3   ISBN 978-3-030-25197-0   (eBook)
https://doi.org/10.1007/978-3-030-25197-0

Cover illustration: aberCPC / Alamy Stock Photo
Cover design: estudioCalamar

This Palgrave Macmillan imprint is published by the registered company Springer Nature
Switzerland AG.
The registered company address is: Gewerbestrasse 11, 6330 Cham, Switzerland

For Tony, Charlotte and Mila

FOREWORD[1]

In 2018–2019, the Creative Margins network held five events around the UK in performance spaces, museums and youth centres. These were places and gatherings for critically chatting about how the traditions of a youth work that is voluntary, improvisatory, associative, without guarantees might reconnect in the future with performance practice and with the visual arts. Last up was Tate and Circuit—Tate's programme connecting galleries and young people to spark change.

In these gatherings we have explored themes about partnership; the politics of space and the space of politics; time and trust; and, over and over again, class. The initial inspiration for these network gatherings was the work which Nicola Sim initiated during her PhD studies at the University of Nottingham and based with Tate and Circuit, which forms the basis of this book. The AHRC funded Creative Margins network is one of the legacies of this research and especially of the associated seminars, which brought together practitioners from the youth sector and the arts sector, starting with the 2015 BERA event on Youth Work and the Arts.

There have been some wonderful moments. The opening event, in which an actor dressed in an elephant costume got everyone singing to

---

[1] Part of this foreword is an adapted version of the blog post: Batsleer, Janet. 2018. Radical youth, community and arts practice in dialogue. *In Defence of Youth Work*. https://indefenceofyouthwork.com/2018/12/03/radical-youth-community-and-arts-practice-in-dialogue/.

Oasis; 'Don't Look Back in Anger,' was one of them. The elephant was speaking testimonies gathered for the performance about being working class and finding a way into theatre as a performer or even more unimaginably as a director and what that's like now. This provoked a sharp set of conversations about 'CLASS: The Elephant in the Room'.

'Class' as a topic has never been far away in these gatherings. Some of the theorists invoked—Raymond Williams and Pierre Bourdieu—explored structures of feeling and practices of distinction, enabling questions about how these create companionable or exclusionary atmospheres. Sometimes it is Brian Massumi's thinking-feeling that enlivens the conversation, when it turns to matters of co-creation and living knowledges. In recognising the role of youth workers, gatekeepers, necessary to the whole project of 'socially engaged arts practice', the divide between part-time youth workers and those other precariously employed young people trying to make their way as 'creatives' has been present one way or another at every gathering. It is often articulated in a sense of the limited nature of youth work practice, from the point of view of those practicing as artists. They speak of a failure of expectation to surprise, to entertain something new, which artists encounter in youth work projects. They often express a preference with many reasons given for working with schools. I have started to feel that I am living with and hearing the consequences of the discrediting of youth work as a practice and its disappearance as a profession. But there is more to it than this: for many years now, I have been teaching youth work courses to people who arrive with a strong sense of lack of entitlement to be at University. They may develop a certain dislike for 'academia' (associated with an overvaluing of reading and writing, which they see as 'not their strong suit') and, somehow linked to this, these students have a very limited range of experiences in relation to a wide cultural offer. With Nicola Sim's work in mind, and selected from a very rich flow of conversation, here are some things I have heard in the network meetings:

> Two young women (both working on close to a minimum wage, as artists) …'Do we need to do all the support work as well?…the youth workers don't do anything….we want to do the art-based practice but the young people need us to do the support stuff even more. They need help with accessing benefits, they don't know where to go to get help with stuff…..'
>
> A dance practitioner: 'Youth workers are scared of offering anything other than DJ workshops or street dance to young people; they don't have confidence themselves for a wider set of offers.'

Someone running a radio workshop/digital arts project: 'We see the value of short-term projects; youth workers turn away from things that aren't long term.'

And I hear casually repeated class-based prejudice about people who 'lack aspiration.' 'Mums just want to get houses, have children, get married, claim benefits…' from staff working on heritage projects who see their offer of engagement as a form of moral rescue.

Because of the relative absence of youth workers from the conversations, there has been little talking back from youth workers about their experience of such 'co-produced projects.' This absence is often explained as a reluctance and unavailability on the part of youth workers, but I think it may speak of a deeper tension that has something to do with a fear of being put down and excluded. It is therefore with much gratitude that I recommend the current book: *Youth work, galleries and the politics of partnership* to both youth workers and creative practitioners. Nicola Sim's account of these tensions as systemic offers the basis for an enormous leap in our understanding. Simply the fact that she uses a systematic approach and offers theorisation of a systemic problem immediately enables a shift in understanding of what is at stake. The heart of the matter is the class-based distribution of positional cultural wealth and the symbolic violence which is enacted to preserve it. Bourdieu's theoretical framing of practice, habitus, fields and doxa guides the analysis in ways which create new illumination. After reading this account, it is really no longer possible to persist in the often-stated belief that fruitful collaborative work depends largely on whether individuals get on well with one another.

This is rich ethnographic writing about both how wonderful and how appalling youth work practice can be (sometimes in the space of a single session). Many 'in the moment' as well as reflective insights by this self-styled 'modest witness' are crafted into a powerful argument for the necessity for a new way of thinking about the partnership between the gallery sector and the youth sector, which recognises the impact of an inherited power dynamic, and consciously strives to move away from it. Youth organisations often tend to be framed as the beneficiaries, and art organisations as the benefactors in cross sector partnerships. The historic imbalance of assets has reinforced a particular power dynamic, which typically locates authority and agency in the hands of the arts partner, leads the youth partner to feel dominated and to each developing behaviours associated with those positions in a power dynamic.

One of the paradoxical realities is that, whilst Nicola Sim argues for the establishment of enduring partnerships at local, regional and national levels, based on mutual recognition, many of the moments of lively energetic engagement appear in her account as moments of 'pop-ups' and of relatively fleeting practice created with and alongside temporary communities of artists and others. In this, the arts practice is similar to moments in detached youth work, which have often been described as improvisatory, in the moment or 'on the wing'. Perhaps the temporary programmatic and collaborative field which Nicola Sim analyses so acutely, in which such joyful moments have occurred throughout the Circuit programme, needs such a sustained infrastructure as a condition of possibility. But we live in liquid modernity and still under conditions in which the corporate turn usually trumps the educational and the relational and the aesthetic turn. In conditions such as these, the analytic resources of this book are important. Alongside the well-grounded pessimism about current conditions, they offer an equally well-grounded hope that the temporary collisions and collaborations analysed here—acted out of solidarity and a sense of justice in spaces beyond the gallery walls (presented as vital evidence throughout this book)—will be events that continue to provoke and connect. Such margins beyond the gallery walls are not places in need of redemption through art, but they can be creative margins and as such, roomy places for collaborative practices of cultural democracy and for meetings based on equality between youth workers, gallery educators and creative practitioners and many others. Let's continue to declare these meetings open.

Manchester, UK   Janet Batsleer
29 April 2019

ACKNOWLEDGEMENTS

This research was made possible through a Collaborative Doctoral Partnership supported by the Arts and Humanities Research Council and jointly hosted by Tate and the School of Education at the University of Nottingham. A huge thanks goes to the gallery practitioners, youth workers, young people, artists and evaluators involved in Circuit who contributed and welcomed me into the programme and into their organisations. I am particularly grateful that Circuit (led by Mark Miller), associated partners and Paul Hamlyn Foundation provided such a supportive environment to talk openly and critically about challenging issues. I am forever grateful to my incredible doctoral supervisors Professor Pat Thomson and Dr Emily Pringle for their critical insights, invaluable guidance and endless encouragement. Thanks also go to the youth work academics and external youth and cultural sector practitioners I met and collaborated with during my research, especially Janet Batsleer who generously agreed to write the foreword for this book. I am grateful to the peer reviewers who offered vital advice in the writing and editing stages. I also want to thank Charlotte Winters for her wisdom and for keeping me laughing throughout the process. And finally, thank you to my incredible family Dan Weill, Mila Sim Weill, Sue, Stuart and Tony Sim, and Georgia, Matt and Kit Cooper for always being there and cheering me on.

Some parts of this publication are taken and adapted from the PhD thesis: *"Like oil and water"? Partnerships between visual art institutions and youth organisations* (2018).

CONTENTS

About the Author

Nicola Sim is a freelance researcher and evaluator who works in arts, youth and play settings across the UK. Nicola previously worked as Curator of Public Programmes at Whitechapel Gallery and in 2017, she completed an AHRC-supported Collaborative Doctoral Partnership with Tate and the University of Nottingham.

CHAPTER 1

Introduction: The Problem of Partnerships Between Galleries and Youth Organisations

This is a book about the tensions, pleasures and confusions that lie behind the rhetoric of 'partnership'. Specifically, this text looks at the partnership working between youth organisations and galleries, and the unique characteristics of these relationships. Partnership is a term so heavily inscribed across funding applications, within programmes, and throughout public sector work, that its very utterance often sends eyes rolling. And yet as human beings, we also instinctively gravitate towards partnerships. In work, play and leisure, we have a natural impulse to cooperate and collaborate (Sennett, 2013). And digital communication has given us new platforms to work together beyond conventional physical boundaries (Brown, 2012). Yet invariably the notion of partnership has become tainted and dulled by its overuse in policy directives, funding literature and corporate rhetoric. Those who have worked on cross-organisational partnerships know them to be hard work and full of complex power dynamics (Isaacs, 2004; Miessen, 2010). This is a book that seeks to unravel that complexity, using theoretical tools and stories of practice.

Workers in the youth and visual art sectors are particularly familiar with the dominant discourse of partnership (Douglas, 2009). They are also often deeply passionate about working with others in creative, democratic ways. But while there is a long history of cross-organisational work between galleries and youth services, relationships are frequently short-lived or troubled by different issues—such as the retention of marginalised

© The Author(s) 2019
N. Sim, *Youth Work, Galleries and the Politics of Partnership*, New Directions in Cultural Policy Research,
https://doi.org/10.1007/978-3-030-25197-0_1

young people. The stakes are exceptionally high in this area of work. If a partnership gets derailed, the hard-earned trust between a youth worker and young person might be at risk. A young person who has been let down countless times in their life may end up feeling disappointed, disempowered or perhaps worse—abandoned and excluded. But if a partnership is successful, a young person might gain new access to enriching cultural experiences that motivates a life-long engagement with the arts, or that changes their worldview, or that enables their own creativity and confidence to thrive. As I have witnessed first-hand on multiple occasions, a young person might develop a relationship with a cultural institution that is so personally significant that the institution becomes their "home" or sanctuary.

Youth and arts organisations and practitioners also stand to gain and lose a great deal from partnership working. A problematic relationship may consume precious time and waste organisational resources. It can damage professional confidence, exacerbate inequalities or tarnish a practitioner's perceptions of art practice or youth work. But a meaningful partnership can invigorate, inform and expand practice. Organisations and workers can exchange knowledge and share experiences of working with young people, youth cultures, the institutional visual arts and practicing artists. In some instances, this type of work has the potential to change the nature of organisations and push practice forward into new, innovative spaces.

Drawing and expanding on the findings of a four-year PhD and parallel evaluation work since 2013, this book offers a framework for understanding the challenges that frustrate partners, and raises issues that often go under-discussed when practitioners and young people from different backgrounds and sectors work together. Using Pierre Bourdieu's connected concepts of 'habitus', 'capitals' and 'fields', this framework outlines the factors that consciously or unconsciously guide individuals' actions when working with others. Questions around why people end up working or socialising in a particular field, and why they might experience discomfort when engaging with other fields may seem basic, but they are fundamental to understanding where conflict or difficulty originates. Bourdieu's theory of fields encourages detailed analysis of the histories, traditions and cultures of different professional fields, so it is possible to identify what types of social and educational capital are valued within them. This book presents insights into the nuances and journeys of youth work and gallery education, and the professional identities of the youth worker and gallery practitioner. One aspiration of this project is to support practitioners in either field to be better informed about their partners—their needs, strengths, values, internal conflicts and the logic that drives the way they work.

The youth and gallery practice discussed throughout this book is limited to the UK context (England and Wales in particular). However, the learning and messages about partnership working are relevant to practitioners and researchers operating internationally. The political and economic conditions affecting practice in the UK are felt to varying degrees across Europe and further afield (Alldred et al., 2018). The cultures and policies of neoliberalism and the effects of austerity have led to widespread changes and cuts across the public sector. In the last decade in the UK, funding reductions, youth centre closures and job losses have consistently threatened youth work as a professional field (UNISON, 2018). Meanwhile the boundaries of 'gallery education' have been tested over the past decade as participatory work has in many cases moved from being confined to specific departments to being at the centre of cultural institutions' work (Matarasso, 2019). These shifts in institutional practice are by no means restricted to the UK, but are part of a broader pattern of curatorial engagement with collaboration and social action across the contemporary art world (Byrne et al., 2018). The arguments made in this publication should therefore speak to both UK-based readers, and an international audience.

This is also a time when the global labour market and workforce is dramatically changing. The concept of the 'multi-hyphen' career suggests that the traditional pathway of training and remaining a specialist in one field is becoming outdated (Gannon, 2018). Partly driven by job insecurity and partly motivated by new technologies and the proliferation of more flexible ways of working, greater numbers of people are diversifying their skills and adopting composite professional identities. Rather than carve out a career for life in a single sector, this type of new professional identity demands that the (often self-employed) worker operate seamlessly across different sectors. With these conditions in mind, this book is orientated towards practitioners who are rooted in either youth work or in gallery education, as well as those who are active across and between these fields of practice, including artists, evaluators and facilitators.

Another ambition of this book is to lay bare (in ethnographic detail) the fundamental inequalities and power imbalances underpinning partnership work between galleries, youth organisations and young people. By mapping out the policy histories of gallery education and youth work in the

UK, it is possible to identify how galleries have benefitted from a greater affordance of agency and autonomy than youth organisations. Unequal distributions of power are shown to have an effect on every relationship in a partnership—at organisational and human levels. By exploring the expectations of peer-led programming and partnership projects involving cultural institutions, I highlight instances of what Bourdieu calls 'symbolic violence' in these relationships. Symbolic violence is not an overt violence but a subtle, often completely unacknowledged or well-intentioned set of forces that can make individuals (who lack specific forms of knowledge and privilege) feel inadequate and out of place. In the context of gallery/youth organisation partnerships, there is typically an orchestrated encounter between young people who have experienced social disadvantage and an art institution that is symbolically wealthy, and that is populated by predominantly white middle class audiences, behavioural codes and cultural references. Projects or events are sometimes set up in a way that unintentionally alienates (particularly working class) young people, whose own cultures and knowledges may not be represented or valued.

The examples of practice and interviews cited in this book offer an account of how this symbolic violence affects youth workers and young people and why gallery projects often struggle to enable the long-term independent engagement of marginalised young people in their wider programmes. At the centre of these examples is the thorny issue of how different communities interpret culture and creativity. Differing tastes, differing experiences of art education and differing levels of creative confidence are all signifiers of social disparities, but they are also factors that tend not to be discussed at the onset of a partnership. Throughout this text, I present evidence of the challenges involved in partnership development and suggest ways for practitioners and young people to get to know one another's worlds in advance of project work. By creating opportunities for acknowledging difference and building mutual respect, I argue that partners and organisations can learn to understand and value different types of cultural capital, which can promote diversity and spread agency within a partnership.

Despite the challenging outlook, this book is written from a place of optimism about the ongoing potential for the youth and visual art sectors to work together in meaningful, inclusive ways. While the situation for open access youth work is bleak, the arts sector is one area where youth and community engagement is growing in importance and where creative, critical and democratic relationships with young people are (at least in theory) prioritised. During the time the research for this book was in progress (between 2013 and 2019), there was also a popular explosion of conversation across social and traditional media around structural racism, the class divide and intersectionality—in other words the intersecting oppressions experienced by marginalised communities (Mckenzie, 2015; Hanley, 2016; Eddo-Lodge, 2017). The call to "check your privilege" became widely mobilised online (Freeman, 2013) and a new generation of young critics began calling out institutional elitism in galleries and museums (Ruigrok, 2018). In many ways, we are living in a new era of consciousness around hidden or unspoken inequalities and oppression. Although in other ways, political and social divisions fuelled by the lasting effects of austerity make current conditions for partnership more sensitive than ever. Hopefully this book provides some actionable ideas for arts and youth workers, as well as those involved in strategic roles. Experimental models of partnership practice are revealing alternative ways for youth organisations and galleries to work together that could summon real change in different localities, and it is this prospect of change that nourishes my interest and guides this text.

CONTEXT

The research that has largely informed this book was generated through a Collaborative Doctoral Partnership between the School of Education at the University of Nottingham and Tate galleries. Funded by the Arts and Humanities Research Council (AHRC) and guided by supervisors Dr Emily Pringle, then Head of Learning Practice and Research at Tate, and Professor Pat Thomson at the University of Nottingham, I was recruited to investigate partnership work through a Tate-led programme called Circuit. Running across four years, from March 2013 to March 2017, Circuit was one of the most ambitious and well-resourced programmes of its kind. It aimed to connect 15–25 year olds to the arts in galleries and museums through working in partnership with the youth sector. Originally conceived by the Learning team at Tate, the programme was supported by the Paul Hamlyn Foundation with a grant of five million pounds.

Circuit involved ten visual arts organisations in eight regions around England and Wales: Tate London (comprising Tate Britain and Tate Modern), Tate Liverpool and Tate St Ives; Firstsite in Colchester; MOSTYN in Llandudno; Nottingham Contemporary; The Whitworth in Manchester; and Wysing Arts Centre and Kettle's Yard in Cambridge.

These organisations vary in scale and remit. Five are museums that house collections of historic, modern and contemporary art; four are galleries that mainly present modern and contemporary art exhibitions and one is an artist residency and studio campus with an exhibitions programme. Some of these organisations had prior experience of running youth programmes, while others did not. Through Circuit, each of these organisations built relationships with youth organisations, youth groups, youth services and independent youth practitioners in their cities and towns.

The idea behind Circuit grew out of Tate's long-term experience of informal youth programming work, which began at Tate Liverpool in 1994 and continued to develop across the four Tate sites (Horlock, 2000). The Tate London Learning team had spent years developing partnerships with local Leaving Care services and other youth organisations, and they had also built on Tate Liverpool's 'peer-led' programming, by hosting and supporting core groups of young people within the galleries (Tate, 2012). These collectives of 15–25 year olds would meet regularly and be responsible for co-curating projects, exhibitions, digital content and events, including large-scale festivals attracting thousands of young people. In doing so, they would gain valuable creative, professional and social experiences and the chance to work up-close with artists and museum workers at the centre of a high profile institution. Circuit represented efforts to step up and roll out a successful programming model in collaboration with organisations around the UK. The programme was also framed as Tate's response to the 2011 summer riots in London, Manchester, Nottingham and other English cities (Clark, 2012). Coupled with increasing cuts to youth services, these riots were seen as a symptom of the lack of provision available for young people, and Tate's leadership recognised the role their galleries and networks might play in this context.

This multi-sited programme presented a timely and important opportunity to focus critical research and attention on the vexed history of partnership work between visual arts organisations and youth organisations. Circuit would provide a receptive setting through which to look at partnership design, development and practice, as well as the barriers to, and facilitators of, good partnership working. I wanted to interrogate what a programme such as this (with ample funding and a learning-orientated approach) might reveal about the nature of youth/arts partnerships, and about what could be done to improve relationships.

In many ways, the aims of the programme chimed with my own desires to make some difference to practitioners, organisations and diverse groups of young people who are underrepresented in cultural organisations. Circuit's aims were:

- *To make a positive difference with and for young people*
- *To improve access and opportunities for harder-to-reach young people through extending and developing sustainable networks between the arts and youth sector*
- *To develop and change practice within and across cultural organisations*
- *To change attitudes and behaviours towards and about young people* (Circuit, 2013a)

The arts organisations involved sought to meet these aims through a cross-disciplinary programme that would bring together young people, art and artists in a range of different situations. Four main delivery strands (modelled on Tate's Young People's Programmes) provided an overarching structure to the activity and budgets at each Circuit site. These strands focused on building profile and engagement through a large-scale festival; embedding work with young people through peer-led groups; building sustainable networks through partnerships with youth organisations and reaching wider audiences through new digital content (Circuit, 2013a).

While 'Partnerships' was identified as one of four strands, the ambition of the programme was to encourage young people engaged through youth organisations to contribute to and participate in all of Circuit's activity (Circuit, 2013a). Supporting so-called 'hard-to-reach' young people to engage with all elements of the programme was a central priority for the Circuit galleries. The key objectives related to partnership working reflected this aspiration to position youth sector partnerships as a route into other opportunities for young people. These objectives were:

1. *To develop strong partnerships between the youth and cultural sectors and thereby open dialogue and opportunity for those young people with least access and voice*
2. *To engage hardest-to-reach young people through opportunities, entry points and pathways into cultural activities*
3. *To open up progression routes for a greater diversity of young people*
4. *To create a lasting impact and legacy with regard to extending and developing sustainable networks* (Circuit, 2013b)

Circuit therefore presented an opportunity to look at an important set of assumptions around partnership work between galleries and youth organisations. One of these assumptions is that this type of work can lead to marginalised young people becoming independently engaged with an arts organisation's wider offer. The broader theory behind this concept is that young people can benefit from a sense of attachment to an institution and peer group, and they can be supported to develop active roles and have their voices heard and ideas realised. The logic is that youth organisations will also gain from seeing their young people progress emotionally, socially, creatively and professionally, and arts organisations will be improved by having a more diverse cohort of young people participating in and contributing to their programmes.

Throughout this text, I offer a critique of the logic of gallery/youth partnerships and question whether the expectations that surround this type of work are realistic or even appropriate in practice.

WHY INVESTIGATE PARTNERSHIPS BETWEEN GALLERIES AND YOUTH ORGANISATIONS?

Over the past decade in the UK there have been copious research projects, publications and network initiatives all dedicated to exploring partnership, or its close relatives: 'collaboration', 'co-production' and so on. In the cultural sector these activities have included the AHRC's Connected Communities programme (2010–) investigating academic/community collaboration (Facer and Enright, 2016; Facer and Pahl, 2017); King's College's 2015 cultural enquiry into the role of partnership in publicly funded arts institutions (Ellison, 2015); the Paul Hamlyn Foundation's Our Museum programme, which tested the ability of communities and museums to work together as active partners (Bienkowski, 2016); explorations of 'non-arts partnerships' in the England-wide Creative People and Places programme (ECORYS, 2016) and the Museum Association's pilot scheme Partnerships with Purpose, which seeks to connect museums with third sector organisations (Steel, 2018). Publications have covered relationships with community organisations and groups (Butler and Reiss, 2007; Lynch, 2011; South London Gallery, 2011; Francke, 2012; Graham et al., 2012; Steedman, 2012), with schools (Smithens, 2008; A New Direction, 2013), with other cultural institutions (Bak Mortensen and Nesbitt, 2012) and with the health sector (Daly, 2012) for example.

However, only a few publications concentrate on the specific nuances of partnership working between galleries and youth organisations or services (Edmonds, 2008; Wheeler and Walls, 2008; Tate, 2012; National Portrait Gallery, 2014). The period in which I conducted my research coincided with a relative surge in interest and activity around connections between the youth and cultural sectors (Creating Change, 2013; Walsh, 2014; Strong Voices, 2015; Slater et al., 2016). Much of this activity was however focused on theatre and performance contexts as opposed to museums and galleries.

A review of youth work literature unearthed very few examples of studies from a youth sector perspective looking at relationships between youth organisations and galleries. Where the arts did feature in youth work publications and events, this was usually in reference to *youth arts* organisations, or non-institutional arts activity (Morford, 2009). Creativity and arts-based practice in youth work was also discussed in practitioner books (Batsleer, 2008), as were partnerships between youth workers and independent artists (Patel, 2010). But visual arts institutions or gallery education practice were seldom mentioned in the literature. What *was* evident within the literature was anxiety over the potential erosion of creativity and imagination in youth work practice in a political climate that seemed to increasingly value targets over play and improvisation (Batsleer, 2008; Taylor, 2014). Youth work lecturers and academics I met during my fieldwork spoke about the need for a more critical, less instrumentalised basis on which to debate the intersections between youth work practice and art practice (Belton, 2015; Howard, 2017). Some individuals were vocal about the need to move beyond discussion of DJ-ing, spray painting and street dance as typical tropes of arts-based youth work, and to encourage practitioners to consider the more uncomfortable territory of the cultural institution as a space for practicing youth work. There was also recognition of the 'need for a critical and reflective examination of partnership' in this area of work (Patel, 2010, p. 64).

All of these factors combined meant there was a clear gap for a piece of research that represented the perspectives of youth workers, and that could find a youth work readership. So much of the literature in this field is generated by the cultural sector, for the cultural sector. Similarly, conferences on the subject of partnership between cultural institutions and youth or community organisations tend to be arranged by the arts sector and populated by arts practitioners. One of the major objectives of this publication is to highlight the thoughts of youth workers and to present findings that are of equal use to the youth and cultural sectors.

Personal Positioning

While I make this claim to want to forefront the critical voice and knowledge of youth work in this publication, it would be remiss of me to ignore the fact that I am not a youth worker. Nor did I grow up engaged with the types of youth services that I interacted with throughout Circuit. I write from the perspective of a middle class, white, non-disabled, heterosexual, London-based, highly educated female gallery practitioner. Acknowledging the capitals we do and don't possess and the way these impact upon our behaviour is part of the project of this book, so it is vital that I include myself in this process of transparency and recognition.

My privileged background is relatively consistent with that of the majority of cultural sector workers—many of whom have at least one parent who went to university and at least one parent who worked in a managerial role (Create, 2015). It is no coincidence that I felt able to cope with social challenges; that I was driven to achieve academically and that I never felt pressure to pursue a well-paid profession. My happy, stable home life and strong adult influences provided the conditions to build confidence and resilience, and my exposure to extra-curricular cultural experiences reinforced the legitimacy of a creative career. Like many cultural sector workers, I also pursued an arts degree. These degrees rarely provide vocational training for gallery work—rather they are shaped around developing students' visual literacy, critical thinking abilities and knowledge of cultural and political contexts. Arts subjects provide a broad and pleasurable intellectual grounding for a wide range of possible careers. The decision to undertake this type of degree is therefore itself underpinned by privilege, because the subject matter's value is derived from a belief in the currency of a particular type of cultural knowledge. This form of education is quite distinct from the vocational character of youth and community work education, which is much more directed towards developing pedagogical practice and equipping students with professional qualifications for the workplace (Gibson and Wylie, 2015).

So the advantages of my upbringing meant that I would be comfortably situated in the gallery education field. Cultural institutions are familiar spaces for me because the social and cultural capitals acquired throughout my childhood were congruent with the practices and values of these spaces (Connell et al., 1982; Thomson, 2002). Through various experiences, including adoption and voluntary or paid work in a range of youth and community settings, I have built a greater understanding of the systemic barriers and social inequalities facing many young people. But I cannot fully know what it is to resist or feel excluded by cultural institutions, either as a young person or as a practitioner. I am also conscious that my early engagements as a volunteer were often motivated by philanthropic impulses and a desire to build my CV. Both of these motivations are loaded with power relations, which is something I became more aware of as my personal politics evolved. The philanthropic inflection of gallery education is a feature of the practice that I have grappled with and that I know has troubled other practitioners (Smith, 2012; Sayers, 2014). I acknowledge that my professional accomplishments and personal fulfilments are partly products of high quality cultural activities introduced by my family, at school, or in after-school drama, music and art classes. And I am politically aggravated by the idea that so many are denied access to similar types of provision.

The other key element of my personal experience that is relevant to this text is the way in which I received my 'break' into employment in gallery education, through securing an unpaid internship with Tate Britain's youth programme in 2008. While thrilled to be offered this internship after graduating, I recall feeling some anxiety about my legitimacy as a white, middle class 22-year-old working with a group of ethnically diverse Londoners only a few years younger than myself. I recognised Tate's complicity in creating hierarchies between young people through their institutional practice of offering unpaid internships, which required interns to work for free three days a week for three months. I was admittedly only able to pursue this internship alongside a full time Master's course and a part time job due to the financial assistance of my parents. This internship was immensely rewarding and pivotal to my securing subsequent paid work with Tate and other institutions. But even though I took advantage of this opportunity, I was conscious that entrenched institutional inequalities (that privileged the financially secure) had facilitated my entry into gallery education. In the years that followed, activism against the structural unfairness of unpaid internships grew in prominence, which helped to encourage organisations such as Tate to pay interns, and therefore widen access into the gallery sector. So my relationship to Tate's youth programme is complex, because I am the beneficiary of the historical culture of free labour that reinforced inequity and social/economic barriers in arts institutions. In many ways, this project has led me to confront uncomfortable questions about my collusion in the problems revealed by the research.

Rather than perceive this as a sign of weakness, I have tried to utilise my professional discomfort as a source of empathy with research participants—namely gallery practitioners and youth workers—who I frequently asked to open up about their own professional histories (Mills and Morton, 2013). My career trajectory corresponds in many ways to that of other gallery practitioners, and my role as an implicated (but critical) insider is something to be exploited. By acknowledging these aspects of my positionality, and unpicking the privileges and power structures that shape my researcher identity, I am attempting to adopt a critical research stance, which brings to light inequality and injustice in the context of study (Madison, 2012). This approach has its own shortcomings, and I appreciate fellow academics' efforts to highlight the need for reflexivity around critical research and its potential to reproduce problematic power relations (Kuby, 2013; Rogers, 2018). For instance, this text draws upon the contributions of practitioners and researchers with overtly working class positionalities but also recognises that the dominant authorial voice is one of a white, middle class positioning. Consciousness of these types of classed and raced dynamics and identities is fundamental to the task of critically unpacking partnership.

Definitions

There are several terms used throughout this publication that require some clarification. The concepts of the 'gallery education' and 'youth' sectors are explored in Chap. 3. It is worth noting however that the term 'gallery education' is shorthand for an area of practice that takes many different forms in different institutions. Some galleries prefer to use terms such as 'learning and engagement' or 'participation' rather than 'education' for instance. Similarly, the term 'youth work' has seen several evolutions over recent years, and sometimes this area of practice is referred to as 'informal education' or even 'social pedagogy'. But in both cases, the terms 'gallery education' and 'youth work' identify a specific lineage of practice that is widely recognisable to practitioners of all generations.

Also discussed in Chap. 3 are the changing roles of the youth worker and gallery education programmer. It is important to point out that in different organisations, different job titles are used for similar roles. In some of the partnerships I observed, practitioners from youth organisations were called 'advisors' or 'support workers' or 'programme managers' for instance. Similarly, gallery practitioners had a number of job titles—from 'Youth and community officer', to 'Curator, Young people's programmes'. Throughout the text, I often use the generic terms 'youth practitioner' and 'gallery practitioner' to describe workers, as this was necessary to conceal the identities of individuals.

The most contentious collection of terms used throughout the publication are the various descriptors applied to 'young people'. Citing Circuit's literature, I have already used the phrase 'hard-to-reach' in reference to young people who are considered to have least access to arts opportunities. This phrase is regularly critiqued for its apparent disregard for organisational barriers, and in Circuit, it often came under scrutiny and fell out of favour with practitioners. I am conscious of the large body of literature across the arts and social sciences that contests the usefulness of dominant concepts such as Not in Education, Employment or Training (NEET) (Russell, 2013), 'hard-to-reach' (Douglas, 2009, p. 50) and 'at risk' (Kester, 2013; Turnbull and Spence, 2011). Much of this literature argues that these brands of disadvantage individualise social problems and unfairly stigmatise young people (Hall, 2001; Kemshall, 2009). Some critics even consider the category of 'youth' to be a 'social construct' (Lohmann and Mayer, 2009, p. 1; Turnbull and Spence, 2011, p. 940). In this text, I apply the principles of the social model of disability to any discussion about disadvantage (Lisicki, 2017). In other words, my understanding is that individuals are marginalised or disadvantaged by *society*, and the individual is not to blame for their marginalisation, nor does it define them. *Not* to use terms such as 'disadvantaged' or 'marginalised' would be to ignore the social conditions that create challenges for young people.

What all of the above issues hopefully illustrate is that this is a complex and sensitive area of practice, which is laden with imperfect language and uncomfortable power relations. This is an equally flawed text, which inevitably contains biases and blind spots. The following chapter sets out how a critical ethnographic approach to the field and a Bourdieusian theoretical framework can help the practitioner or researcher to see with greater clarity the prejudices and structural conditions that underpin partnerships between galleries and youth organisations.

References

Alldred, Pam, Fin Cullen, Kathy Edwards, and Dana Fusco. 2018. Introduction. In *The Sage handbook of youth work practice*, ed. Pam Alldred, Fin Cullen, Kathy Edwards, and Dana Fusco, xxix–xxxvi. London: Sage Publications.

A New Direction. 2013. Schools forum: Effective partnership working. *A New Direction*. Accessed 25 April 2014. http://www.anewdirection.org.uk/knowledge/resources/a-new-direction-schools-forum-effective-partnership-working.

Bak Mortensen, Marie, and Judith Nesbitt, eds. 2012. *On collaboration*. London: Tate.

Batsleer, Janet. 2008. *Informal learning in youth work*. London: Sage Publications Ltd.

Belton, Brian. 2015. The impact of art analysis and interpretation on the role and practice of youth work. *Youth work, informal learning and the arts: Exploring the research and practice agenda*, The University of Nottingham, 18 November 2015.

Bienkowski, Piotr. 2016. *No longer us and them: How to change into a participatory museum and gallery: Learning from the Our Museum programme*. London: Paul Hamlyn Foundation.

Brown, Colin. 2012. Six degrees of collaboration. In *On collaboration*, ed. Marie Bak Mortensen and Judith Nesbitt, 94–103. London: Tate.

Butler, David, and Vivienne Reiss, eds. 2007. *Art of negotiation*. London: Arts Council England.

Byrne, John, Elinor Morgan, November Paynter, Aida Sánchez de Serdio, and Adela Železnik, eds. 2018. *The constituent museum: Constellations of knowledge, politics and mediation: A generator of social change*. Amsterdam: Valiz.

Circuit. 2013a. *Circuit programme handbook*. London: Tate.

———. 2013b. *A guide to Circuit evaluation framework*. London: Tate.

Clark, Nick. 2012. Riots spark £5m Tate arts project for the young. *The Independent*, December 13. Accessed 7 April 2014. http://www.independent.co.uk/arts-entertainment/art/news/riots-spark-5m-tate-arts-project-for-the-young-8411694.html.

Connell, Raewyn, Dean Ashenden, Sandra Kessler, and Gary Dowsett, eds. 1982. *Making the difference: Schools, families and social division*. Sydney: Allen & Unwin.

Create. 2015. *Panic!* Create London. Accessed 3 December 2015. http://www.createlondon.org/panic/survey/.

Creating Change. 2013. Creating change: A network for targeted youth arts. Accessed 13 May 2014. http://creating-change.org.uk/.

Daly, Eileen, ed. 2012. *Engage 30 Arts and healthcare*. London: Engage.

Douglas, Anthony. 2009. *Partnership working*. Oxon: Routledge.

ECORYS. 2016. *Non-arts partnerships*. Creative People and Places.

Eddo-Lodge, Reni. 2017. *Why I'm no longer talking to white people about race.* London: Bloomsbury Publishing.

Edmonds, Kathy. 2008. Making connections: Widening participation in the arts for young people through dynamic partnerships. *Engage 22 Young People and Agency*, 57–62.

Ellison, Jane. 2015. *The art of partnering.* London: King's College London.

Facer, Keri, and Bryony Enright. 2016. *Creating living knowledge.* Bristol: The University of Bristol and AHRC Connected Communities programme.

Facer, Keri, and Kate Pahl, eds. 2017. *Valuing interdisciplinary collaborative research: Beyond impact.* Bristol: Policy Press.

Francke, Andrea. 2012. *Invisible spaces of parenthood.* London: The Showroom.

Freeman, Hadley. 2013. Check your privilege! Whatever that means. *The Guardian*, June 5. Accessed 3 February 2019. https://www.theguardian.com/society/2013/jun/05/check-your-privilege-means.

Gannon, Emma. 2018. *The multi-hyphen method.* London: Hodder & Stoughton.

Gibson, Alan, and Tom Wylie. 2015. Albemarle years and the emergence of modern youth and community education. *One hundred years of youth and community work education: A celebration*, YMCA George Williams College, London, 8 October 2016.

Graham, Janna, et al., eds. 2012. *On the Edgware road.* London: Serpentine Gallery; Koenig Books.

Hall, Roz. 2001. Tailor-made practice. *Engage 11 Inclusion Under Pressure*: 43–49.

Hanley, Lynsey. 2016. *Respectable: The experience of class.* London: Penguin Random House UK.

Horlock, Naomi, ed. 2000. *Testing the water: Young people and galleries.* Liverpool: Liverpool University Press and Tate Liverpool.

Howard, Frances. 2017. The arts in youth work: A spectrum of instrumentality? *Youth & Policy*. Accessed 20 July 2017. http://www.youthandpolicy.org/articles/the-arts-in-youth-work/.

Isaacs, Hedy Leonie. 2004. The allure of partnerships: Beyond the rhetoric. *Social and Economic Studies* 53 (4): 125–134.

Kemshall, Hazel. 2009. Risk, social policy and young people. In *Work with young people: Theory and policy for practice*, ed. Jason Wood and Jean Hine, 154–162. London: Sage.

Kester, Grant H. 2013. *Conversation pieces: Community and communication in modern art.* 2nd ed. London: University of California Press.

Kuby, Candace R. 2013. *Critical literacy in the early childhood classroom: Unpacking histories, unlearning privilege.* New York: Teachers College Press.

Lisicki, Barbara. 2017. Social model of disability. *Shape Arts*. Accessed 1 July 2017. https://www.shapearts.org.uk/News/social-model-of-disability.

Lohmann, Ingrid, and Christine Mayer. 2009. Lessons from the history of education for a "century of the child at risk". *Paedagogica Historica* 45 (1): 1–16.

Lynch, Bernadette. 2011. *Whose cake is it anyway?: A collaborative investigation into engagement and participation in twelve museums and galleries in the UK.* London: Paul Hamlyn Foundation.

Madison, D. Soyini. 2012. *Critical ethnography: Methods, ethics, and performance.* Los Angeles: Sage.

Matarasso, François. 2019. *A restless art: How participation won, and why it matters.* London: Calouste Gulbenkian Foundation.

McKenzie, Lisa. 2015. *Getting by: Estates, class and culture in austerity Britain.* Bristol: Policy Press.

Miessen, Markus. 2010. *The nightmare of participation.* Berlin: Sternberg Press.

Mills, David, and Missy Morton. 2013. *Ethnography in education.* London: Sage.

Morford, Roger. 2009. *Arts work with socially excluded young people.* Leicester: The National Youth Agency.

National Portrait Gallery. 2014. *Domino effect: Engaging NEET young people through photography.* London: NPG.

Patel, Raj. 2010. Creativity and partnership. In *What is youth work?* ed. Janet Batsleer and Bernard Davies, 61–72. Exeter: Learning Matters.

Rogers, Rebecca. 2018. Literacy research, racial consciousness, and equitable flows of knowledge. *Literacy Research: Theory, Method, and Practice* 67: 24–43.

Ruigrok, Sophie. 2018. The White Pube are the world's freshest, funniest art critics. *Dazed*, May 17. Accessed 4 February 2019. https://www.dazeddigital.com/art-photography/article/40004/1/the-white-pube-are-the-worlds-freshest-funniest-art-critics.

Russell, Lisa. 2013. Researching marginalized young people. *Ethnography and Education* 8 (1): 46–60.

Sayers, Esther. 2014. *Making 'culture vultures': An investigation into the socio-cultural factors that determine what and how young people learn in the art gallery.* PhD thesis, Goldsmiths, University of London.

Sennett, Richard. 2013. *Together: The rituals, pleasures and politics of cooperation.* London: Penguin Books.

Slater, Imogen, Chrissie Tiller, and Alison Rooke. 2016. *Taking risks: An evaluation of the Ovalhouse Future Stages programme methodology and impact.* London: Ovalhouse.

Smith, Emma. 2012. What does community mean? In *Gallery as community: Art, education, politics,* ed. Marijke Steedman, 19–42. London: Whitechapel Gallery.

Smithens, Renee. 2008. Building partnerships. *A New Direction.* Accessed 5 May 2014. http://www.anewdirection.org.uk/knowledge/resources/building-partnerships.

South London Gallery. 2011. *The cat came as a tomato: Conversations on play and contemporary art practice.* London: South London Gallery.

Steedman, Marijke, ed. 2012. *Gallery as community: Art, education, politics.* London: Whitechapel Gallery.

Steel, Patrick. 2018. MA launches pilot scheme to connect museums with third sector. *Museums Association*, July 4. Accessed 13 March 2019. https://www.museumsassociation.org/news/04072018-ma-launches-pilot-scheme-to-connect-museums-with-third-sector.

Strong Voices. 2015. Strong Voices archive. Accessed 20 December 2015. https://strongvoicesarchive.wordpress.com/.

Tate. 2012. *Seeing through: The practice, process, delivery and value of working with young people in care*. London: Tate.

Taylor, Tony. 2014. IDYW statement 2014. *In Defence of Youth Work*. Accessed 5 October 2015. https://indefenceofyouthwork.com/idyw-statement-2014/.

Thomson, Pat. 2002. *Schooling the rustbelt kids: Making the difference in changing times*. Stoke on Trent: Trentham Books.

Turnbull, Gavin, and Jean Spence. 2011. What's at risk? The proliferation of risk across child and youth policy in England. *Journal of Youth Studies* 14 (8): 939–959.

UNISON. 2018. Axing millions from youth work puts futures at risk, says UNISON. *UNISON*, December 3. Accessed 11 March 2019. https://www.unison.org.uk/news/press-release/2018/12/axing-millions-youth-work-puts-futures-risk-says-unison/.

Walsh, Aylwyn. 2014. *Creating change, imagining futures: Participatory arts and young people 'at risk'*. London: Centre for Urban and Community Research, Goldsmiths, University of London.

Wheeler, Jo, and Amber Walls. 2008. *Envision: A handbook, supporting young people's participation in galleries and the arts*. London: Engage.

CHAPTER 2

Fields of Practice: Theorising Partnership

This chapter outlines a methodological approach for navigating the different conceptual and literal geographies of partnership and theorising what happens when partners from different fields work together. These 'geographies' of partnership exist in relations between humans, between organisations and between sectors. In contemporary working life, partnership also exists across multiple sites: in meetings, in workshops, in contracts, on email and through social media for instance. Some partnerships in this area of practice involve multiple stakeholders spread around a particular locality—with activity taking place in youth settings, galleries, temporarily occupied spaces and the wider public realm. Examining partnership therefore demands that attention is paid to all of these different sites of engagement. As suggested in the introductory chapter, any researcher or evaluator of partnership also needs to recognise their own positioning within this landscape. In research and in partnership individuals bring preconceptions and predispositions that inflect their reading of situations (Charmaz, 2014). By acknowledging these, it is possible to appreciate how partnership involves diverse perspectives and numerous subjectivities and truths (Denzin, 1997). The multiplicity of partnership is a condition of the practice, and the following chapter seeks to offer tools for understanding and analysing this layered environment.

© The Author(s) 2019
N. Sim, *Youth Work, Galleries and the Politics of Partnership*, New
Directions in Cultural Policy Research,
https://doi.org/10.1007/978-3-030-25197-0_2

MULTI-SITED ETHNOGRAPHY

In the case of Circuit, 10 galleries and over 50 youth organisations were involved in partnerships of different kinds across various time periods and regions. The dispersed nature of the programme, operating in large urban centres as well as small coastal or rural towns, provided a platform to observe partnership working in a range of contexts. In light of the distribution of activity in Circuit and considering the dialogic, engaged nature of youth work and gallery education, I decided to conduct a multi-sited ethnography, which would focus mainly on hanging out at different sites, making observations and hosting interviews.

While traditional understandings of 'ethnography' are associated with the idea of a researcher embedding themselves within a community over months or years, multi-sited ethnography accommodates the fragmented, networked, temporary spatialities of current working practices (Marcus, 1995; Hannerz, 2003). The fieldwork of multi-sited ethnography can therefore legitimately take place at events, online or through other fluid and virtual 'sites' (Hannerz, 2003; Falzon, 2009; Nicolini, 2009). Ethnographic places may even be abstract, imagined and socially constructed, as well as 'bounded' localities such as neighbourhoods, buildings or national and regional space (Massey, 2005; Ingold, 2008; Pink, 2012, p. 118). This open approach to the spatial definition of the 'field' makes it possible to think through the emotional, administrative and physical geographies of partnership.

Multi-sited ethnography also provides tools for approaching and interrogating different professional sectors—as was necessary in my research context. In order to understand the current dynamic of a professional sector, the multi-sited or 'multi-event' ethnographer can explore events such as conferences, workshops and festivals—otherwise referred to as 'field-configuring events' (Delgado and Cruz, 2014, p. 44). These events gather together practitioners and researchers representing different organisations, to debate issues that are pertinent to the field. As such, they are ideal spaces to get to know the internal politics of a professional sector, the key tensions and issues and the leading voices shaping the sector's agenda. Zilber (2014, p. 102) advocates that ethnographers of inter-organisational spaces should also explore 'trans-organisational structures' such as professional membership bodies, field-wide events and field-wide publications, to analyse the composition of sectors. For the research that informs this book, I attended numerous youth sector and gallery sector events across two years. Some of these events (particularly those in the gallery field) included cross-sector interaction, or debates about cross-sector work. Several of these events were organised by membership bodies that represent workers and organisations throughout the youth and art sectors.

My engagement with Circuit itself involved both in-depth and more fleeting observations of different areas of partnership. Sometimes I was able to be part of the very early process of relationship development, while in other cases I entered projects that were already underway. I took part in meetings, events, joint away days, workshops, exhibitions and several off-site initiatives. I worked in four of the regions regularly, making weekly visits to two sites over several months, while I continued to have less concentrated contact with institutions in the other four Circuit regions. During observations, I would often join in with activity or take on an assistant role—taking time to form connections and have friendly conversations with practitioners and young people. Over 80 people took part in semi-structured interviews for the research, including youth sector partners, gallery staff, young people, board members, consultants, artists and the main funder contact.

It is impossible to fully observe and understand all features and dynamics of a partnership. I had, for instance, to come to terms with the difficulties of accessing the usually private and sensitive space of early partnership negotiation. I learnt over the course of my fieldwork that an ethnographer has to walk a thin line between being an amenable research partner and a persistent interrogator. It was also sometimes difficult to present full findings or field notes back to participants if these included sensitive comments made by one partner or colleague about another partner or colleague. From an ethical standpoint, researching partnership is fraught with risks, and it is part of the researcher's job to avoid creating or exacerbating problematic relations (Campbell and Lassiter, 2015). Ultimately, ethnography encourages the researcher to see practice up close and to inhabit the same space as projects and participants. And with careful and respectful trust building, ethnographic practice can represent voices that are otherwise marginalised or underrepresented (Neyland, 2008; Down, 2012). In studying ethnographic traditions, I came to acknowledge that ethnography presents a picture that is *always* partial and never complete (Clifford and Marcus, 1986). I would have to embrace my status as a 'modest witness' (Haraway, 1999) and accept the constructed, often mysterious or semi-visible conditions of partnership working.

A Spatial Lens

This text makes a case for thinking about partnership through theories of space. There are numerous symbolic and physical geographies represented through relationships between galleries and youth organisations. With Circuit as an example, partnership activity literally took place in different regions—in towns and cities with varying levels of wealth, social need and cultural status. Within these regions, organisational partnership was also situated in different localities and physically contained within a series of highly coded built environments—each defined by particular assets, or lack of assets. Notably, the galleries involved in Circuit were all large sites of architectural significance. They housed expensive art works and were destination venues for UK and international visitors. Many of the youth organisations or services involved in Circuit operated in relatively modest (and often underfunded) spaces that were sometimes used for other purposes. The profile and reach of most of these organisations was also usually limited to the local area and a targeted population of young people. The unequal distribution of social and economic power across and through space is fairly clear when these types of organisations are paired together. There is also obviously an expectation within this type of programming for young people and practitioners from one set of social and organisational territories to interact with and ultimately attach to another set of social and organisational territories. Pierre Bourdieu's writings suggest how mapping and conceptualising the socio-cultural properties of these spaces can help to make sense of the politics surrounding their interactions.

In *The weight of the world: social suffering in contemporary society* (1999), Bourdieu highlights the importance of recognising the relationship between 'social agents' (people) and the 'social space' that they occupy (p. 124). Social space is said to be constituted through the differences and exclusions that distinguish it from other sites. According to Bourdieu, social space is also expressed in physical space—that is, in buildings, neighbourhoods and other places—which are designated as the locus for certain goods, practices and communities. In some circumstances, social space is home to rich cultural goods and privileged populations, whereas other social space is the site of congregation for marginalised groups. These spaces are therefore characterised by 'hierarchies and social distances', and the agency and power of a social agent is revealed through their position in relation to and within social space (Bourdieu et al., 1999, p. 124). Bourdieu's interpretation of space provides a useful explanatory device with which to frame the key subjects of this book—galleries and youth organisations—and their different accumulations of resources, people and status.

Bourdieu understands the varying degrees of power in space in terms of capital. He posits, for instance, that the capital city is 'the site of capital' (Bourdieu et al., 1999, p. 125). It is the place where power is both figuratively and actually located. This idea was reproduced through the organisation of Circuit, where the management of the programme was centralised in London, and specifically at Tate London, which occupied the most dominant position in Circuit's order of authority, and in the wider UK art world. The prestigious venues of Tate Modern and Tate Britain exemplify the 'profits of occupation' (Bourdieu et al., 1999, p. 127), where agents with sufficient capital to inhabit these spaces are rewarded through the enjoyment of grand, socially exclusive surroundings. For Bourdieu, the capital required to enter particular social space is largely symbolic. While Tate Modern and Tate Britain are free for anyone to visit, these galleries project particular types of (predominantly middle class) cultural behaviour that can feel alien to some individuals and groups (Cousins, 2014). They contain works of art that may only seem decipherable to highly educated audiences (Grenfell and Hardy, 2007). Equally, they may be geographically too distant or inaccessible for less mobile communities to reach. As such, even though these spaces claim to be open to all, they have the capacity to exert what Bourdieu calls 'symbolic violence' on communities who do not possess the types of capital necessary to belong (Bourdieu, 1977). An encounter with an art gallery could for instance confirm an individual's sense of intellectual inferiority or social undesirability through the feeling of being out of place (Bourdieu, 1985; Silva, 2008; McKenzie, 2015). Agents from different social spaces can physically enter the 'habitat' of other agents, but their social proximity to that habitat is determined by a much more complex set of structural considerations (Bourdieu et al., 1999, p. 128). It is these considerations that hold relevance for an analysis of partnership between galleries and youth organisations, which typically stages an encounter between the art institution and young people from working class, ethnically diverse or disadvantaged backgrounds.

Another way of phrasing the idea of social space or spheres of social activity is through Bourdieu's concept of 'fields'. These fields function with their own internal logic, but they are also affected by other fields and forces, and more specifically by the 'overall field of power' (Thomson, 2017, p. 8). In relation to this area of research, the 'field' can be ascribed to several different overlapping spatialities. The youth sector and gallery sector are two such fields, within which pedagogical *sub*-fields reside— namely youth work and gallery education. These spaces also host a vast litany of further sub-fields—some of which are considered areas of practice (e.g. open access youth work, youth mental health services etc.), and some of which are singular organisations, or even programmes within organisations. These fields also regularly come into contact with the political fields of the local authority or national government, which often set the conditions and policy environment for different organisations and sectors, and the agents that populate them. By naming these interrelated geographies, it is possible to identify how partnership exists within a network of spaces that function at various scales. In Bourdieu's framework, micro and macro phenomena are tightly associated, and the actions of the individual cannot be read in isolation from societal movements and structures (Grenfell and Hardy, 2007; Thomson, 2017).

This text therefore moves through these different spaces of attention— starting with the policy histories and social changes that have created, shaped and governed the youth and gallery education sector fields. This first step of analysis aligns with Bourdieu's suggestion that the researcher must first understand the position of the field in relation to the field of power (Bourdieu and Wacquant, 1992). Chapter 3 identifies the extent to which these fields are impacted differently and similarly by policy shifts, and explores to what degree these fields are dominated by, or autonomous from, regimes of governance. These issues tell us things about the relative agency of the fields, which is important in a study of partnership. Bourdieu contends that the overall field of power works to service the governing agenda, and in the case of youth work and gallery education the forces of neoliberalism are shown to have cast significant influence over the development of the sectors, and over the changing concept of 'partnership'.

From a Bourdieusian perspective, each field also has its own mode of being or ways of doing things. Agents have to learn how to play the 'game' of their field and adapt to its protocol if they are to advance their position (Bourdieu, 1985; Bennett, 2010, p. xxi). According to Bourdieu, each field values and legitimates particular cultural and social capitals in its agents that pertain to the logic of that field. Cultural capital refers to the experiences and knowledge accumulated by an individual, as well as the signifiers of this capital—that is, the possessions and qualifications that demonstrate their status (Bourdieu, 1985). Social capital refers to the social assets acquired through connections with specific groups, organisations and localities. Objectified or economic capital refers to the material assets and monetary wealth of the agent (Bourdieu, 1985). Playing the game of the field is a process of accumulating capitals that are deemed valuable in the context of that field (Thomson, 2017). The following two chapters outline how understandings of prized professional capitals have shifted within the sectors, and contemplate to what extent these sectors differentiate themselves through their distinctive ideas of what constitutes significant cultural and social capital. In this sense, the chapters enact what Bourdieu refers to as the second mode of field analysis—by charting the competing discourses between groups of agents within the respective fields—as they strive to legitimate their agendas (Bourdieu and Wacquant, 1992). This process of analysis provides insight into the ways in which specific professional knowledge becomes elevated and devalued depending on the dominant belief system of the field—characterised by Bourdieu as 'doxa' (Bourdieu, 1977; Bourdieu and Wacquant, 1992).

While 'doxa' is described as the received, 'taken for granted' way of doing things, Bourdieu stressed that fields are not homogenous spaces, and not all agents are willing to play the game required of them by higher authorities (Bourdieu, 1977, p. 164). In many fields, the doxa is a site of contestation, and Bourdieu's methodology asks the researcher to shed light on these contests. There are for instance conflicting factions within the youth sector that hold opposing ideas about the purpose and activity of youth work. Some mainstream state-funded youth work is sometimes seen as adhering to an outcome-based practice that propagates the notion that young people can overcome personal challenges and be improved through 'individual socialisation' into wider society (Coussée, 2008, cited in Cooper, 2012, p. 54). This is in contrast to the more critical faction, which rejects the role of the market and associated targets in youth work in favour of democratic, open-ended relationships on young people's terms (Taylor, 2014). This faction seeks to defend youth work from a doxic narrative that pathologises young people and limits their ability to perceive and act against wider structures of oppression exercised by political power (Cooper, 2012). This is a crass illustration of the disparities between different fields of youth work, and in reality, there are many who occupy an in-between position of critical compliance. However, for many critically engaged youth workers, submission to the national policy discourse is an example of symbolic violence—where the imposition of a dominant worldview disguises systemic inequality produced by authorities

(Cooper, 2012). Symbolic violence is said to be enacted in youth work when young people are contained in apparent 'safe spaces' and not supported to participate in 'radical' action and debate (Cooper, 2012, p. 56). The emphasis of many youth programmes on positive messaging (Baillie, 2015) and developing individuals to become responsible citizens suggests that those who fall outside of this vision are accountable for their own failings (Fitzsimons et al., 2011). Bourdieu refers to this type of situation as 'misrecognition'—where education initiatives are designed to privilege certain forms of capital in young people, and therefore perpetuate division and exclusion.

Recognising these conflicting traditions and battles for power is vital to any analysis of partnership. This process enables the researcher to comprehend both the politics of the field and the tensions embodied by individual practitioners as they perform their roles. In a Bourdieusian study of partnership, the 'partner' comprises a series of interconnected fields, and agents at different positions in the hierarchy of their field. These fields are complex and changing and cannot be conceived as fixed entities, which has clear implications for partnership sustainability. A youth sector partner or a gallery sector partner cannot be easily defined and generalised, and what counts as good practice in one youth sector setting may differ in another youth sector setting. The doxic frictions of the field also produce dilemmas in cross-sector alliances. Partners from other sectors need to make strategic decisions and judgements about which faction they wish to align with—that is, whether they subscribe to (or resist) the prevailing doxa of the partner field. This area of enquiry is one of the key concerns of Chap. 6, where I explore the compatibility of relationships between selected Circuit galleries and different types of youth organisations and services. Also of interest in this analysis of partnership is the positioning of different partner agents within the programmatic field. In Chap. 5, I discuss how Circuit created horizontal and vertical structures of positioning within its own programme design (noting for instance that youth practitioners were not included in the managerial centre of the programme).

The third major step in a Bourdieusian understanding of the field of practice is the analysis of 'habitus' (Bourdieu, 1984; Bourdieu and Wacquant, 1992). A person's 'habitus' represents the dispositions, tastes and unconscious thought processes they assume which guide their actions, behaviour and motivations. Habitus is a congregation of sentiments, personal qualities and attitudinal leanings that give agents a sense of belonging to a field. These collective dispositions are generally shaped through an individual's position in social space, which is often governed by educational background and social origin. In developing these attributes, people build an inclination to work within a particular field, and they build capital that is relevant to their occupation. Their occupational field also continues to produce and shore up communal patterns of thought and behaviour. This cyclical set of movements related to habitus and capitals helps to explain why communities of practitioners often originate from similar backgrounds, or possess similar types of academic, economic and cultural capital (Bourdieu, 1985). In youth work for instance, a lived experience of disadvantage is often considered valuable embodied capital. In gallery education, a degree in the arts qualifies as standard institutional capital. The social identity of a professional field and the associated habitus of the practitioner are therefore established through a complicated assembly of class influences, upbringing, geographic location, education and other cultural conditioning. Gender, ethnicity, sexuality, health and ability are also factors that shape the character of the agent and form their professional mentality (Thomson, 2017). Habitus is not a tangible thing that can be straightforwardly passed on from an agent in one field to an agent in another. Nor is it possible in social space to 'group *anyone* with just *anyone* while ignoring the fundamental differences, particularly economic and cultural ones' (Bourdieu, 1985, p. 726). This is an issue I explore in the Chap. 7, which details the challenges involved in managing clashes of culture when practitioners from the youth sector were recruited to work on Circuit.

Bourdieu's 'habitus' also supports analysis around the different approaches towards art practice that are often seen in youth work contexts and gallery contexts. Attitudes towards art reveal various things about an individual's habitus—their tastes, perceptions, interpretations, privileges and prejudices. Bourdieu's seminal research in *Distinction* (1984) speaks directly to the dispositions of arts workers and initiated participants, who are so closely affiliated with institutions of so-called legitimate culture (i.e. galleries and museums). His research into cultural preferences denotes how aesthetic judgements and tastes vary in relation to class groupings, and how different art forms and genres are classified within hierarchies of legitimacy. Bourdieu implies that these value systems (reinforced by peer consensus and validation, or rejections and exclusions), can act as divisive as well as unifying forces (Bennett, 2010). Recent studies examining the contemporary application of Bourdieu's *Distinction* have confirmed that the visual arts continue to act as a key marker of social position, and class division in particular. Silva (2008) indicates how taste and attitude in relation to visual art (more than any other art form) manifests exclusivity, tension and instances of defensiveness amongst people.

In my fieldwork then, I looked to explore how aesthetic attachments and inherited cultural values differed amongst practitioners and contributed to tension. In interviews (as is consistent with a Bourdieusian methodology) I asked participants to reflect on their personal histories and career trajectories, their reasons for entering their field, their relationship to art and creativity more broadly, and their core values and pedagogic principles. These conversations allowed me to gather a multi-layered perspective on the key divergences in language and approach that were often identified as signals of cultural clashes between practitioners operating in the youth and gallery sectors. The conversations also revealed how several practitioners involved in Circuit had moved between the fields of youth work and gallery education throughout their careers. While each participant held nuanced ideas about the value of engagement with the arts, there were clear and revealing patterns of difference between the attitudes of practitioners whose background was primarily located in youth work, and those practitioners whose background was primarily located in the visual arts.

If the visual art world is known to incite degrees of discomfort and to reproduce elitist tendencies, it follows that symbolic violence and misrecognition can also be attributed to gallery youth programmes. Subsequently, one of the major areas of interest in my research was the doxa of Circuit and its effects on partnership working. In Chap. 7, I explore the competing agendas at play in the programme and accompanying processes of recognition and misrecognition. Bourdieu is commonly mobilised in gallery education studies to question hierarchical or elitist assumptions behind institutional programming. These assumptions relate to the characterisation of galleries and museums as stores of significant cultural capital, and to the deficit-oriented framing of uninitiated communities who are often considered to be lacking cultural capital (Sayers, 2014). Bourdieu's work has helped gallery education researchers to articulate the exclusionary behaviour of institutions, and their capacity to reinforce alienation through prioritising the cultural tastes of a privileged minority (Pringle, 2008). In the case of this research, I look at the discourse of 'peer-led' as the core means of youth engagement in galleries. As explained in the introduction, one of the chief goals of

Circuit was to provide 'entry points and pathways' for 'hard-to-reach young people' to access the cultural activity of the gallery (Circuit, 2013). There was an explicit ambition that young people from partnership groups might join peer groups at each gallery, and become involved in producing events, projects, exhibitions and festivals for their peers. Utilising data from cross-site observations and interviews, I reflect on the inclusivity of the peer-led pedagogy and contemplate the charge of some practitioners and young people that this way of working reproduced institutionalised practice and fostered limited class diversity. I use Bourdieu to determine the reasoning behind examples of disengagement, as well as exceptional examples of transition between partnership and peer groups, and ask whether expectations for assimilation into gallery programmes represent subtle, unconscious forms of symbolic violence. I also explore how the action research framing of the programme provided space for critical reflection around these issues, and how some galleries worked in ways that did accommodate diversity, inclusivity and difference within their programmes.

By analysing these doxic struggles in both sectors, I am not placing blame on particular organisations, practitioners and programmes—rather I am demonstrating how these agents and fields are themselves conditioned by a much wider, market-oriented political doctrine that entrenches ideas about what constitutes valuable capital in society. While partnership often appears to boil down to interpersonal relationships, Bourdieu's theory of practice teaches the researcher to look beyond interpersonal chemistry, and to contextualise individual behaviour with the 'present and past positions in the social structure that biological individuals carry with them, at all times and in all places' (Bourdieu, 1977, p. 82). By remaining attentive to the structural effects influencing the actions of the individual, the researcher can perceive the impact of the broader field of power on the construction of partnership (Bourdieu et al., 1999).

POSSIBILITIES FOR ACTION AND CHANGE

While Bourdieu's theoretical framework seems to imply that hegemonic forces make change impossible, there are a number of ways in which his methodology can be used to suggest possibilities for action and resistance. Bourdieu proposed for instance that fields are always in flux and 'in tension', and as such they create openings for change (Thomson, 2017,

p. 21). In my fieldwork, I looked for examples of these tensions and opportunities for disruption, and became particularly interested in partnership initiatives that took place in offsite, temporary, outsider spaces. In these sites there was potential for typical power geographies to be destabilised, and for doxic boundaries to be renegotiated.

Bourdieu noted that changes in the dominant political order are also possible, and the political upheaval of 2016–2019 (consumed by 'Brexit' and the election of Donald Trump) confirmed this to be true. While these seismic shifts may not have resulted in more socially just systems, the volatility of the time precipitated a moment of global disruption, which arguably injected new political energy and appetite for activism into youth engagement programmes. In my research, I wanted to understand how youth organisations and galleries might unite around a shared commitment to informal education, and work together at regional and national levels to preserve spaces for creative, democratic and politically/socially engaged youth provision.

The ability of agents to adopt positions of reflexivity and criticality within their respective fields is a further indicator of conceivable change, according to Bourdieu (Grenfell, 2012; Decoteau, 2016; Thomson, 2017). Circuit's focus on reflective practice generated a culture of collective analysis and peer accountability, and supported practitioners to critique their own programming and act upon/embed learning. Bourdieu also saw researcher reflexivity as a vital element of his methodological toolkit (Grenfell, 2012). In interview situations, Bourdieu suggests that while the researcher usually controls the terms of the conversation, steps can be taken to even up the power dynamics and reduce the intrusions inherent in the researcher-participant alliance. These steps include: creating the ideal circumstances for the participant to speak freely and honestly, and adhering to the practice of 'active and methodological listening' (Bourdieu et al., 1999, p. 609). Bourdieu proposes that the process of active and methodological listening compels the researcher to get to know participants and the 'social conditions of which they are a product' in advance, to enable a 'constant improvisation of pertinent questions' (Bourdieu et al., 1999, p. 613). Bourdieu suggests that this sociological approach to interviewing supports participants to unravel the full complexity of their responses. In building these methodological principles, Bourdieu sought to demonstrate that effective, rigorous research could become a catalyst for action and change (Thomson, 2017).

BEYOND BOURDIEU

While a Bourdieusian methodology lends itself well to the analysis of partnership, other theoretical resources are cited throughout this text, where there is demand for more in-depth analysis into specific phenomena. For example, my findings establish that partnerships between youth organisations and galleries are greatly enhanced if they build upon the existing cultural tastes of young people, and find ways to support all participants to have creative agency. Bourdieu's work is however critiqued for not recognising the diversity and agency of dominated working class culture and communities (Bourdieu, 1993; Bennett, 2013). In the Rancierian and Freirean traditions, this conception of a hierarchy of knowledge is understood to reinforce inequality, and marginalised communities should be considered as having equal but different intelligences to non-marginalised populations (Sayers, 2014). In response to these debates, I draw upon a range of literature that has attempted to bring critical analytic rigour to the cultural engagements and productions of oppressed and marginalised young people, beyond typical redemption or deficit narratives (Willis, 1990; Yosso, 2005; Hickey-Moody, 2013; Pringle, 2014, McKenzie, 2015; Hanley, 2016). Critical Race Theory (CRT) for instance, offers an alternative perspective on conventional interpretations of cultural capital, and argues for the recognition of the 'aspirational, navigational, social, linguistic, familial and resistant capital' of 'Communities of Colour' within education institutions (Yosso, 2005, p. 69). CRT is deployed as a means to redefine these communities as culturally wealthy and critically active, rather than being culturally deficient through the lens of the white middle class status quo. This type of work demonstrates the importance of acknowledging young people's own social fields, and of valuing their embodied cultural capital—often derived from knowledge of place, of sub/popular cultures and local youth communities (France et al., 2013). By mobilising this work, it is possible to position spaces and issues of marginality as generative, critical and creative sites of co-production.

Leading on from this, another area of enquiry that some critics suggest is under-developed in Bourdieu's work is the concept of relations and interactions between different fields (Rawolle, 2005). Bourdieu's writing tends to focus on the logics, products, forces and tensions that are specific to individual fields, rather than extensively investigate the intersections and exchanges between them. Analysing the capacity for cross-pollination between fields is obviously centrally important to this research. I also searched for descriptive tools to meaningfully explain the space created by galleries and youth organisations coming together in collaboration. The work of Lingard and Rawolle (2004) and Rawolle (2005) has been useful in these respects, as they build upon Bourdieu's 1998 publication *On television and journalism*, to convey the potential for 'cross-field effects' and 'temporary social fields'. Their premise is that social fields interact with one another in various ways, and that logics of practice can have cross-field significance. Similarly, agents can operate across different fields, and in some cases, they can 'readily convert their capitals to gain advantage in other fields' (Lingard and Rawolle, 2004, p. 366). They understand that there are different reasons for fields to interact (e.g. dependency) and that some fields are better equipped at doing this cross-field work than others. These ideas prompt exploration about which logics of practice and which capitals have been shown to have 'purchase' both in the fields of gallery education and youth work (Lingard and Rawolle, 2004, p. 378). Their writing also helps to guide analysis around more external effects (e.g. 'structural', 'temporal', 'systemic' and 'event effects') that have impacts across multiple fields (Lingard and Rawolle, 2004, p. 368). In my research I looked for cross-field effects and examples of particular incidents, such as negative press about young people that directly impacted both the gallery partner and the local youth service, and which consolidated their rationale for working together.

In addition to these ideas, Rawolle's development of the 'temporary social field' concept offers a means of defining the social space that is generated in the alliance of separate fields that 'share common stakes' (Rawolle, 2005, p. 712). The temporariness of these social fields is due to the fact that the association is usually motivated by a particular event. The notion of a temporary social field is useful in this context as partnerships between galleries and youth organisations are often seen to emerge out of the 'event' of a funded programme, a public initiative or a local issue. However I also want to explore how the concept of a temporary social field might be pushed further to imagine permanent cooperative or collaborative fields based on systemic change and structures of integrated practice.

In summary, I intend to use Bourdieu's framework to construct a series of ideas for cultivating both a mutual respect for practice between the youth and gallery sectors, and a mutually productive recognition of difference and diversity. I do this work in the hope that these moves untangle the complex reasons behind the challenges that have historically frustrated these types of alliances, and to highlight new ways of thinking about partnership. Brought together, these arguments illustrate how exclusions, inclusions, agency, collaboration and power relations are spatialised in partnership. By framing these spaces as being socially produced, and performed through the 'repetitious enactment of particular social norms' (Glass and Rose-Redwood, 2014, p. 16), this text attempts to communicate how it is that these spatialities can be constructed and performed differently.

A brief summary of key terms
Fields: Social or professional spaces of interaction or practice
Agent: An individual acting within a field
Capitals: Experiences, connections, assets and qualifications that agents accumulate and that give them legitimacy in particular fields
Doxa: The dominant belief system of the field
Habitus: The attitudes and tastes that an individual develops as a result of their upbringing and educational and professional background
Symbolic violence: An exertion of damaging or marginalising forces, usually generated by structural inequalities and felt by individuals whose capitals are not valued within a particular field

An interpretation of Bourdieu's toolkit, adapted for partnership research

- Understand the position of the partner fields in relation to the field of power, to comprehend differences in agency.
- Explore competing agendas within partner fields, including conflicts around the logic of practice and the types of capital that counts.
- Analyse the habitus of practitioners in the partner fields, to understand the attitudes and preconceptions agents bring to a partnership.
- Get acquainted with the doxa of the partnership programme. Look at the positioning of agents and knowledge and identify which partner holds the dominant position, and where power is located.

- Observe the compatibility of different fields by looking at partnership models in practice.
- Interrogate the capacity for misrecognition and symbolic violence within a partnership and how this is dealt with.
- Pay attention to moments of critical reflexivity and offer recommendations for change.

REFERENCES

Baillie, Robin. 2015. The UNTITLED: The difference between young people and contemporary art. Presented by Richie Cumming at *Youth work, informal learning and the arts: Exploring the research and practice agenda*, The University of Nottingham, 18 April 2015.

Bennett, Tony. 2010. Introduction to the Routledge Classics edition. Pierre Bourdieu, 1984. In *Distinction: A social critique of the judgement of taste*. London: Routledge.

———. 2013. *Making culture, changing society*. London: Routledge.

Bourdieu, Pierre. 1977. *Outline of a theory of practice*. Cambridge: Cambridge University Press.

———. 1984. *Distinction: A social critique of the judgement of taste*. London: Routledge.

———. 1985. The social space and the genesis of groups. *Theory and Society* 14 (6): 723–744.

———. 1993. *Sociology in question*. London: Sage.

Bourdieu, Pierre, and Loïc Wacquant. 1992. *An invitation to reflexive sociology*. Cambridge: Polity Press in association with Blackwell Publishers.

Bourdieu, Pierre, et al. 1999. *The weight of the world: Social suffering in contemporary society*. Malden: Polity Press.

Campbell, Elizabeth, and Luke Eric Lassiter. 2015. *Doing ethnography today: Theories, methods, exercises*. Chichester: Wiley-Blackwell.

Charmaz, Kathy. 2014. *Constructing grounded theory*. 2nd ed. London: Sage.

Circuit. 2013. *A guide to the Circuit evaluation framework*. London: Tate.

Clifford, James, and George E. Marcus. 1986. *Writing culture: The poetics and politics of ethnography*. Berkeley: University of California Press.

Cooper, Charlie. 2012. Imagining 'radical' youth work possibilities—Challenging the 'symbolic violence' within the mainstream tradition in contemporary state-led youth work practice in England. *Journal of Youth Studies* 15 (1): 53–71.

Cousins, Mark. 2014. Middle-class rules deaden too many arts venues. Let's fill them with life and noise. *The Guardian*, August 10.

Decoteau, Claire Laurier. 2016. The reflexive habitus: Critical realist and Bourdieusian social action. *European Journal of Social Theory* 19 (3): 303–321.

Delgado, Natalia Aguilar, and Luciano Barin Cruz. 2014. Multi-event ethnography: Doing research in pluralistic settings. *Journal of Organizational Ethnography* 3 (1): 43–58.

Denzin, Norman K. 1997. *Interpretive ethnography: Ethnographic practices for the 21st century.* London: Sage.

Down, Simon. 2012. A historiographical account of workplace and organizational ethnography. *Journal of Organizational Ethnography* 1 (1): 72–82.

Falzon, Mark-Anthony. 2009. *Multi-sited ethnography: Theory, praxis and locality in contemporary research.* Oxon: Ashgate Publishing Group.

Fitzsimons, Annette, Max Hope, Charlie Cooper, and Keith Russell. 2011. *Empowerment and participation in youth work.* Exeter: Learning Matters.

France, Alan, Dorothy Bottrell, and Edward Haddon. 2013. Managing everyday life: The conceptualisation and value of cultural capital in navigating everyday life for working-class youth. *Journal of Youth Studies* 16 (5): 597–611.

Glass, Michael R., and Reuben Rose-Redwood. 2014. Introduction: Geographies of performativity. In *Performativity, politics and the production of social space,* ed. Michael R. Glass and Reuben Rose-Redwood. Oxon: Routledge.

Grenfell, Michael. 2012. *Pierre Bourdieu: Key concepts.* London: Routledge.

Grenfell, Michael, and Cheryl Hardy. 2007. *Art rules: Pierre Bourdieu and the visual arts.* Oxford: Berg.

Hanley, Lynsey. 2016. *Respectable: The experience of class.* London: Penguin Random House UK.

Hannerz, Ulf. 2003. Being there… and there… and there!: Reflections on multi-site ethnography. *Ethnography* 4 (2): 201–216.

Haraway, Donna J. 1999. *Modest witness@secondmillenium: Femaleman meets oncomouse.* London: Routledge.

Hickey-Moody, Anna. 2013. *Youth, arts and education: Reassembling subjectivity through affect.* London: Routledge.

Ingold, Tim. 2008. Bindings against boundaries: Entanglements of life in an open world. *Environment and Planning A* 40 (8): 1796–1810.

Lingard, Bob, and Shaun Rawolle. 2004. Mediatizing educational policy: The journalistic field, science policy, and cross-field effects. *Journal of Education Policy* 19 (3): 361–380.

Marcus, George E. 1995. Ethnography in/of the world system: The emergence of multi-sited ethnography. *Annual Review of Anthropology* 24: 95–117.

Massey, Doreen. 2005. *For space.* London: Sage.

McKenzie, Lisa. 2015. *Getting by: Estates, class and culture in austerity Britain.* Bristol: Policy Press.

Neyland, Daniel. 2008. *Organizational ethnography.* London: Sage.

Nicolini, Davide. 2009. Zooming in and zooming out: A package of method and theory to study work practices. In *Organizational ethnography: Studying the complexities of everyday life*, ed. Sierk Ybema, Dvora Yanow, Harry Wels, and Frans H. Kamsteeg. London: Sage.

Pink, Sarah, ed. 2012. *Advances in visual methodology*. London: Sage.

Pringle, Emily. 2008. *The artist as educator: An examination of the relationship between artistic practice and pedagogy within contemporary gallery education*. Thesis, Institute of Education, University of London.

———. 2014. Exploring the 'Cs': Cultural capital, critical race theory and Circuit. *Circuit*. Accessed 2 September 2014. https://circuit.tate.org.uk/2014/09/exploring-the-cs-cultural-capital-critical-race-theory-and-circuit/

Rawolle, Shaun. 2005. Cross-field effects and temporary social fields: A case study of the mediatisation of recent Australian knowledge economy policies. *Journal of Education Policy* 20 (6): 705–724.

Sayers, Esther. 2014. *Making 'culture vultures': An investigation into the socio-cultural factors that determine what and how young people learn in the art gallery*. Thesis, Goldsmiths, University of London.

Silva, Elizabeth. 2008. Cultural capital and visual art in the contemporary UK. *Cultural Trends* 17 (4): 267–287.

Taylor, Tony. 2014. IDYW statement 2014. *In Defence of Youth Work*. Accessed 5 October 2015. https://indefenceofyouthwork.com/idyw-statement-2014/

Thomson, Pat. 2017. *Educational leadership and Pierre Bourdieu*. London: Routledge.

Willis, Paul. 1990. *Common culture*. Buckingham: Open University Press.

Yosso, Tara J. 2005. Whose culture has capital? A critical race theory discussion of community cultural wealth. *Race Ethnicity and Education* 8 (1): 69–91.

Zilber, Tammar B. 2014. Beyond a single organisation: Challenges and opportunities in doing field level ethnography. *Journal of Organizational Ethnography* 3 (1): 96–113.

CHAPTER 3

(Un)common Ground: Parallel Histories and Policy Contexts

To grasp what it means for the youth and gallery education sectors to work together, it is first necessary to understand these fields, both as separate occupational territories and as areas of practice with clear common ground. This is how Bourdieu suggests fields (and the relationships between them) can be explored and analysed (Thomson, 2017). Bourdieu also suggests that to understand the comparative position of social fields, they must be considered in relation to the broader field of power, or wider society (Bourdieu and Wacquant, 1992). By charting the origins and major policy movements of the youth and gallery education sectors it is possible to identify the key debates and issues at stake in their interactions, and to determine the scope of each field's political, social and economic agency when working in partnership. This historical account of the sectors' development also highlights the ways in which conceptions of 'partnership' have been defined and redefined as a tool of governance by successive political parties. This chapter focuses on the UK context, but the paradigms and policy conditions discussed have international parallels and significance.

It is impossible to arrive at universally recognised definitions of gallery education and youth work. The nebulousness of the youth sector in particular is an essential dimension of its character (Banks, 2010; Bright, 2015). There are in existence numerous types of youth organisations, services and programmes, which sit under the umbrella of the 'youth

© The Author(s) 2019   37
N. Sim, *Youth Work, Galleries and the Politics of Partnership*, New
Directions in Cultural Policy Research,
https://doi.org/10.1007/978-3-030-25197-0_3

sector'—from local authority services and faith-based youth clubs, to uniformed, voluntary or detached youth work agencies. Many of these initiatives include provision with an established arts offer. However when the terms 'youth work' or 'youth sector' are used in this book, they refer to an area of practice where the core concern is building relationships with and between young people for their personal and social development (Jeffs and Smith, 2010). The term 'gallery education' meanwhile, is used to refer to a specific field of practice that has its roots in the visual arts, and that is chiefly concerned with enabling people to learn and engage with art through institutions and artists. The contested identity of youth work is a feature that has left the state-supported section of the profession especially exposed to the whims of policy makers (Bright, 2015). The gallery sector enjoys (to some extent) the benefits of the arms-length principle of government funding for the arts, which has partially buffered the sector from direct government influence. However, both sectors have felt the effects of shifting policy agendas, and so, researching their approach to partnership requires an appreciation of the policy lenses through which their activity has been framed.

This chronologically arranged chapter is shaped around six key phases of UK governance that signify meaningful changes in the histories of the two sectors—from the eighteenth century to 2019. While these policy narratives are complex, this timeline points to the wider ideological trends and the conflicts that have accompanied the development of the youth and gallery education sectors. These trends are characterised by a general shift from democratic, informal, grassroots movements, towards an increasingly formalised and instrumentalised environment, as the welfare state has expanded and contracted under new political regimes. The remedial emphasis of this work has also evidently become more entrenched across the late twentieth and early twenty-first centuries (Matarasso, 2013). Growing levels of social inequality and financial austerity form the backdrop to this chronology, but while youth work has been 'dismantled' in many areas of England (Davies, 2019), the practices associated with gallery education and participatory art have become progressively centralised and celebrated in institutions across the UK and globally (Matarasso, 2019). These differences point to the fundamental conditions of inequity that colour relationships between youth organisations and galleries. But they also highlight obvious opportunities for alliance.

Pre-1960s: Common Origins

The 1960s represent an important foundation moment for contemporary understandings of the gallery education and youth sectors. Nonetheless, it is worth briefly retracing their journeys preceding this formative period, to build a more detailed picture of the institutions, principles and struggles that sit behind the respective fields of work.

The histories of arts education and youth work in the UK have arguably been intertwined since their origins. The Foundling Hospital (now a museum) in central London lays claim to representing both Britain's first children's charity (established in 1739 for children in care) and Britain's first public art gallery, under the patronage of William Hogarth (*The Foundling Museum*, 2016). The hospital, which supported the upbringing of abandoned children, worked closely with artists and used exhibitions and concerts to entice benefactors and complement the moral education of the resident 'Foundlings'. This is one of the earliest examples of art being used as a pedagogical, 'civilising' force for the purpose of the personal and social development of vulnerable young people in Britain (Mörsch, 2016). These endeavours were symptomatic of the times, which were punctuated by much wider debate around the health and education of society, taste, class, the democratisation of culture and paternalistic, colonial discourses of the 'other' (Mörsch, 2016). The history of public museums is therefore caught up in broader societal concerns that also formed the foundations for the development of youth provision outside of formal school-based education.

Some of the earliest accounts of 'youth work' in Britain stretch back to the efforts of evangelical Christians through the emergence of Sunday Schools in the late eighteenth century and volunteer-run 'ragged' schools for disadvantaged children in the early nineteenth century (Smith, 2013). The concept of youth clubs for boys and girls gained familiarity in the mid-to-late nineteenth century, and some of these initiatives seemingly adopted a more radical, political mission—including the furtherance of women's rights. Youth work did however continue to develop as a largely Christian endeavour, with the founding of the YMCA (the first international youth organisation) in London in 1844 and with the formation of the Scouting and Guiding movements in the early twentieth century (Smith, 2013; Bright, 2015).

While most galleries and museums in Britain are notably secular in origin (Duncan, 1995) it is also possible to identify a clear relationship between the early history of arts education, religious virtue, altruism and social reform. Whitechapel Gallery in east London is a key example of the outputs of these combined histories. Founded in 1899 by Anglican cleric Samuel Canon Barnett alongside his wife and fellow social reformer Henrietta, the gallery sought to bring great art to the impoverished communities of Whitechapel, and promoted the idea that art could help to 'empower' and educate the public, and offer 'hope' to those in challenging circumstances (Yiakoumaki, 2012). In its cycle of temporary exhibitions, the gallery presented yearly shows of work by children (mainly from schools) as early as 1902. Henrietta Barnett was also hugely influential in developing support initiatives for young people and adults, such as the Metropolitan Association for the Befriending of Young Servants (founded in 1876) and the Country Holiday Fund (1877), which provided rural holidays for poor slum-based children (Smith, 2007). So it is evident that during this period of social reform—which predates the materialisation of youth and arts 'sectors'—arts engagement and work with young people occupied similar and overlapping spaces.

The state gradually established its involvement in youth work after the First World War with the introduction of Juvenile Organising Committees in Local Authorities to tackle 'delinquency', however it took the advent of the Second World War (and concerns about young people's preparedness for service) to motivate the development of a formalised youth service (Smith, 2013; Bright, 2015). Government interest in youth work apparently cooled following the end of the war, when universal schooling for under 15s was established, but it intensified again with the birth of teenage culture in 1950s Britain, and associated 'moral panics' linked with adolescent behaviour (Smith, 2013). The post-war period also witnessed the formation of the Arts Council, which included in its founding statements an expressed desire to advocate for the 'civilising arts' and to open up the enjoyment of cultural experiences to all (Doeser, 2015a, p. 10). The aim of engaging young people in the arts was also part of the Arts Council's founding mission, but there was little formal legislation or infrastructure to support this until the 1960s (Doeser, 2015a). The Arts Council also encouraged collaboration with local authorities, and started to utilise the term 'partnership' in its reporting from 1951 (Doeser, 2015b).

The early histories of youth and arts organisations in Britain reflect some of our contemporary understandings of the tensions inherent in the fields of arts education and youth work. Both practices grew out of a contested space populated by those individuals and organisations with emancipatory, democratic ideals, and those with a more regulatory social agenda aimed at controlling so-called problem communities. The arts and youth work were both perceived in different ways to offer opportunities for personal betterment and civic development. This history also highlights the beginnings of the youth sector's strong voluntary tradition in the Victorian era, when the middle classes in particular were driven by a sense of moral obligation to offer philanthropic support to less privileged communities (Bright, 2015). It is worth noting that this support did sometimes include engagement with music and other arts-based pursuits. National youth initiatives such as Robert Baden-Powell's Scouting movement drew from a combination of militaristic, educational, religious, survivalist, and cultural influences, in its attempt to focus on the self-improvement of the working classes (Savage, 2008). The origins of the arts education and youth sectors are collectively rooted therefore, both in particular concepts of social justice and the democratisation of opportunity, and in assumptions about the primacy of bourgeois values, cultures and behaviours.

1960s–1970s: Formalisation of the Sectors and Countercultural Collaboration

Pre-1960s, neither arts education nor youth work had received a great deal of policy attention in the UK. This situation was to change with the publication of the Albemarle Report on the youth service in 1960 and the first arts policy White Paper in 1965.

The arrival of mass youth culture, a population growth and the ending of young people's involvement in the war effort created a renewed need for an organised youth service within the emerging welfare state (Bradford, 2015). A sense of urgency built up around negative media representations of young people, instances of race riots and youth-led crime, which compelled the Ministry of Education to form a committee (chaired by Countess Albemarle), to advise on government strategies as a means to address the perceived threats posed by rapidly changing societal conditions. The Albemarle Report highlighted the weak, underfunded status of youth work in England and Wales, and strongly supported the extension of a government-funded, professionalised youth service. As a consequence, the Albemarle Report accelerated the development of formal training programmes for youth workers, and led to state investment in youth centres, clubs and projects (Bradford, 2015).

Within the discourse generated by the report, young people were framed as requiring both guidance and discipline to navigate their roles as conscientious citizens, however the report also demonstrated an appreciation of the value of unstructured, friendly and socially responsive forms of youth work (Smith and Doyle, 2002). While the service's capacity to act as a coherent, unified body of organisations was relatively limited due to the small and varied workforce, the Albemarle Report did mark a turning point in the conception of youth work as a professional sector, and this in turn mobilised considerably more practitioners to study and adopt youth work as a career (Bradford, 2015).

Just as the increased political focus on youth work came about partly in response to social anxieties about the rise of the teenager and the creative revolutions that accompanied this moment, the Arts Council was considered (at least by its Chairman in 1966) to champion high art, as a counterpoint to the growth of popular, entertainment-based or experimental culture, commonly associated with danger and deviance (Savage, 2008; Doeser, 2015a). This is not to suggest however, that arts education and youth work were tethered to these reactionary and often elitist ideas of the political and cultural establishment. To the contrary, in the 1960s and 1970s both practices were prominently situated in community-led, radical spaces of activity. The community development movement of the 1970s, largely located in disadvantaged areas of the UK, drew together community development workers from grassroots organisations with artists and theatre makers associated with the burgeoning Community Arts Movement (Matarasso, 2013). These interwoven movements were embedded in the localities from which they derived, and they were politically engaged and committed to enabling active participation. Involving different age groups, the creative undertakings of the Community Arts Movement included festivals, mural-making, adventure play, music, dance and radical writing (Matarasso, 2013). While at this time these endeavours were often set in resistance to the activities of formalised arts institutions such as galleries and museums, many significant figures who eventually helped to establish gallery education had a background in community arts (Allen, 2008; Pringle, 2016; Steedman, 2016).

Community arts activity often took place outdoors in the streets, in housing estates and public parks; however, it is also important to acknowledge the vital role played by community centres, which often acted as hubs where youth work and community arts would meet. An example of this is Centreprise—a Hackney-based community centre founded by youth worker Glenn Thompson that opened in 1971 and accommodated a bookshop, youth club, legal advice service, cafe, reading centre, publishing project, crèche and community arts projects (Berger and Busby, 2001; On the record, 2014). Influenced by his childhood experiences of homelessness and the ideas of Paulo Freire and Ivan Illich, Thompson believed in the potential of literacy, poetry and publishing to empower working class communities, who were culturally underserved due to authorities' low expectations of their intellectual and creative capacities (Berger and Busby, 2001). Hackney had a history of fostering strong leftist, activist movements and organisations, and in this context, community arts and concepts of cultural democracy were said to have flourished (Worpole, 2013). In these spaces, practitioners were not aspiring to establish their credentials as high profile artists, rather they were largely concerned with people, social injustice, the politics of place—and fun (Gefter and Young, 2013; Worpole, 2013).

There are a number of contemporary research projects invested in retracing, archiving and analysing the history of the community arts movement in recognition of the paucity of material available (Jeffers and Moriarty, 2014, 2017; Unfinished histories, 2016; Matarasso, 2016). These types of histories signal how, in the 1960s and 1970s, youth and community clubs were places where working class young people might encounter radical art forms or generate their own cultural experiences (Hanley, 2016). They also suggest that the roles of play workers, youth workers, community organisers and arts practitioners were often interchangeable. These movements were not based upon a middle class elite facilitating access to institutional assets and canonised knowledge, but on the idea that everyone possessed cultural resources and had the capacity to be an artist, and that grassroots cultural/youth engagement held emancipatory power (Willis, 1990; Worpole, 2013; Jeffers and Moriarty, 2014).

While the Arts Council and Gulbenkian Foundation did fund some community arts programmes, the movement was largely marginalised by Arts Council leaders (Doeser, 2015a). As proponents of community arts championed the notion of 'cultural democracy' (which opposed the cultural hierarchies of dominant, bourgeois value systems) the General Secretary of the Arts Council argued for the democratisation of high culture for all (Kelly, 1985). The Community Arts movement has since been credited with ensuring the arts were 'part of a common experience', in a way that the post-war Arts Council and exclusionary arts institutions failed to do (Willis, 1990, p. 4). But the stigmatisation and criticism of the Community Arts movement (particularly around the issue of quality) is important to acknowledge, because this area of arts education practice was closely affiliated with youth and community work.

Allen (2008) contends that as a practice, gallery education is intrinsically allied to the principles and values of the liberation movements of the 1960s and 1970s—particularly feminism and the consciousness raising activities of the women's movement. The artists and practitioners active in the early years of gallery education sought to engender an approach that favoured critical, dialogic, experimental and open-ended processes, that valued cross-disciplinarity and that worked to deconstruct power relationships in institutions (Allen, 2008). Children and young people would be positioned as active participants rather than recipients, and their insights valued—in opposition to the notion that their engagements might represent a 'dumbing down' of arts practice (Allen, 2008, p. 5). The anti-establishment alignment of gallery education extends to its relationship with formal education. From its inception in the 1970s, it was evident that many gallery education practitioners were resistant to the strictures of a curriculum, and aimed to carve out a pedagogical space of engagement beyond the authority and regulations of the school (Allen, 2008). The vast majority of practitioners were (and still continue to be) women, partly due to the origins and character of the practice and the part time working conditions that attracted women otherwise shut out of male-dominated roles in the art world (Allen, 2008).

In the 1970s then, both youth work and gallery education were operating in positions of (both deliberate and imposed) marginality, they were connecting with different forms of localised activism, and they were developing loose networks and critical thinking around the activity of informal education. Collaboration, cooperation and generosity were hallmarks of the practice of community work and early gallery education at this time (Sillis, 2015). The concept of partnership was therefore not yet positioned as a top-down idea; rather it was seemingly a natural condition of practice for organisers, artists, small-scale organisations and local authorities. However, if the 1970s represented a radical, democratic moment for these practices, the following years would be marked by increasing attention towards professionalisation, managerialism and individualism, as a new political orthodoxy gained ground.

1979–1996: THE NEOLIBERAL TURN

The Conservative government under Margaret Thatcher from 1979 ushered in a radically different relationship between government and the welfare state—one that sought to diminish the role of public funding and privilege a mixed economy model (Bradford, 2015). This new era of neoliberalism saw public services, organisations and education institutions pressured into emulating private business models and adopting managerial, enterprising behaviour—a trait that would become commonplace in the youth sector and many areas of the art sector for the following decades (Gielen, 2012; Harvie, 2013).

These changes made an inevitable impression on the nature of youth work training, which became the subject of critique, both from government inspectors, who found the professional skills of youth work to be ill defined, and from grassroots groups, which argued that the professionalisation and academisation of youth work education alienated those more suited to practice-based training (Bradford, 2015). There are long-held debates within youth work about the value of lived experience of disadvantage versus professional training, and the logic presented by those critical of the creeping bureaucracy and focus on theory in youth work was that these movements undermined the potential for working class practitioners to advance into the field. These different arguments about the professional identity of the good, authentic youth worker ultimately helped to shape the future of youth work training around practice-based competencies rather than knowledge/theory-based learning—framing youth work as an accessible vocation rooted in hands-on experience (Bradford, 2015).

The distinct education and training cultures of the arts and youth sectors are important in this respect, because they prioritise different skillsets. As a result of the emerging critical factions of the 1970s and 1980s, youth work developed a strong commitment to equity of opportunity amongst workers, and to valuing the expertise of adults who had experienced challenges as young people at first-hand. However, this characterisation of youth work as an anti-intellectual practice has also since permeated the field, with sometimes-negative consequences. A common stereotype cited by youth workers is that their practice is regarded as essentially hanging out and playing pool or table tennis with young people (Brent, 2013). This is also partly why the label of 'youth work' has lost authority and currency over decades.

Practitioners working in participatory arts (even since the Community Arts movement of the 1970s and 1980s) have tended to emerge from higher education—training at either art schools or universities (Jeffers and Moriarty, 2017). Gallery education also became more professionalised as an area of work in the 1980s, as it received greater political and institutional attention. Following rising unemployment due to the decline in manufacturing, and racial tensions in inner city areas, the early 1980s witnessed rioting and considerable economic deprivation in deindustrialised regions. One outcome of this was the injection of funding into capital projects for new regional galleries and museums in an attempt to develop the cultural economy and kick-start regeneration in deindustrialised areas (Allen, 2008; Matarasso, 2013). The creation of Tate Liverpool in the 1980s was one such institution—conceived in the wake of the 1981 Toxteth riots and designed for the derelict Albert Dock. Local opposition towards the gallery was said (by Toby Jackson, then Head of Education), to have compelled the institution to re-examine and prioritise its engagement strategies and 'develop a critical understanding of the role of the museum in society' (Dewdney et al., 2013, p. 25). Tate Liverpool was subsequently the first of the Tate galleries to establish a peer-led youth programme. This period signalled the beginning of three decades of considerable regeneration-focused investment in regional galleries and museums, which inevitably helped to expand and consolidate the position of gallery education in the arts sector. The Arts Council also published its first education policy statement in 1983 and allocated increasing amounts of funding to education programmes, which helped to motivate galleries and other arts organisations to employ permanent education staff (Doeser, 2015a). In the later 1980s, the concept of a national association of gallery educators (now known as 'engage') was born (Sillis, 2015).

While the spaces and places that hosted gallery education activity were growing rapidly (alongside gallery audiences) in the 1980s, the sites that typically housed youth provision were experiencing a sharp decline in use (Smith, 2013). Much debate in youth work has centred upon the relevance of drop-in youth centres—often branded as 'open access' or universal provision—which typically offers opportunities for all young people (of a particular age bracket) to engage in leisure-based activities, and to talk to youth workers in a safe, non-judgemental, non-targeted environment (Brent, 2013). Proponents of this type of work argue that its retention is fundamental to the informal, radical traditions of youth work, and is tied to the premise that meaningful relationships with young people should be developed on voluntary (rather than compulsory) terms (Taylor, 2014). The fall in membership of youth organisations in the 1980s and early 1990s was in large part due to the changing social habits of young people, who had more access to home entertainments and commercial leisure opportunities and less need or desire to socialise in youth centres (Jeffs, 2014). Cuts to state funding also left these clubs lacking the ability to modernise, and the dwindling numbers attending made it difficult for youth services to advocate for further resources. The seemingly outmoded and uncompetitive nature of these services meant there was a loss of confidence amongst politicians (and some practitioners) in the effectiveness of open access, club-based provision (Brent, 2013).

In many senses, the Thatcher/Major years brought about a key moment of divergence for the gallery education and youth sectors. Though the visual arts sector was the beneficiary of major investment (as politicians capitalised on the potential of cultural industries and destination galleries to lever regeneration), the profile and funding of the youth sector was simultaneously waning. In relation to youth policy, the government also largely focused its efforts on schooling and further education rather than informal education. This was reflected in the policy statements from the Arts Council in the 1980s, which explicitly concentrated on arts provision in state education (Doeser, 2015a). As described earlier, this period of professionalisation additionally triggered wider debate about the skills and experiences required to operate as a youth worker, which resulted in the promotion of a practice-based training regime that supported those with experience of disadvantage to enter youth work. These changes likely contributed to the progression of the increasingly working class identity of youth work (Batsleer, 2014). Under the advancing neoliberalism that characterised the late 1980s, the concept of community fell out of fashion, and the collaborative, pluralist climate that nurtured the community development and community arts movements was replaced by a more fiscally aggressive and individualised set of social conditions (Matarasso, 2013).

1997–2010: Partnership as a Tool for Governance

The election of a Labour government in 1997 was initially well received by the youth sector, which throughout history has most commonly aligned with left-leaning politics and socialist principles as a result of its frontline engagement with young people whose lives are affected by structural inequalities (Sercombe, 2015a). Rather than embrace the politics of socialism however, Tony Blair's centrist New Labour platform sought to entrench a neoliberal, pro-marketisation agenda across all forms of public life, through the adoption and promotion of New Public Management techniques (Sercombe, 2015a). New Public Management is a system driven by a belief in the benefits of applying private sector managerial methods to the running and administration of public sector institutions, and by the understanding that the market is the most effective mechanism for achieving best outcomes in the public sector (Entwistle et al., 2007; Sercombe, 2015b). This concept precipitated a fundamental reframing of the relationship between public sector workers and members of the public towards a transactional model based on inputs and outputs. Organisations would be tasked with evidencing the value of their outputs via the accumulation of data, and government (now reframed as 'purchaser' of provision rather than 'provider'), would contract out services to those organisations most able to quantify and qualify their worth and to meet government priorities (Sercombe, 2015a).

These reforms to the organisation and delivery of public services under New Labour were to have a profound and lasting impact on the status of the youth sector and on conceptions of 'partnership' (a favoured buzzword), as the government sought to create a climate of competition between public and private agencies and to remodel national youth associations as 'partners' of the state (Davies, 2010). Successive youth ministers in this Labour government criticised the youth service for its perceived patchiness, and as part of the New Labour agenda to modernise the welfare state, strove to instil New Public Management approaches across the sector (Davies, 2010). State-funded provision (e.g. in local authorities) had to shift its emphasis towards achieving statistical targets and outcomes, while in some areas, contracts for providing youth services were open to bids from external 'for-profit' organisations. Adapting to this funding environment, larger scale bodies representing voluntary and community organisations worked to professionalise their operations and developed increasingly business-like practices in readiness to secure contracts. These bodies, conceived as part of the 'Third sector', were regular recipients of government grants (Davies, 2010). These changes weighted responsibility for the creation of youth policy in the hands of state, as opposed to charitable organisations, and reduced the autonomy of the sector from government.

The notion of 'partnership' in this period became heavily politicised as some practitioners regarded its usage to be a veil for government's tightening oversight and monitoring of all aspects of the public sector (Davies and Wood, 2010; Davies, 2018). Those organisations in pursuit of government funding would have to participate in procurement, out-sourcing and commissioning processes and demonstrate their ability to perform government policy through extensive evaluating and reporting (Davies, 2018). 'Partnership' since the late 1990s therefore, seems to have had an association with performativity, competition and a loss of freedom and trust for grassroots youth workers (Young, 1999; de St Croix, 2016). Critics of the encroachment of neoliberal values in youth work remarked upon the shifts in the practice 'from voluntary participation to more coercive forms; from association to individualised activity; from education to case management; and from informal to formal and bureaucratic relationships' (Jeffs and Smith, 2010, p. 11). This critical faction argued that resources were being redirected away from practice-based, person-centred work to managers and administrators, and that measurement indicators failed to grasp the human qualities of youth work. The treasured concept of open access was also felt to be under even greater threat by New Labour's focus on specific social issues such as teenage pregnancy and youth unemployment. The governance orientation of partnership (Glendinning et al., 2002; Geddes, 2006) was grounded in the need to bring greater levels of efficiency and accountability and a more rigorous, coherent evidence base to areas such as youth work that had previously operated in relative isolation from state direction.

Another key development in the use of partnership as a signifier of governmental concerns was the initiation of programmes that encouraged 'joined-up working' across youth policy. In England in 2000, Labour launched the £420m Connexions youth service, as a response to findings from its Social Exclusion Unit that there was a lack of cooperation between the various agents implicated in supporting young people—including youth and health services, schools and careers agencies (Sercombe, 2015a). Ironically, the service focused on universal access, although it concentrated efforts on unemployed and disadvantaged young people, and it utilised youth work methods to engage young people and provide guidance on careers, education, housing and health matters through relationships with personal advisers. While this initiative seemed to portray an endorsement of youth work approaches, it received criticism for its perceived use of young people's personal data as a mode of surveillance (Smith, 2000, 2007).

The 2002 Department for Education and Skills publication *Transforming youth work* married the Connexions strategy with a series of other plans, including developing a curriculum for youth work, accreditation opportunities and performance indicators related to Connexions targets (Smith, 2002). Contemporary critique of these moves centred upon the seemingly formalised, bureaucratic, school-like nature of the policies and the tendency to target and label young people according to risk categories (Smith, 2002). The requirements of this new regime, which focused attention towards the supervision and guidance of individuals rather than group engagement, were seen (at least by youth studies academics and grassroots practitioners) to be in conflict with the practices and concerns of good youth work (de St Croix, 2010).

Connexions was not sustained long term as a national initiative for a number of reasons, including doubts over effectiveness and funding constraints (Smith, 2000, 2007). Joined-up working (particularly involving the police) was also highlighted as being problematic for youth workers, who derived their legitimacy amongst young people on the basis of a relationship of trust and discretion (Mason, 2015). The history of Connexions offers some further insight into youth work's fraught associations with cross-sector partnership, which has tended to result in the compromising of core youth work values and ethics. One of the other contributing factors said to have indirectly limited the longevity of the Connexions programme, was the restructuring of children's services under proposals from the 2003 government Green Paper *Every child matters*. This new initiative also called for greater levels of integration across services and increased the coordination and commissioning powers of local authorities, which ultimately became responsible for deciding how the scheme would be funded (Mason, 2015). The 2005 Green Paper *Youth matters* ushered in an enhanced tranche of ring-fenced funding (£115 million) for local authorities to spend on youth programmes, which represented 'the first capital funding for youth work in over 30 years' (Mason, 2015, p. 57). Nevertheless, Labour's restructuring led to many dedicated local authority youth services being amalgamated with children and young people's departments, and subsumed within multi-disciplinary teams (Davies, 2013). And in return for funding, state-supported agencies at local authority level were also obligated to meet centrally defined objectives. This period of relatively plentiful support for youth initiatives paradoxically helped to advance the erosion of the professional identity and autonomy of the youth worker.

The New Labour years produced mixed fortunes for the youth sector. While young people were in many respects the subjects and recipients of key policies and investments, the government's deficit–driven agendas and poor regard for the youth service soured an already tense relationship between grassroots youth work and the state. This also contributed to a further loss of unity in the sector, and to divisions between those agencies seen as complicit with the government's agenda, and those organisations and individuals who pledged to resist or challenge policy directives. The In Defence of Youth Work Campaign was founded in 2009 towards the end of Labour's second term to bring together critical voices and champion the types of practices deemed to be under threat by the prevailing governing parties. Academics and practitioners involved sought to advocate for the value of the 'voluntary principle' and democratic practice in youth work; the importance of starting from the concerns of young people, recognising their diversity and 'attending to the here-and-now of young people's experience rather than just focusing on "transitions"' (Taylor, 2016). Their activities congregated around conferences, seminars, publications and social media platforms including a blog and Facebook group. Its continuing presence serves to illuminate the persistent fragmentation of the sector, and youth work's almost permanent status of vulnerability.

Similar apprehensions were felt in the arts in this era, as generous funding for gallery education was understood to be coexistent with an increase in government influence and outcome-driven approaches to practice. However, the professional context in which these tensions arose was quite different to the occupational context of youth work. When Labour was elected on a wave of excitement about 'Cool Britannia', artists and pop culture took centre stage within the political narrative, and contemporary art and its institutions were championed as being good for society (Ballard et al., 2015). The opening of Tate Modern in 2000 was an important symbol of this energy and emotional investment. At the turn of the Millennium the Tate galleries represented the advent of a new era in the arts, where dialogues with new publics were prioritised through audience development policies, branding, the improved profile of education work and an orientation towards the 'language of experience' (Dewdney et al., 2013, p. 41). The early 2000s saw the beginnings of permanent peer-led youth programmes—then named 'Raw Canvas' at Tate Modern and 'Tate Forum' at Tate Britain—and the publication of *Testing the water: young people and galleries* (Horlock, 2000), which reflected on learning from the first six years of Tate Liverpool's peer-led programme 'Young Tate'.

Even though Tate had worked with young people beyond a schools context since 1988, this period of time marked a step-change in the institutional standing of peer-led youth programmes (Sinker, 2008). As well as employing many members of staff to its dedicated education departments, Tate and other organisations began titling education staff as 'Curators' of young people's programmes, schools programmes and so on, which helped to elevate the prominence of these roles in the broader arts sector (Charman, 2005). Engage, the National Association for Gallery Education also facilitated 'envision'—a cross-gallery programme resulting in a major resource about gallery education practice, policy and agendas (Wheeler and Walls, 2008). In the 2000s, with further investment from Lottery funds and the Clore Duffield Foundation into programmes and learning spaces, gallery educators enjoyed a heightened sense of status (Howell, 2009).

Whereas youth work entered the new Millennium as a relatively embattled practice requiring modernisation and dealing with decreasing numbers of young people—public art institutions, buoyed by the 'Tate effect', were welcoming growing first-time audiences for contemporary art (Nittve, 2016). While the opening of Tate Modern would also reinforce a new system of managerialism in public galleries, for those working in the relatively young field of gallery education, the institutionalisation of the practice would bring job security, employment rights and strong leadership to the profession (Allen and Raney, 2015). This then marks another point of divergence between the youth and arts sectors. As smaller visual arts organisations benefitted from the success of Tate Modern, and the generally collegial gallery education community strengthened, in the youth sector there was a rising culture of disunity amongst youth organisations, as competition intensified and larger agencies became the main recipients of funding. These distinctions are useful indicators of the source of some of the power imbalances that characterise the relationship between the arts and youth sectors.

However, there were, by the early-2000s, comparable debates being played out within the arts and youth sectors around the political imperative to focus on 'social exclusion', or to target young people 'at risk of social exclusion' (Jermyn, 2001; Sandell, 2003, p. 45; Watson, 2007). Just as the youth sector was tasked with redirecting its efforts towards the engagement of 'NEETs' (young people not in education, employment or training), or young people involved in 'anti-social behaviour' (Davies and Wood, 2010), museums and galleries would also be seen as potential vehicles for the tackling of entrenched societal issues (Douglas, 2009). At the same time, in recognition of evidence that participants for the arts were largely white, educated and middle class, the Arts Council under New Labour pursued a cultural diversity agenda, and encouraged its grantees to implement strategies to remove barriers to participation and broaden their audience base (Panayiotou, 2006). While the definition of 'diversity' was broad, there was a specific focus on racial and ethnic diversity, and on countering institutional discrimination (Panayiotou, 2006).

In relation to an understanding of partnership, the emphasis on diversity created a major incentive for galleries to seek out associations with specific youth organisations and services that might be able to provide access to so-called harder-to-reach young people. Research by the Gulbenkian Foundation in the late 1990s had shown that there were fewer instances of engagement work between galleries and youth services, as opposed to with the formal education sector, and that youth agencies were 'a comparatively under-used support system in terms of widening young people's attendance at cultural venues' (Harland and Kinder, 1999, p. 32). While galleries were not generally set up with the in-house expertise required to do the direct work of engaging marginalised young people via street based methods or referrals, youth organisations represented an opportunity to connect with an existing captive membership of young people from diverse backgrounds. Partnership working with the youth sector was therefore understood to be one of the most effective means of reaching socially excluded young people, who were more likely to be drawn to informal and alternative education provision than their less marginalised peers (Edmonds, 2008).

While partnership working between arts and youth organisations increased, it is worth noting that the vast majority of these partnerships were being initiated by arts organisations rather than by youth organisations (Jermyn, 2004). The motivation to connect with more diverse participants and to make a difference to the lives of young people through the arts was clear on the part of cultural workers (Edmonds, 2008). But for youth workers—galleries, museums and the visual arts were not recognised as natural sites of engagement for socially excluded young people. From a youth sector perspective, it seems there was a more consistent tradition of youth services working together with *youth arts* organisations (i.e. organisations where the core mission is youth participation). The National Youth Agency's (2009) publication: *Arts work with socially excluded young people* for instance limited its case studies to: music projects run as an integrated part of council youth services; community charities with arts provision and independent arts programmes targeting groups of young people (Morford, 2009). Galleries are seldom mentioned in this rare publication of arts based youth work and partnerships. This was (and still is) quite typical of academic and practice-based literature on arts engagement from a youth work perspective. In many publications, the arts are not mentioned at all, but where they are, the focus tends to be on the performing arts or street arts—for instance rap and other popular music, dance and graffiti. Interest has predominantly resided in art forms that young people are likely to be familiar with in their everyday lives, and in practices that young people can pick up themselves in a youth setting, rather than engagement with formal arts institutions.

For those organisations and services that did work together, one of the key concerns for practitioners was building capacity to develop measurements and evaluation techniques for assessing the social value of this work, and particularly its impact on young people's progression (Morford, 2009; Crossick and Kaszynska, 2016). Funders, local authorities and government expected to see evidence of outcomes from 'interventions' (as projects sometimes became known), and ideally evidence that provided clear confirmation that the work had made a positive difference to people's lives. This was particularly important in areas such as criminal justice work, where practitioners had to demonstrate the impact of arts projects on crime prevention, or on the reintegration of young offenders (Hughes, 2005). These pressures triggered a number of impact studies on arts and community participation (Hamilton et al., 2003; Argyle and Bolton, 2005; Macnaughton et al., 2005; Hacking et al., 2006; Daykin et al., 2008). The year 2005 also saw the launch of the Arts Award, which provided an accredited system of achievement for young people, designed for use by arts and youth organisations and schools, to provide tangible outcomes from arts engagements.

From an early stage in the development of this type of approach, concerns were being raised in the arts sector about qualifying and quantifying the arts in terms of non-arts related outcomes such as social, economic or health benefits (Holden, 2004; Belfiore and Bennett, 2008). For many academics and practitioners in the arts, this issue boiled down to a well-worn debate about the instrumental vs. intrinsic value of the arts (Belfiore, 2002; Sandell, 2004; Belfiore and Bennett, 2007; Gray, 2007; Vuyk, 2010; Crossick and Kaszynska, 2016). Critics argued that ambitions to deliver social change through the arts were not only highly questionable, but they also had the potential to compromise and supersede artistic ambitions, and therefore result in poor practice—both social and creative (Mirza, 2006). There were also concerns raised about the equity of the relationships between arts and community partners, the unrecognised power hierarchies embedded in institutions and the class-based divisions between programmes, which seemed to promote 'aesthetic values for the middle classes, instrumental outcomes for the poor and disadvantaged' (Lynch, 2001; Holden, 2004, p. 25). Some arts education practitioners were particularly wary of the paternalistic language deployed in engagement work with targeted groups of young people, and the potentially stigmatising effects of imposing policy labels such as 'hard-to-reach' or 'at risk', which seemed to ignore the cultural agency of young people and reinforce their marginalisation (Hall, 2001; Kester, 2013). These arguments reveal some of the enduring conflicts that lie behind partnerships between galleries and youth or community organisations, and that form the background to this text.

The international curatorial and academic art community also involved itself in theoretical debate about the shift towards socially engaged practice and the 'ethics of engagement' (Downey, 2009, p. 593), in the wake of the so-called 'collaborative turn' in contemporary art (Lind, 2007, p. 15; De Bruyne and Gielen, 2011; Jackson, 2011; Thompson, 2012). During this period, gallery education workers pushed harder for their field to be recognised as having initiated much of the dialogue and practice around institutional critique and social engagement, and they made the case for more integrated programming models, which would aim to position education staff on equal terms to exhibition staff in galleries and de-silo their work from the rest of the institution's activities (Tallant, 2008; Allen, 2008; Graham, 2008). From 2008 onwards, a number of landmark offsite projects accompanied these moves, including *The Street*, led by Marijke Steedman at Whitechapel Gallery (2008–2012); *The Edgware Road Project* (2008–present) led by Janna Graham and Sally Tallant at Serpentine Gallery and *Making Play*, managed by Frances Williams at South London Gallery (2008–2011). This generation of gallery education practitioners, most of whom came of age professionally under the neoliberal conditions of the late 1990s, sought to challenge the dominant instrumentalisation agenda by working in venues outside of their respective galleries, with communities of place and self-defined (sometimes politicised) communities such as market traders, migrant workers, housing associations and estate residents. These projects situated education staff and artists within socially diverse communities on a long-term, everyday basis—not as outreach—but as a gesture of commitment to working towards achieving 'equitable relations' in projects and privileging un-prescribed, critically responsive associations with people and contexts (Graham, 2012). While this type of approach was not commonplace across mainstream gallery education, these projects were duly celebrated by the gallery sector as innovations in participatory curatorship—and publica-tions, conferences, exhibitions and press attention were to follow (South London Gallery, 2011; Graham et al., 2012; Steedman, 2012).

The critical turn in gallery education is important because the ethos and arguments motivating certain sections of gallery education practice and dialogue in 2008 are similar to those of the In Defence of Youth Work campaign, which launched just one year later. By examining these parallel critical turns side-by-side, it is possible to discern a shared understanding in some areas of the youth and gallery education sectors, about the inher-ent value of voluntary relationships with different communities, and about the disempowering potential of adhering to dominant political rhetoric. Crucially however, while in youth work this critical stance was in defensive mode, in galleries it was praised as being new and exciting, and came with the backing of major funding from trusts and foundations (Townley and Bradby, 2009; The Museum Prize Trust, 2011; Seligman, 2012). The gal-lery sector, because of its broad remit, its 'arms-length' distance from gov-ernment and its ability to look elsewhere for funding, was able to effectively circumvent many of the directives that seemed to so profoundly affect the character of youth provision (Allen, 2008). If gallery education might have been a sympathetic, radical ally to critical, democratic youth work though, there is scant evidence that much dialogue was happening to this effect. From my own experience, entering the gallery education sector in 2008, partnerships with youth organisations and services were still associ-ated with instrumentalised practice and youth workers were not generally identified as politically coherent, radical communities.

The financial crisis of 2008 and consequent years of recession and aus-terity politics were to foster even greater waves of change, particularly for the youth sector, as budget cuts, club closures and workforce contraction fundamentally altered the landscape of youth provision in the UK (UNISON, 2014). Within this climate, and following the England street riots of summer 2011, there was a widespread social reawakening to the political disenfranchisement of young people, and gallery educators would seek to bolster their efforts towards working with marginalised young people and youth partners. In the meantime, the government discourse around partnership facilitated a new and increasingly destructive agenda: to shift funding obligations away from the state and in the process to de-professionalise many public services.

2010–2015: AUSTERITY AND THE BIG SOCIETY

The legacy of New Labour neoliberalism continued to be felt during the years of the Conservative/Liberal Democrat Coalition government from 2010 to 2015, as ministers embraced the project of marketisation through contracting out youth services and encouraging competition (Davies, 2013). However while the Labour government implemented national frameworks, the Coalition government prioritised a localism strategy—premised on the concept of power devolution, and designed to reorient the way public services were financed and delivered (Kraftl et al., 2012). The cornerstone of the dominant Conservative party's political ideology at the time was the 'Big Society' (Cabinet Office, 2010)—a cross-departmental mantra that brought together the government's claim to want to encourage community-led volunteerism and social action. The Big Society plan was pitched as a response to the economic crisis that was used to justify major cuts, and it pledged to 'introduce new powers to help communities save local facilities and services threatened with closure, and give communities the right to bid to take over local state-run services' (Cabinet Office, 2010, p. 1). It therefore signalled a clear aspiration to transfer local services from the public sector to the voluntary and private sectors (de St Croix, 2015).

The Coalition approach to youth policy, as detailed in the 2011 *Positive for youth* paper, committed to a focus on local partnerships and local leadership, and on handing responsibility to local authorities to identify areas of need, commission programmes and distribute resources. This policy document suggested that young people should be involved and consulted throughout the coordination and delivery of youth services, and that services should be accountable to local authorities rather than central government (Cabinet Office and Department for Education, 2010). The *Positive for youth* strategy put the onus on community leaders, voluntary groups, local youth organisations, charities, statutory bodies, commissioners and businesses working together to maximise resources and develop new funding opportunities. This proposal seemingly promoted a less top-down approach to youth policy implementation, however the wider reduction in funding to local authorities and removal of ring-fencing around youth service budgets meant that in reality, many councils significantly reduced or cut their youth service offer and redirected funding towards areas where there was greater statutory pressure to sustain services (McGimpsey, 2015). The partnership model prescribed in *Positive for youth* essentially utilised the language of community collaboration in order to absolve central government of its responsibility to invest in youth services.

Despite the Coalition's localism agenda, the government did funnel substantial funding into some flagship national initiatives, including the National Citizen Service (NCS) youth volunteering and residential programme, and the Youth Contract scheme aimed at 16 and 17 year olds out of work and education. The NCS in particular represented David Cameron's vision to create a programme that would be seen as a rite of passage for school leavers, and that would encourage young people lacking direction to become socially conscious and responsible citizens (Davies, 2018). Nevertheless the NCS encountered significant criticism for diverting funds from youth services towards short-term projects with the already-engaged (Taylor, 2013; Murphy, 2014) and the Youth Contract was scrapped early, amid reports that it also failed to meet its targets (Pickard, 2014). Youth work received a further blow in 2013 when the then Secretary of State for Education Michael Gove (who had shown little interest in the youth service) decided to shift responsibility for the youth service onto the Cabinet Office—regarded by some as the 'dustbin department' (Jeffs, 2015, p. 12)—thus apparently underlining the government's lack of faith in the pedagogical, professional capacities of youth services.

By 2014, the impact of the austerity-related cuts on council-run youth services was becoming clear. The Connexions service had ended; the youth service lost at least £60 million of funding between 2012 and 2014; around 350 youth centres were closed and more than 2000 youth workers were made redundant (UNISON, 2014). Some councils that retained funding for youth services would need to adapt to a capacity building model, where youth workers would be recast as commissioners, and tasked with training volunteers to do the work previously carried out by qualified youth workers (Buckland, 2013). The identity of the youth sector was being remodelled, and as such, its identity as a partner (and ability to work in partnership) was in constant flux.

From 2009, arts and culture funding was also hit by significant cuts to local authority budgets, Department for Culture, Media and Sport (DCMS) and the national Arts Councils—however partly because of its mixed funding model, the gallery sector was relatively safeguarded from closures or widespread job losses. As with the youth sector, 'partnership' and its social and economic incentives were at the centre of Arts Council England's policies during the Coalition government. The national schools programme Creative Partnerships stopped receiving government funding in 2011, but many of the associated regional hubs became Arts Council-funded Bridge Organisations from 2012—taking on a remit to help connect the cultural sector with the education and youth sectors in ten regions across England. The Arts Council's vision was one of 'Grand Partnerships', where arts organisations might work strategically within their wider locality through enterprising alliances with councils, planning bodies, education institutions, public sector services, commercial businesses and other cultural agencies. The 'Grand Partnership' was talked about as a 'transformative opportunity', which had the power to unlock funds for the regions (Bazalgette, 2013, p. 8).

In order to further develop frameworks for establishing connections with local authorities, Arts Council England also invested in the Cultural Commissioning Programme, delivered in partnership with the National Council for Voluntary Organisations (NCVO), which aimed to better prepare the arts sector to work with commissioners and secure contracts to 'deliver' elements of local public services in areas such as crime prevention or mental health (Bagwell et al., 2014). Arguably, the government and the Arts Council were advocating for arts organisations to engage in contractual relationships as service providers, in order to 'fill in the gaps' left open by cuts to social services (Osborne, 2016). These developments represented efforts to formalise and marketise the work of cross-sector partnership. While this overt instrumentalisation agenda was contentious, some leading figures in the arts believed that the concept of connecting artists with public sector provision and civic diplomacy held powerful subversive potential (Garrard, cited in Caines, 2014).

One result of all the aforementioned issues around government cuts and policy decisions that disproportionately and negatively affected the young was a renewed desire in the gallery education sector to work together with the youth sector, and to focus programming energy towards young people from disadvantaged backgrounds, who seemed to have borne the brunt of the Coalition's cuts. Tate's four year, £5 million programme Circuit was conceived both as a reaction to the circumstances that contributed to the 2011 riots, and as a response to calls from service providers for there to be a more 'sustained offer for young people who are hardest to reach' (Suntharalingam, 2012). For Tate in 2012, collaboration had 'never been more important' (Serota, 2012, p. 5), and its newly launched Plus Tate initiative would link the institution to a national network of regional galleries, which multiplied its collaborative capacity. Discourses of 'partnership' and 'collaboration' would also not go unchallenged during this period, and Tate was involved in developing more nuanced, critical discussion around these concepts (Bak Mortensen and Nesbitt, 2012).

Beyond Tate and the policy context, funders such as the Paul Hamlyn Foundation (PHF) were also playing a key role in the advancement of research and critical practice around partnership. In 2011, PHF published an influential report, *Whose cake is it anyway?* (Lynch, 2011), which became the driver for a subsequent programme: *Our Museum: communities and museums as active partners* (2012–2015). Lynch's uncompromising findings revealed that museums were frequently engaged in a cycle of short-term relationships; that alliances with community partners were not embedded, and that claims made to empower and include partners in decision-making were disingenuous. Lynch's report charged some of the museums involved in the study with treating community organisations as 'passive beneficiaries' rather than 'active partners' (Lynch, 2011, p. 14, 7). This report and the *Our Museum* programme argued that active partnership should exist at the centre (rather than the periphery) of an arts organisation's priorities. They also precipitated a body of interrogatory work examining organisational barriers to equitable partnership practice (Bienkowski, 2015, 2016). With these ideas circulating in the art sector, Paul Hamlyn Foundation funded a number of other projects, specific to the arts and youth sectors, which involved action research around cross-sector partnership working. They included *Future Stages* at Ovalhouse theatre in London (2013–2015) and an associated network for youth and arts practitioners called *Creating Change*, as well as Circuit from 2013.

Simultaneously, the Department for Education funded *Strong Voices*, which ran concurrently to Circuit for two years (2013–2015) and involved five regional Bridge organisations. This action research programme addressed the question: 'Are there mutual benefits to professionals from the arts and youth sectors working in partnership to deliver arts provision in youth clubs?' (Stavrinou, 2015). The resulting investigation produced a number of programmes, reports, events, and an online archive of material, some of which I draw upon later.

Projects such as these offered evidence of the rising levels of attention in arts and funding organisations towards partnership working with the youth sector. By 2015, there were calls—across both the arts and youth sectors—to develop a more rigorous understanding of partnership methodologies, and to bring greater levels of intelligibility to ambiguous and uncritical conceptualisations of collaboration (Davies, 2015; Doeser 2015b; Cunningham, 2016).

2016–2019: Division, Activism and New Moral Panics

Across the UK and internationally, 2016 saw the start of a series of major democratic upheavals that seemed to indicate deep discontent amongst communities who were feeling disenfranchised by globalised neoliberal politics and economically neglected by years of austerity. The decision (by a slim majority) of the UK's voting public to leave the European Union, and the election of Donald Trump in the United States were seen as key symptoms of volatile social division between classes, generations, ethnic groups and geographies. The campaigns and media circuses around these events propelled views around nationalism and anti-immigration into the public consciousness. These political movements appeared to underline critical divergences between the likes of art world communities (stereotypically associated with pro-EU, metropolitan elitism) and marginalised communities (stereotypically associated with anti-EU sentiment and being 'left behind') (Harris, 2018). While the reality of the situation was and is much more complex, the polarising referendum debates stoked a climate of discord and resentment across communities and the outcome fuelled increasing concern over young people's futures and the prosperity of the arts and youth sectors (Coburn and Gormally, 2017; Brown, 2018; Jones, 2019).

Between 2016 and early 2019, it was reported that UK youth services budgets were cut by £13.3 million, which (although less than previous years) would bring total cuts since 2010 to £400 million. At least 160 youth centres closed between 2016 and early 2019 and 892 youth worker jobs were lost (UNISON, 2019). Youth worker surveys revealed that a majority of respondents felt a lack of confidence around the financial stability of their organisation or service and the quality of support provided (UNISON, 2019). Between 2016 and 2018, the Conservative government did invest £40 million in a Youth Investment Fund to develop youth facilities and £11 million in an 'Early Intervention Youth Fund'. These initiatives, and other investments connected to young people's mental health, employment and uniformed youth services were seen by critics in the youth sector as 'gesture policies'—papering over the problems created by widespread cuts to youth provision (Davies, 2018, p. 355). Depleted budgets and the rising costs of social care also led to further arts cuts in local authorities. Since 2010 £400 million has reportedly been cut from local authority spending on arts and culture—the exact same figure as has been cut from youth services (Butler, 2019). As previously stated, the mixed income model of museums and galleries protected most institutions from closure, but the loss of arts officers and arts services in local authorities dismantled some of the infrastructure that would have supported regional partnership (Romer, 2016).

While there is awareness within the art sector about the extent of the cuts facing youth services in the name of austerity, there is less awareness about evolving forms of service delivery based on the reshaping of youth provision financing. In what has been characterised as 'late-neoliberal' policy, funding for the youth sector is being directed towards newly created bodies able to claim an ability to produce a social return on investment (McGimpsey, 2018). The social return approach involves a cost-benefit analysis where a monetary value is assigned to the future societal benefits and potential savings made as a result of a service investment. Where local authorities once acted as the main distributors of funding sources for the youth sector, large social investment intermediary bodies are now receiving and distributing funds to a range of delivery partners (McGimpsey, 2018). The organisational makeup of the youth sector has changed to reflect this new landscape and there is a growing focus on predefined aims and targets, 'fixed term interventions' and the 'datafication' of young people (McGimpsey, 2018, p. 236). In this reformed market, local grassroots and open access youth services are once again being deprioritised by the field of power, as funding is increasingly channelled towards investment-ready consortia, larger charities and social enterprises.

An example of this redirection of capital is the case of the NCS, the national youth programme initiated by David Cameron with a multi-million pound annual budget, piloted in 2011. When Cameron resigned as Prime Minister following the EU Referendum, the first role he took up was as Chair of Patrons at NCS (Weakley, 2016). This move coincided with the introduction of the NCS Bill to Parliament, which would go on to ensure that the service was given royal assent and made 'statutory'—a status that has been repeatedly denied to local authority youth services

(Davies, 2018). While the NCS is in some cases delivered through local youth services, criticisms have consistently been raised about the high costs per young person allocated for NCS engagement versus the (lower) costs per young person of providing year round provision (Davies, 2018). In 2018, it emerged that the government was spending 95% of its funding for youth services on NCS, even though in some years (e.g. 2016) take up was as low as 12% of eligible young people (Walker, 2018). Announcing that it would be spending £1 billion between 2017 and 2020 with £10 million going towards a rebrand in 2019, the NCS continued to attract criticism from the media, youth sector and council leaders, who noted the injustice of the government investing heavily in a programme that was failing to meet its targets while youth clubs around the country were closing and youth workers were losing jobs (Lepper, 2019).

From a partnership perspective, NCS links with the Arts Award to support young people to gain accredited qualifications through their creative social action projects. However, there seems to be minimal evidence of interaction between NCS and the gallery and museum sector. While I have heard of galleries providing space for NCS events, it is much more common to see galleries partnering or collaborating with local services or organisations than youth consortia or citizenship schemes such as NCS, the Duke of Edinburgh's Award or the Scout Association for instance. Moreover, the discourse of social investment is not only little understood in the arts, but the very amalgamation of social impact and finance capital is repellent to many in the cultural sector. Attempts made to produce standardised metrics to quantify the value of artistic quality or social impact in the sector for instance have met with considerable resistance (Hill, 2017). While some arts and community projects are using the social return on investment model, the majority attitude towards these types of measurements tends to be one of deep scepticism, and there is not the same level of pressure to apply these models in the arts as there is in youth services. The visual arts sector (like the more critical faction of the youth sector) is willingly engaged in rigorous evaluation, research and critical discussion of its impact, but the political desire to frame impact in economic terms is consistently problematised (Belfiore, 2015). It could be argued that in order to work sustainably with the youth sector in its current state, arts organisations should play the game of demonstrating the long-term fiscal value of their partnership work. A counter argument could be that the policy landscape is shifting so rapidly and the political future is so uncertain that collaborative resistance and creative rethinking of the value debate may be a more worthwhile collective endeavour.

By way of evidencing the changeability of the landscape, in 2016 it was confirmed (after three years of being moved to the Cabinet Office), that responsibility for national youth policy would be transferred to the Department for Culture, Media and Sport (DCMS). National youth sector bodies such as UK Youth and then Youth Minister Rob Wilson welcomed the opportunity to form stronger links between the youth, arts and sporting sectors as a result of this move (Offord, 2016; Davies, 2018). However, the move also seemed to have the effect of stalling progress on a specific youth strategy (Puffett, 2017). With plans for a youth policy statement abandoned in 2017, DCMS instead released a Civil Society Strategy, which reiterated the government's vision for greater levels of collaboration between communities and private and public sector organisations and for cross-sector partnership and increased commissioning to improve opportunities for young people (DCMS, 2018). The strategy also reinforced concern about the quality of the youth sector's data and evidence base and pledged to invest more in evaluation through the Youth Investment Fund. A review of the statutory guidance provided to local authorities was promised to address the deprioritisation of youth services in councils. Across the youth sector there was a mixed response to the strategy, with endorsement for the review but disappointment expressed at the lack of new commitments and lack of attention given to the structural barriers facing disadvantaged young people (Howell, 2018; NYA, 2018; UK Youth, 2018). Following the release of the strategy an All-Party Parliamentary Group (APPG) of Youth Affairs presented findings sourced from consultation across the youth sector about the direction of youth provision in the UK, and this too revealed a catalogue of shortcomings. The APPG reported that the funding and policy conditions had nearly decimated open access or universal provision in some regions (leading to many young people being 'overlooked'); that there is poor coordination and understanding of youth provision at local and national levels; that there are huge disparities between regional offers for young people; that much of the current work is short term and targeted in nature and that there is inconsistent support and training standards for the youth sector workforce (APPG, 2018). A key message coming from the sector focused on the need to sustain universal or open access provision. And one of the key recommendations of the report was that youth work be recognised as a form of education and that responsibility for youth policy should be placed with the Department for Education.

If we consider all of these issues in relation to Bourdieu's concept of fields, it appears evident that the youth sector 'field' is incoherent and disjointed in its composition. Funding and policy conditions have created internal conflicts, reduced infrastructure and produced a weakened professional space that is difficult for external fields to understand. The movement of the youth policy remit from the Department for Education to the Cabinet Office and then to DCMS (with calls for it to be moved again) reveal that the youth sector also doesn't sit easily with broader fields of power. The visual arts sector is a more confident and seemingly coherent field, with ties to different fields of power such as commerce, the art market, corporate and individual philanthropy, trusts and foundations, academia, celebrity, media, as well as government (Grenfell and Hardy, 2007; Thorpe, 2019). Although in recent years, there has been increased critical scrutiny of the ethical conduct of benefactors and the entanglement of the arts with big business and gentrification (Bishop, 2013; Pritchard, 2018; Neate, 2019). While the visual arts sector (and the artists working within it) may have a licence to work in ways that are oppositional, risky, open-ended, activist and community-focused, the sector is still accountable or beholden to the agendas of multiple fields. Bourdieu was himself vocal about the problem of artists' interdependence with critics and collectors, and the effects this could have on their freedom to be antagonistic (Grenfell and Hardy, 2007). Perhaps the difference is that the concepts of critical autonomy and integrity in art practice are fiercely cherished and in many ways respected by the fields of power that support and govern it. There is a culture of healthy internal critique and debate that emboldens the arts and artists and also holds them to account.

The practices associated with gallery education specifically (whether labelled as participatory, socially engaged or collaborative etc.) have continued to ascend in value in the fields of power relevant to the art world. The Culture White Paper released in 2016 put public engagement, partnership, inclusion and diversity at the forefront of its messaging (DCMS, 2016). Former heads of education teams now sit as directors of major institutions (e.g. Caro Howell at the Foundling Museum in London, Esme Ward at Manchester Museum and Sally Tallant at Queen's Museum, New York). When the expanded Tate Modern opened in 2016, this also launched the start of the institution's 'open experiment' Tate Exchange, which would position over 65 organisations as 'Associates', who would co-programme activity within the gallery to 'explore the role of art in society' (Wilmot, 2017, p. 7). Meanwhile new grant funding has been announced to support The Whitworth Art Gallery in Manchester and Van Abbemuseum in Eindhoven, the Netherlands to embark upon a joint project called 'The Constituent Museum' which seeks to reframe the role of the museum and position relationships with visitors and communities as the core purpose of their activity (McGivern, 2019). This turn towards experimental co-production and the extension of the listening, collaborative function of the visual arts institution to its managerial centre is becoming more and more commonplace in contemporary practice (Byrne et al., 2018). Across Europe, calls for arts institutions to support social change, represent marginalised voices and engage in practices of cultural democracy have arguably never been louder (Bishop, 2013; Calouste Gulbenkian Foundation, 2017).

So while the youth and arts sectors both continue to be used as vehicles for neoliberal government policy, there are forces of resistance and subversion at play in both fields, and there is a common aspiration to focus energies on grassroots activity and localised collaboration and to redefine traditional hierarchies of knowledge and cultural value. The histories of these sectors show that this current turn is not particularly 'new'. Rather the definitions of what is constituted 'radical practice' have shifted within the broader neoliberal context (Ball et al., 2015). For the reasons described above however, the logic of the youth sector is particularly vulnerable to instrumentalisation. By 2018 for instance, the moral panic surrounding increased knife crime (particularly in London) had put conversations about cuts to youth services onto the top of the news agenda. But the discourse had positioned the role of youth work as 'soft policing'—as a preventative intervention to tackle violent crime rather than as a pedagogical practice in its own right (Taylor, 2018). These misinterpretations (and misrecognitions of structural problems) are also nothing new in the field of youth work.

The years between 2016 and 2019 have been marred by the political chaos precipitated by 'Brexit' that has diverted attention from domestic issues and slowed legislative progress. What the EU Referendum *did* do was destabilise the global field of power and undermine the political orthodoxy that has established neoliberal concepts of partnership as an accepted good. Other significant events in 2017 and 2018 such as the devastating Grenfell Tower fire, the bankruptcy of Conservative-led

Northamptonshire county council and the liquidation of construction company Carillion amplified public critique around the effects of outsourcing contracts to profit-making companies (Williamson, 2017; Davies, 2018; Jones, 2018). The groundswell of activist movements on all sides of the political spectrum revealed an appetite for grassroots organising and a yearning for a sense of community that has eroded over recent decades (Harris, 2018). In these unpredictable circumstances, it is possible to imagine that the dominant neoliberal ideology could be re-thought and a less instrumentalised, more progressive policy landscape might emerge. But there is also the possibility for hostility and economic conditions to worsen further, and for organisations to be forced into ever more constricting and compromised relationships.

CONCLUSION

This chronology of the intersecting histories of youth work and gallery education tells a story of convergences and disparities—illustrating how the fields emerged out of similar social and political movements and have since fostered similar critical and moral values. It is notable that the history of youth work is written by more male than female voices, and the history of gallery education is conveyed predominantly by women. This reflects the gender differences of the two workforces—which also differ along class lines. While youth work has (since its beginnings as a pursuit of the middle classes) become a progressively working class occupation and more recently de-professionalised (Batsleer, 2014) the gallery education workforce has become increasingly professionalised, and its workforce consistently middle class, white, economically secure and highly educated (Needlands et al., 2015, p. 35; Create, 2015).

There are ongoing internal contests for dominance and resistance in the youth and art sectors, with conflicting 'systems of value' in both fields, driven by neoliberal ideology on the one hand, and emancipatory, radical traditions on the other (Bishop, 2013, p. 61). This climate of antagonism is common to both practices; however, in relative terms, gallery education has experienced a gradual elevation of its status, while youth work's position in relation to the field of power has become increasingly unstable. Throughout modern history in the UK, youth work has fallen in and out of favour with governments of the day, and is ironically most likely to receive attention when moral panics or negative social attitudes towards young people intensify. The practices associated with gallery education however have become steadily more visible and embedded in institutional programming and cultural policy as part of growing interest in the civic role of the institution. This unequal distribution of power and agency makes galleries the more privileged partner in a youth/arts organisational relationship.

Potentially most revealing however is the evidence accrued throughout this history that the idea of cross-field partnership has become a construct, where it was once a normalised and necessary state of being for youth and arts practitioners. The professional distancing of these fields has led to a patchy and (in some senses) problematic record of collaborative work. The broader instability of the youth sector and lack of appreciation for the value of youth work as a discipline has led to many youth services compromising their values and servicing the agenda of other organisations through partnerships (Young, 1999). But there is also clear opportunity for alliance and common ground to draw upon. The fact that government policy for arts and youth now lies under the same department could provide the basis for more strategic links between the sectors. And the growing critique of neoliberal concepts of partnership presents the opportunity to reinvent collaborative associations on more grassroots terms.

REFERENCES

Allen, Felicity. 2008. Situating gallery education. In *Tate Encounters—[E]dition 2*. Accessed 20 February 2014. http://www2.tate.org.uk/tate-encounters/edition-2/tateencounters2_felicity_allen.pdf.

Allen, Felicity, and Karen Raney. 2015. Maintaining a radical vision. *Engage 35: The International Journal of Visual Art and Gallery Education: Twenty-five Years of Gallery Education*: 20–30.

APPG. 2018. APPG on youth affairs: Youth work inquiry. Recommendations and summary.

Argyle, Elaine, and Gillie Bolton. 2005. Art in the community for potentially vulnerable mental health groups. *Health Education* 105 (5): 340–354.

Bagwell, Sally, David Bull, Iona Joy, and Marina Svistak. 2014. *Opportunities for alignment: Arts and cultural organisations and public sector commissioning*. NCP Cultural Commissioning Programme.

Bak Mortensen, Marie, and Judith Nesbitt, eds. 2012. *On collaboration*. London: Tate.

Ball, Malcolm, Tania De St Croix, and Louise Doherty. 2015. Creating spaces for radical youth work? In *Innovation in youth work*. London: YMCA George Williams College.

Ballard, Liz, Lawrence Bradby, Croose Myhill, Bethan Lewis, and Natalie Zervou. 2015. Five terms from the lexicon of gallery education. *Engage 35: The International Journal of Visual Art and Gallery Education: Twenty-five Years of Gallery Education*: 41–48.

Banks, Sarah. 2010. Ethics and the youth worker. In *Ethical issues in youth work: Second edition*, ed. Sarah Banks, 3–23. Oxon: Routledge.

Batsleer, Janet. 2014. Educating for a disappearing profession? The case of youth and community work. *BERA Conference*, London, 23–25 September 2014.

Bazalgette, Peter. 2013. *Sir Peter Bazalgette's inaugural lecture as Chair, Arts Council England at the RSA*, 20 March 2013.

Belfiore, Eleonora. 2002. Art as a means of alleviating social exclusion: Does it really work? A critique of instrumental cultural policies and social impact studies in the UK. *International Journal of Cultural Policy* 8 (1): 91–106.

———. 2015. 'Impact', 'value' and 'bad economics': Making sense of the problem of value in the arts and humanities. *Arts and Humanities in Higher Education* 14 (1): 95–110.

Belfiore, Eleonora, and Oliver Bennett. 2007. Rethinking the social impacts of the arts. *International Journal of Cultural Policy* 13 (20): 135–151.

———. 2008. *The social impact of the arts: An intellectual history*. Basingstoke: Palgrave Macmillan.

Berger, John, and Margaret Busby. 2001. Glenn Thompson. *The Guardian*, September 12.

Bienkowski, Piotr. 2015. *Museum Association seminar: Take your partners: Creating sustainable participation*. Millennium Centre, Cardiff, 16 June 2015.

———. 2016. *No longer us and them: How to change into a participatory museum and gallery: Learning from the Our Museum programme*. London: Paul Hamlyn Foundation.

Bishop, Claire. 2013. *Radical museology: Or, what's 'contemporary' in museums of contemporary art?* London: Koenig Books.

Bourdieu, Pierre, and Loïc Wacquant. 1992. *An invitation to reflexive sociology*. Cambridge: Polity Press in association with Blackwell Publishers.

Bradford, Simon. 2015. State beneficence or government control? Youth work from circular 1486 to 1996. In *Youth work histories, policy and contexts*, ed. Graham Bright, 22–37. London: Palgrave Macmillan.

Brent, Colin. 2013. Lost in the middle: Reappraising the role of the youth centre in youth work provision. *Youth Policy*. Accessed 4 November 2016. http://www.youthpolicy.org/blog/youth-work-community-work/lost-in-the-middle-reappraising-the-role-of-the-youth-centre/.

Bright, Graham. 2015. The early history of youth work practice. In *Youth work histories, policy and contexts*, ed. Graham Bright, 1–21. London: Palgrave Macmillan.

Brown, Mark. 2018. Brexit is black cloud for UK arts, says former National Theatre boss. *The Guardian*, October 12.

Buckland, Lesley. 2013. Positive for youth. A critique. *The Encyclopaedia of Informal Education*. Accessed 1 October 2016. http://infed.org/mobi/positive-for-youth-a-critique/.

Butler, Patrick. 2019. Councils say more arts cuts inevitable amid rising social care need. *The Guardian*, January 28.

Byrne, John, Elinor Morgan, November Paynter, Aida Sánchez de Serdio, and Adela Železnik, eds. 2018. *The constituent museum: Constellations of knowledge, politics and mediation: A generator of social change*. Amsterdam: Valiz.

Cabinet Office. 2010. Building the Big Society. *Gov.uk*. Accessed 2 July 2015. https://www.gov.uk/government/publications/building-the-big-society.

Cabinet Office and Department for Education. 2010. Positive for youth: A new approach to cross-government policy for young people aged 13 to 19. *Gov.uk*. Accessed 3 October 2015. https://www.gov.uk/government/publications/positive-for-youth-a-new-approach-to-cross-government-policy-for-young-people-aged-13-to-19.

Calouste Gulbenkian Foundation. 2017. *Rethinking relationships: Inquiry into the civic role of arts organisations. Phase 1 report*. London: Calouste Gulbenkian Foundation UK Branch.

Charman, Helen. 2005. Uncovering professionalism in the art museum: An exploration of key characteristics of the working lives of education curators at Tate Modern. *Tate Papers No. 3*. Accessed 3 March 2014. http://www.tate.org.uk/research/publications/tate-papers/03/uncovering-professionalism-in-the-art-museum-exploration-of-key-characteristics-of-the-working-lives-of-education-curators-at-tate-modern.

Coburn, Annette, and Sinéad Gormally. 2017. Beyond Brexit: The impact of leaving the EU on the Youth Work Sector. *Youth & Policy*. Accessed 8 August 2018. https://www.youthandpolicy.org/articles/beyond-brexit-the-impact-of-leaving-the-eu-on-the-youth-work-sector/.

Create. 2015. Panic survey. *Create London*. Accessed 3 December 2015. http://www.createlondon.org/panic/survey/.

Crossick, Geoffrey, and Patrycja Kaszynska. 2016. *Understanding the value of arts and culture: The AHRC cultural value project*. Swindon: Arts and Humanities Research Council.

Cunningham, Jocelyn. 2016. A spectrum of change. *People place power conference*, Cast, Doncaster, 28 September 2016.

Davies, Bernard. 2010. Policy analysis: A first and vital skill of practice. In *What is youth work?* ed. Janet Batsleer and Bernard Davies, 7–19. Exeter: Learning Matters.

———. 2013. Youth work in a changing policy landscape: The view from England. *Youth and Policy* 110: 6–32.

Davies, Bernard. 2018. *Austerity, youth policy and the deconstruction of the youth service in England*. Cham, Switzerland: Palgrave Macmillan.

———. 2019. Decade of cuts: The policies that have dismantled youth work. *Children & Young People Now*, January 29.

Davies, Bernard, and Emily Wood. 2010. Youth work practice within integrated youth support services. In *What is youth work?* ed. Janet Batsleer and Bernard Davies, 73–89. Exeter: Learning Matters.

Davies, Richard, 2015. Partnership: A philosophical consideration. *BERA conference 2015*, Queen's University Belfast, 17 September 2015.

Daykin, Norma, Ellie Byrne, Tony Soteriou, and Susan O'Connor. 2008. The impact of art, design and environment in mental healthcare: A systematic review of the literature. *The Journal of the Royal Society for the Promotion of Health* 128 (2): 85–94.

DCMS. 2016. *The culture white paper*. DCMS.

———. 2018. *Civil society strategy: Building a future that works for everyone*. DCMS. Accessed 23 March 2019. https://www.gov.uk/government/publications/civil-society-strategy-building-a-future-that-works-for-everyone.

De Bruyne, Paul, and Pascal Gielen, eds. 2011. *Community art: The politics of trespassing*. Amsterdam: Valiz.

de St Croix, Tania. 2010. Youth work and the surveillance state. In *What is youth work?* ed. Janet Batsleer and Bernard Davies, 140–152. Exeter: Learning Matters.

———. 2015. Volunteers and entrepreneurs? Youth work and the big society. In *Youth work histories, policy and contexts*, ed. Graham Bright, 58–79. London: Palgrave Macmillan.

———. 2016. *Questioning the youth impact agenda. Evidence and impact essay collection*. London: The Centre for Youth Impact.

Dewdney, Andrew, David Dibosa, and Victoria Walsh. 2013. *Post-critical museology: Theory and practice in the art museum*. Oxon: Routledge.

Doeser, James. 2015a. *Step by step: Arts policy and young people 1944–2014*. London: King's College London.

———. 2015b. The drive to partner. In *The art of partnering*, ed. Jane Ellison, 32–38. London: King's College London.

Douglas, Anthony. 2009. *Partnership working*. Oxon: Routledge.

Downey, Anthony. 2009. An ethics of engagement: Collaborative art practices and the return of the ethnographer. *Third Text* 23 (5): 593–603.

Duncan, Carol. 1995. *Civilizing rituals*. Oxon: Routledge.

Edmonds, Kathy. 2008. Making connections: Widening participation in the arts for young people through dynamic partnerships. *Engage 22 Young People and Agency*: 57–62.

Entwistle, Tom, Michael Marinetto, and Rachel Ashworth. 2007. Introduction: New Labour, the new public management and changing forms of human resource management. *International Journal of Human Resource Management* 18 (9): 1569–1574.

Garrard, Hadrian. 2014. In Matthew Caines. Arts head: Hadrian Garrard, director, Create. *The Guardian*, September 2.

Geddes, Mike. 2006. Partnership and the limits to local governance in England: Institutionalist analysis and neoliberalism. *International Journal of Urban and Regional Research* 30 (1): 76–97.

Gefter, Asya, and Pete Young. 2013. *Radical community arts centres in 1970s and 1980s Hackney: What legacy?* Open School East, London, 21 November 2013.

Gielen, Pascal. 2012. Artistic praxis and the neoliberalization of the educational space. In *Teaching art in the neoliberal realm*, ed. Pascal Gielen and Paul De Bruyne, 15–31. Amsterdam: Valiz.

Glendinning, Caroline, Martin Powell, and Kirstein Rummery. 2002. *Partnerships, New Labour and the governance of welfare*. Bristol: Policy Press.

Graham, Janna. 2008. Un-role-ing the Educational Role of the Museum: Toward a radical diplomacy? *Situating Gallery Education*. Association of Art Historians Annual Conference, Tate Britain, London, 2–4 April 2008.

———. 2012. Inherent tensions. In *Gallery as community: Art, education, politics*, ed. Marijke Steedman, 197–219. London: Whitechapel Gallery.

Graham, Janna, et al., eds. 2012. *On the Edgware road*. London: Serpentine Gallery; Koenig Books.

Gray, Clive. 2007. Commodification and instrumentality in cultural policy. *International Journal of Cultural Policy* 13 (2): 203–215.

Grenfell, Michael, and Cheryl Hardy. 2007. *Art rules: Pierre Bourdieu and the visual arts*. Oxford: Berg.

Hacking, Sue, Jenny Secker, Lyn Kent, Jo Shenton, and Helen Spandler. 2006. Mental health and arts participation: The state of the art in England. *The Journal of the Royal Society for the Promotion of Health* 126 (3): 121–127.

Hall, Roz. 2001. Tailor-made practice. *Engage 11 Inclusion Under Pressure*: 43–49.

Hamilton, C., S. Hinks, and M. Petticrew. 2003. Arts for health: Still searching for the holy grail. *Journal of Epidemiology and Community Health* 27: 401–402.

Hanley, Lynsey. 2016. *Keynote: People place power: Increasing arts engagement: A national conference*, Cast, Doncaster, 28 September 2016.

Harland, John, and Kay Kinder, eds. 1999. *Crossing the line: Extending young people's access to cultural venues*. London: Calouste Gulbenkian Foundation.

Harris, John. 2018. Britain's insecure towns aren't 'left behind'. They hold the key to our future. *The Guardian*, September 17.

Harvie, Jen. 2013. *Fair play: Art, performance and neoliberalism*. Basingstoke: Palgrave Macmillan.

Hill, Liz. 2017. "Only a fool or a knave" trusts quality metrics, say academics. *Arts Professional*, June 2. Accessed 22 March 2019. https://www.artsprofessional. co.uk/news/only-fool-or-knave-trusts-quality-metrics-say-academics.

Holden, John. 2004. *Capturing cultural value: How culture has become a tool of government policy*. London: Demos.

Horlock, Naomi, ed. 2000. *Testing the water: Young people and galleries*. Liverpool: Liverpool University Press and Tate Liverpool.

Howell, Caro. 2009. Education tower: Space: The final frontier. In *A manual for the 21st century institution*, ed. Shamita Sharmacharja, 142–155. London: Koenig Books.

Howell, Samuel. 2018. Our summary of the government's civil society strategy. *London Youth*. Accessed 21 March 2019. https://londonyouth.org/ our-summary-government-civil-society-strategy/.

Hughes, Jenny. 2005. *Doing the arts justice: A review of research literature, practice and theory*. The unit for the arts and offenders centre for applied theatre research. Accessed 3 October 2016. http://www.artsevidence.org.uk/evaluations/doing-arts-justice-review-research-literature-prac/.

Jackson, Shannon. 2011. *Social works: Performing art, supporting publics*. Oxon: Routledge.

Jeffers, Alison, and Gerri Moriarty. 2014. Where have we come from? Community arts to contemporary practice. *Community Arts Unwrapped*. Accessed 2 November 2016. https://communityartsunwrapped.com/2014/03/24/ where-have-we-come-from-community-arts-to-contemporary-practice/.

———. 2017. *Culture, democracy and the right to make art: The British community arts movement*. London: Bloomsbury.

Jeffs, Tony, 2014. Innovation in youth work—Creative practice in challenging times. In *Creative practice in challenging times*, YMCA George Williams College, London, 13 May 2014.

———. 2015. What sort of future? In *Innovation in youth work: Thinking in practice*, ed. Naomi Stanton, 11–17. London: YMCA George Williams College.

Jeffs, Tony, and Mark K. Smith. 2010. *Youth work practice*. Basingstoke: Palgrave Macmillan.

Jermyn, Helen. 2001. *The arts and social exclusion: A review prepared for the Arts Council of England*. London: Arts Council England.

———. 2004. *The art of inclusion*. London: Arts Council England.

Jones, Owen. 2018. Carillion is no one-off scandal. Neoliberalism will bring many more. *The Guardian*, May 16.

Jones, Gareth. 2019. Brexit has left communities divided and young people isolated. *Third Force News: The voice of Scotland's third sector.* Accessed 20 March 2019. http://thirdforcenews.org.uk/tfn-news/brexit-has-left-communities-divided-and-young-people-isolated#a3W6yY8oHFbpPxED.99.

Kelly, Owen. 1985. In search of cultural democracy. *Arts Express.* Accessed 20 May 2017. https://jubileeartsarchive.com/resources/.

Kester, Grant H. 2013. *Conversation pieces: Community and communication in modern art.* 2nd ed. London: University of California Press.

Kraftl, Peter, John Horton, and Faith Tucker, eds. 2012. *Critical geographies of childhood and youth.* Bristol: Policy Press.

Lepper, Joe. 2019. Council leaders slam £10m NCS rebrand. *Children & Young People Now*, March 15. Accessed 21 March 2019. https://www.cypnow.co.uk/cyp/news/2006475/council-leaders-slam-gbp10m-ncs-rebrand.

Lind, Maria. 2007. The collaborative turn. In *Taking the matter into common hands: On contemporary art and collaborative practices*, ed. Johanna Billing, Maria Lind, and Lars Nilsson, 15–31. London: Black Dog Publishing.

Lynch, Bernadette. 2001. If the museum is the gateway, who is the gatekeeper? *Engage 11 Inclusion Under Pressure*: 12–21.

———. 2011. *Whose cake is it anyway?: A collaborative investigation into engagement and participation in twelve museums and galleries in the UK.* London: Paul Hamlyn Foundation.

Macnaughton, Jane, Mike White, and Rosie Stacy. 2005. Researching the benefits of arts in health. *Health Education* 105 (5): 332–339.

Mason, Will. 2015. Austerity youth policy: Exploring the distinctions between youth work in principle and youth work in practice. *Youth & Policy Special Edition: The Next Five Years: Prospects for Young People* 114: 55–74.

Matarasso, François. 2013. 'All in this together': The depoliticisation of community art in Britain, 1970–2011. *Parliament of Dreams: Thinking about culture as if democracy mattered.* Accessed 2 December 2016. https://parliamentofdreams.com/2013/01/31/all-in-this-together/.

———. 2016. Community arts history. *Parliament of Dreams: Thinking about culture as if democracy mattered.* Accessed 2 December 2016. https://parliamentofdreams.com/free-downloads/community-arts-history/.

———. 2019. *A restless art: How participation won, and why it matters.* London: Calouste Gulbenkian Foundation.

McGimpsey, Ian. 2015. Public Money: A campaign aim for a new political context. *In Defence of Youth Work.* Accessed 1 June 2015. http://indefenceofyouthwork.com/2015/05/26/creating-a-new-vision-of-public-money-and-youth-work-idyw-seminar-june-22-manchester/.

———. 2018. The new youth sector assemblage: Reforming youth provision through a finance capital imaginary. *Journal of Education Policy* 33 (2): 226–242.

McGivern, Hannah. 2019. New £150,000 grant to 'embolden' museums goes to Whitworth and Van Abbemuseum. *The Art Newspaper*, March 14. Accessed 14 March 2019. https://www.theartnewspaper.com/news/new-gbp150-000-grant-to-embolden-museums-goes-to-whitworth-and-van-abbemuseum.

Mirza, Munira. 2006. *Culture vultures: Is UK arts policy damaging the arts?* London: Policy Exchange.

Morford, Roger. 2009. *Arts work with socially excluded young people.* Leicester: The National Youth Agency.

Mörsch, Carmen. 2016. The education/formation of others through art: Art education, colonialism and white femininity. The University of Applied Arts Vienna. Accessed 4 December 2016. https://www.youtube.com/watch?v=yudLfkZoFYI.

Murphy, Sean. 2014. National Citizen's Service: A model for mending youth in 'broken Britain'? *What is radical in youth and community work now?* Newman University, Birmingham, 28 June 2014.

Neate, Rupert. 2019. Austerity forcing arts institutions to accept gifts from billionaires. *The Guardian*, March 22.

Needlands, Jonothan, et al. 2015. *The Warwick commission: Enriching Britain: Culture, creativity and growth.* Coventry: The University of Warwick.

Nittve, Lars. 2016. How Tate Modern transformed London—And beyond. *Apollo: The International Art Magazine.* Accessed 1 December 2016. http://www.apollo-magazine.com/how-tate-modern-transformed-london-and-beyond/.

NYA. 2018. *An NYA response to the Civil Society Strategy.* NYA. Accessed 21 March 2019. https://nya.org.uk/2018/08/an-nya-response-to-the-civil-society-strategy/.

Offord, Adam. 2016. Youth policy set for move to Department for Culture, Media and Sport. *Children & Young People Now*, July 19. Accessed 21 March 2019. https://www.cypnow.co.uk/cyp/news/1158274/youth-policy-set-for-move-to-department-for-culture-media-and-sport.

On the record. 2014. A Hackney autobiography. *On the Record.* Accessed 6 December 2016. http://on-the-record.org.uk/projects/hackney-autobiography-remembering-centerprise/.

Osborne, George. 2016. Nicholas Serota interviews George Osborne. *Artsnight, BBC.* Accessed 13 May 2016. http://www.bbc.co.uk/programmes/p03v1pbd.

Panayiotou, Tony. 2006. Arts Council England. Diversity—The journey. *Engage 19: The International Journal of Visual Art and Gallery Education. Diversity*: 6–10.

Pickard, Jim. 2014. Flagship youth jobs scheme scrapped. *Financial Times.* Accessed 26 July 2015. https://www.ft.com/content/97e40d92-1340-11e4-925a-00144feabdc0.

Pringle, Emily. 2016. Take three: "From community practice to gallery education". *Community Arts? Stages* 5. Accessed 5 June 2017. http://www.biennial. com/journal/issue-5/take-three-from-community-practice-to-gallery-education.

Pritchard, Stephen. 2018. Caught Doing Social Work?—Socially engaged art and the dangers of becoming social workers. *Colouring in Culture*, November 15. Accessed 21 March 2019. http://colouringinculture.org/blog/caughtdoingsocialwork.

Puffett, Neil. 2017. Government ditches youth policy statement. *Children & Young People Now*, November 17. Accessed 21 March 2019. https://www.cypnow.co.uk/cyp/news/2004514/government-ditches-youth-policy-statement.

Romer, Christy. 2016. Local authority arts services continue to be cut. *Arts Professional*, November 11. Accessed 21 March 2019. https://www.artsprofessional.co.uk/news/local-authority-arts-services-continue-be-cut.

Sandell, Richard. 2003. Social inclusion, the museum and the dynamics of sectoral change. *Museum and Society* 1 (1): 45–62.

———. 2004. Put to good use: Museums, galleries and the combating of social exclusion. In *Engage extra Museums and galleries as learning places*. London: Engage.

Savage, Jon. 2008. *Teenage: The creation of youth culture*. London: Pimlico.

Seligman, Isabel. 2012. Art review: Serpentine takes a trip down the Edgware Road. *Artlyst*. Accessed 3 December 2016. http://www.artlyst.com/articles/serpentine-takes-a-trip-down-the-edgware-road.

Sercombe, Howard. 2015a. In the service of the state: Youth work under New Labour. In *Youth work histories, policy and contexts*, ed. Graham Bright, 38–57. London: Palgrave Macmillan.

———. 2015b. The watchmaker's chainsaw: Why New Public Management is the wrong tool for youth work (and most of the professions). *Journal of Applied Youth Studies* 1 (1): 97–122.

Serota, Nicholas. 2012. Foreword. In *On collaboration*, ed. Marie Bak Mortensen and Judith Nesbitt. London: Tate.

Sillis, Jane. 2015. Gallery education: A co-operative community. *Engage 35: The International Journal of Visual Art and Gallery Education: Twenty-five Years of Gallery Education*: 15–19.

Sinker, Rebecca. 2008. Tate Forum: On the evolution of a peer-led programme. *Engage 22 Young People and Agency*: 24–32.

Smith, Mark K. 2000, 2007. The Connexions Service in England. *The Encyclopaedia of Informal Education*. Accessed 4 November 2016. http://www.infed.org/personaladvisers/connexions.htm.

———. 2002. Transforming youth work—Resourcing excellent youth services. A critique. *The Encyclopedia of Informal Education*. Accessed 3 November 2016. www.infed.org/youthwork/transforming_youth_work_2.htm.

———. 2007. Henrietta Barnett, social reform and community building. *The Encyclopedia of Informal Education*. Accessed 4 November 2016. http:// infed.org/mobi/henrietta-barnett-social-reform-and-community-building/.

———. 2013. What is youth work? Exploring the history, theory and practice of youth work. *The Encyclopedia of Informal Education*. Accessed 2 November 2016. www.infed.org/mobi/what-is-youth-work-exploring-the-history-theory-and-practice-of-work-with-young-people.

Smith, Mark K., and Michele Erina Doyle. 2002. The Albemarle Report and the development of youth work in England and Wales. *The Encyclopedia of Informal Education*. Accessed 3 November 2016. http://infed.org/mobi/the-albemarle-report-and-the-development-of-youth-work-in-england-and-wales/.

South London Gallery. 2011. *The cat came as a tomato: Conversations on play and contemporary art practice*. London: South London Gallery.

Stavrinou, Lara. 2015. *Strong Voices: A.N.D. A new direction for arts, culture and young London: An action research report on the key findings of a two year programme*. London: A New Direction.

Steedman, Marijke, ed. 2012. *Gallery as community: Art, education, politics*. London: Whitechapel Gallery.

———. 2016. Take four: "Beyond the mural". *Community Arts? Stages 5*. Accessed 5 June 2017. http://www.biennial.com/journal/issue-5/take-three-from-community-practice-to-gallery-education.

Suntharalingam, Silaja. 2012. *Circuit second stage proposal to the Paul Hamlyn Foundation*. London: Tate.

Tallant, Sally. 2008. Experiments in integrated programming. *Situating Gallery Education*. Association of Art Historians Annual Conference, Tate Britain, London, 2–4 April 2008.

Taylor, Tony. 2013. National Citizen Service saga continues—Overspent and underused! *In Defence of Youth Work*. Accessed 5 December 2016. https:// indefenceofyouthwork.com/2013/08/27/national-citizen-service-saga-continues-overspent-and-underused/.

———. 2014. IDYW statement 2014. *In Defence of Youth Work*. Accessed 5 October 2015. https://indefenceofyouthwork.com/idyw-statement-2014/.

———. 2016. About. *In Defence of Youth Work*. Accessed 3 November 2016. https://indefenceofyouthwork.com/about/.

———. 2018. Reviving youth work as soft-policing: Labour Party policy? *In Defence of Youth Work*. Accessed 24 March 2019. https://indefenceofyouthwork.com/2018/07/31/reviving-youth-work-as-soft-policing-labour-party-policy/.

The Foundling Museum. 2016. The Foundling Museum. Accessed 1 December 2016. http://foundlingmuseum.org.uk/about/the-museum/.

The Museum Prize Trust. 2011. Clore award for learning 2011. Accessed 1 December 2016. http://www.museumprizetrust.org.uk/prize-winners-and-judges/clore-award-learning/2011/.

Thompson, Nato, ed. 2012. *Living as form: Socially engaged art from 1991–2011*. Cambridge, MA: MIT Press.

Thomson, Pat. 2017. *Educational leadership and Pierre Bourdieu*. London: Routledge.

Thorpe, Vanessa. 2019. Beyoncé effect fills galleries with a new generation of art devotees. *The Guardian*, March 24.

Townley and Bradby. 2009. Part 2 of review of Future Perfect: Engage/enquire conference. *a-n*. Accessed 1 December 2016. https://www.a-n.co.uk/reviews/part-2-of-review-of-future-perfect-engageenquire-conference.

UK Youth. 2018. Civil Society Strategy launch: UK Youth's response. *UK Youth*. Accessed on 23 March 2019. https://www.ukyouth.org/2018/08/09/civil-society-strategy-uk-youths-response/.

Unfinished histories. 2016. Welcome to unfinished histories. Unfinished histories: Recording the history of alternative theatre. Accessed 26 November 2016. http://www.unfinishedhistories.com/#.

UNISON. 2014. *The damage. The UK's youth services. How cuts are removing opportunities for young people and damaging their lives*. London: Unison Local Government.

———. 2019. *Youth services at breaking point*. London: UNISON.

Vuyk, Kees. 2010. The arts as an instrument? Notes on the controversy surrounding the value of art. *International Journal of Cultural Policy* 16 (2): 173–183.

Walker, Peter. 2018. Cameron's £1.5bn 'big society' youth scheme reaching few teenagers. *The Guardian*, August 2.

Watson, Sheila, ed. 2007. *Museums and their communities*. London: Routledge.

Weakley, Kirsty. 2016. David Cameron becomes chair of NCS patrons. *Civil Society*, October 13. Accessed 20 March 2019. https://www.civilsociety.co.uk/news/david-cameron-becomes-chair-of-ncs-patrons.html.

Wheeler, Jo, and Amber Walls. 2008. *Envision: A handbook, supporting young people's participation in galleries and the arts*. London: Engage.

Williamson, Chris. 2017. This is how neoliberalism, led by Thatcher and Blair, is to blame for the Grenfell Tower disaster. *Independent*, August 4. Accessed 20 March 2019. https://www.independent.co.uk/voices/grenfell-tower-inquiry-deregulation-thatcher-tony-blair-fire-service-cuts-a7876346.html.

Willis, Paul. 1990. *Common Culture: Symbolic work at play in the everyday cultures of the young*. Milton Keynes: Open University Press.

Wilmot, Hannah. 2017. *Tate Exchange year one evaluation report 2016–2017*. London: Tate.

Worpole, Ken. 2013. *Radical community arts centres in 1970s and 1980 Hackney: What legacy?* Open School East, London, 21 November.

Yiakoumaki, Nayia. 2012. History of the Whitechapel Gallery. *Whitechapel Gallery.* Accessed 1 December 2016. http://www.whitechapelgallery.org/about/history/.

Young, Kerry. 1999. *The art of youth work.* Dorset: Russell House Publishing.

CHAPTER 4

Field Conditions, Attitudes and Relations in Practice

This chapter listens to practitioners. Delving into the literature is just one way to 'understand' a professional field, and existing relations between fields. But in order to get close to understanding the lived experiences and concerns of a sector, a researcher has to spend time in the company of practitioners—hearing debates, observing activity or engaging in conversation. The 'sector' event is arguably an ideal discursive space to provide insights into the disciplinary 'doxa' (or belief system) of the professional field, as well as the composition of the workforce and 'habitus' of practitioners. These events are also often platforms for candid discussion around internal and cross-sector conflict. Recognising competing agendas and positions is a process Bourdieu suggests is necessary for identifying the 'doxic contests' in any given field—in other words, the tensions surrounding how things should be done (Bourdieu and Wacquant, 1992; Grenfell and Hardy, 2003, Thomson, 2017, p. 19). This process also allows the researcher to gather a perspective on the 'relative autonomy' of each field, which is usually shaped by the '"nature" of the constraints' put upon or felt by agents (Hilgers and Mangez, 2015, p. 19). As discussed in the previous chapter, the dissemination of agency and power in partnership is often determined by the freedoms afforded to an organisation and its workers by wider fields of power.

As part of my research, I engaged with the concept of 'multi-event ethnography' (Delgado and Cruz, 2014) and attended numerous youth

© The Author(s) 2019   81
N. Sim, *Youth Work, Galleries and the Politics of Partnership*, New
Directions in Cultural Policy Research,
https://doi.org/10.1007/978-3-030-25197-0_4

sector and gallery education events in Glasgow, Belfast, Cardiff, Leeds, Bradford, Nottingham, Gateshead, Manchester, Birmingham, London, Brighton, Liverpool and other areas of the UK, as well as some international events. Some of the events I attended, presented at and organised were orchestrated to bring together practitioners from both the youth and visual art sectors. These events revealed various things about the dynamics between arts and youth organisations and practitioners. Alongside observations at sector events, I also interviewed youth and arts practitioners from different parts of the UK about their past experiences of partnership, and their relationship with notions of art and culture. I also joined several youth sector groups on Facebook and found these to be essential gateways to knowledge about the urgencies and debates occupying the sector. While the findings from this fieldwork only capture a particular moment in time, many of the issues raised continue to be relevant to present day practice. This chapter presents snapshots from these different interactions to provide empirical evidence about the character of the two fields and their attitudes to partnership, as well as their differing approaches to creativity.

CONFLICT IN THE FIELD: UNDERSTANDING THE YOUTH SECTOR

Broadly speaking, I engaged with two 'types' of youth sector event. One type of event tended to be organised by large-scale youth organisations, consortia or membership bodies. The other type of event tended to be organised by academic organisations such as the YMCA George Williams College, the British Educational Research Association or the campaigning group In Defence of Youth Work. While the former category of event was generally positioned as the space of the official, publicly/privately funded youth sector, the latter type of event would usually be framed as a space of critique and resistance towards perceived 'collusion with the State's imposed and prescribed outcomes-based agenda' (Taylor, 2014).

To give two examples, in November 2014 I attended the Creative Collisions conference, staged in London's Queen Elizabeth Olympic Park, which was organised by ten leading youth organisations including the National Youth Agency, UK Youth, the National Council for Voluntary Youth Services and London Youth. The second event was a seminar held the following day at the University of Birmingham, titled *Creative Resistance: Why? Where? How?* This was organised by the In Defence of

Youth Work campaign. The following field notes illustrate selected moments and comments of significance.

> *I am signed up to attend the Creative Collisions conference: Uniting for Young People. For weeks now the organisers have been sending emails with the agenda, and a reminder to submit questions to ask Rob Wilson, Minister for Civil Society, who will be talking at the event.*
>
> *I arrive at the Copperbox in time for the exhibition and networking section of the day. The venue is a vast arena with a large central sunken space, and thousands of tiered seats reaching up to the ceiling. Around the perimeter of the central space is a walkway populated by a marketplace of bright stands, each representing a different youth agency or charity. The area is already teeming with delegates—mainly adults, with a smattering of people who appear to be in their late teens/early 20s. There are quite a few men wearing suits. I walk around browsing stalls and leaflets. A man from Onside Youth Zones tells me about the work of this national initiative to build state of the art youth centres offering universal and targeted provision for 8–19 year olds. The literature explains that young people have to pay 50p a session. I chat to a very articulate young person from the British Youth Council about their campaign to secure the vote for people aged 16 and 17. He tells me there's a general assumption that young people lean to the left politically, but it's not necessarily true—he's a Conservative. There are stands promoting volunteering opportunities through programmes such as vInspired, and stands featuring content produced and marketed by the Youth Media Agency. The Arts Award also has a presence.*
>
> *At 10am the 700 or so delegates are ushered into the main space, where a stage is set for the first plenary, to be chaired by TV presenter Rick Edwards. The panel for this initial session includes Rob Wilson MP and Lisa Nandy MP, Shadow Minister for Civil Society. Conservative Rob Wilson, who is responsible for the government's youth policy, speaks first. He shares anecdotes about his son attending Cubs and his daughter being a Brownie. He recognises the need to ensure that all young people have access to the cultural, sporting and educational opportunities available in the UK, regardless of background. He acknowledges the life-changing work that youth practitioners do, and the important contribution that the youth sector makes in the UK. Mid-speech, a woman in the audience interjects loudly: "Pay for it then!" There is a ripple of applause and some stifled giggling. Wilson suggests he's getting to that.*
>
> *Wilson goes on to name a series of government priorities. They want to ensure that opportunities exist beyond formal education, so are continuing to support uniformed youth organisations, the Step Up To Serve programme and the NCS. The government is committed to austerity, and the youth sector is expected to "become more resilient" by forming enterprising partnerships between local authorities, businesses and youth organisations. Wilson also stresses the*

importance of impact measurement, and welcomes the launch of the new
Centre for Youth Impact at today's conference. As he concludes, the Minister
apologises because he can't stay as he has other meetings to attend, and as soon
as he finishes the speech he swiftly leaves the stage and exits the venue. I'm taken
aback by this unexpected departure, particularly as we were asked to submit
questions in advance.

   Later in the session, Piers Telemacque, Vice President for society and citizen-
ship at the National Union of Students, stands up in the audience and tells the
rest of the delegates that he ran after Rob Wilson to ask him why he wouldn't
stay and answer questions. Telemacque argues that this government has consis-
tently deprioritised young people, and that statutory protection for youth ser-
vices is needed to ensure their survival.
   [Field notes, 6 November 2014]

The significance of the scarpering Minister was not lost on anyone in
the conference hall that day. Wilson's hasty departure from the room
appeared symbolic of the government's disinterest in listening to youth
workers, and its abandonment of duty towards youth services. The message from the Minister around business-led social investment spelt out the
government's intention to reduce youth organisations' reliance on council
budgets, and to endorse public-private partnership models to capitalise
upon alternative sources of funding. As well as revealing divisions, the
event exposed the youth sector's lack of influence and advocacy power at
a national level. The CEOs of the ten organising partners admitted they
had tried to place a campaign letter in the national press that day, but no
paper or media agency was interested in taking it. The CEO of UK Youth
also admitted that the youth sector has been failing to reach all young
people. The general consensus amongst the main speakers was that the
sector must develop new and better means of collaboration.
   The event held on the subsequent day by In Defence of Youth Work
revealed more about the low morale of the sector, and frustrations of
practitioners.

The following day, I'm heading to Birmingham for the Creative Resistance
seminar. I arrive at the campus and reach the seminar room, which is crammed
full with around 25 participants. I recognise a few attendees from some other
youth work conferences. The NUS Vice-President from yesterday is here too.
Some of the group report back from the Creative Collisions conference. They are
recalling some of the more volatile moments from the day, and referring to the
huge pressure being experienced by youth workers, many of who are feeling
compromised and intimidated by the shifts towards privatisation in youth prac-

tice. Their argument is that youth work should be seen as a discipline in its own right—that it is about developing an empowering and equal relationship with young people. The youth worker is, as one contributor suggests, "not a watered down social worker".

As well as seeing the basic values and professional status of their practice eroded, the group are deeply concerned about the scale of the cuts to youth provision. The NUS Vice-President explains that they have introduced a parliamentary Early Day Motion, which proposes that youth services in the UK should receive ring-fenced, statutory funding, and that responsibility for youth services should sit with the Department for Education. The situation for youth work courses seems bleak. One attendee argues that training agencies are "teaching a subject called youth work that doesn't exist". Another youth worker tells me they have been told not to display In Defence of Youth Work literature at their workplace.

[Field notes, 7 November 2014]

These kinds of conversations and statements were commonplace in my experience of youth sector events. Both examples describe a disempowered, divided sector, struggling to assert its position. The impact of these field conditions on the workforce was also clear. Youth work lecturers spoke about the loss of identity for a practice that is now dispersed in schools, hospitals and other settings (Green, 2014). The perception of youth and community work as a low status occupation—or the "poor relation" of other forms of social and educational work was also raised (Batsleer, 2014). These first-hand accounts, combined with the literature analysis, provide evidence about the diminished autonomy of the field of youth work. The competencies and capitals traditionally required of youth workers have been consistently devalued in favour of managerialist and administrative capitals. Interpretations of the 'game' of youth work lurch between regulation of deficient youth and compliance with new managerialism on the one hand, and concepts of democratic empowerment and consciousness raising on the other (Hughes et al., 2014). These circumstances have created an inhospitable, precarious professional environment, which fosters obvious consequences for the youth sector's ability to constitute itself as a favourable partner.

ATTITUDES TO PARTNERSHIP IN THE YOUTH SECTOR

With growing acknowledgement of the necessity for collaboration across and beyond the youth sector, there has been no shortage of discussion about the politics of partnership at youth sector events in recent years.

Despite the rhetoric, the consensus at many of these events was that the current policy and economic climate had produced a culture of competition rather than collaboration—with organisations vying for the same reduced funding. Youth practitioners noted how fears over job security and orientations towards targets were also causing some organisations to behave protectively with their cohorts of young people. Below is an extract of field notes from an event called *Breaking barriers: where evidence goes next*, organised in London by Project Oracle, a children and youth 'evidence hub'. Their annual conference brought together youth providers, senior figures in public services and London governance, funders and researchers. The breakout session: *Collaboration—more than the sum of your parts*, staged a roundtable conversation about the obstacles to good partnership working and the types of collaborations needed in the youth sector:

> *The afternoon's workshop on collaboration promises to look at the shifts in culture needed to ensure that organisations are prepared to work well in partnership, and able to reflect on challenges. The main speakers are David Warner, Director of London Funders, Sharon Long, Strategic Director of Partnership for Young London, and Rosie Ferguson, Chief Executive of London Youth. This is a very over-subscribed session—the small room is packed full.*
>
> *The event begins with a question to the audience about some of the issues affecting partnership work. One delegate says it's about partners being on the same page; another says her concern is how to build trust between large and small-scale organisations. David Warner proposes four principles that should underpin collaboration: leadership, trust, clarity of shared vision and a focus on the ultimate beneficiaries (young people). He suggests that practitioners need to put aside organisational interests and concentrate on being driven by the moral imperative.*
>
> *Rosie Ferguson highlights that as a Chief Executive of a voluntary organisation, she is constantly incentivised to over-claim. She believes funding structures and other factors encourage organisations to fabricate evidence and to demonstrate that their work is the best, which perpetuates a competitive system. Ferguson argues that they need to be thinking like movements, not institutions, and organisations need to have collaborative, mission-focused leaders who are brave enough to refuse to play the game. She lists a set of conditions that need to be in place to enable these changes in culture:*
>
> 1. *You need to like each other in order to go the extra mile.*
> 2. *Practitioners need to work with different people and organisations. The risk is that if we only work with people who are similar to us, we will end up with lots of like-minded groups.*

3. *A culture of honesty is essential.*
4. *Partners need to relax their organisational ego (some organisations in the sector get hung up on intellectual property and ownership).*
5. *Partners should hold each other to account.*
6. *The balance of power should be as equal as possible, so one organisation is not servicing the other.*

> *Warner agrees that one of the frustrations of the funding community is the inherent imbalance of power between funders and grantees. Funders are interested in honest feedback about their own performance as funders, as well as the performance of funding recipients.*
>
> *Some of the audience members describe the challenges they face in trying to enact these types of practices. One delegate admits that it's hard for organisations to collaborate effectively because "things are shaky". Another delegate believes that if you collaborate too much you can lose your identity as an organisation.*
>
> *The final part of the discussion focuses on fostering local relationships. Warner suggests that the local is going to be an increasingly important place to advocate. Sharon Long agrees that the youth sector is losing connectors and brokerage in local spaces, and there are fewer centralised systems for communicating information. There is agreement amongst the speakers that the needs of localities would be best served by organisations forming local networks, and doing strategic work around horizon scanning and place based evidence.*
>
> [Field notes, 12 October 2015]

This is just one example of a sector discussion on partnership, but it demonstrates the complex performativity that surrounds partnership working and the ways in which fields of power (e.g. funders) influence the collaborative activity of youth organisations. The implicit or explicit pressure to meet targets and evidence success is shown to have encouraged disingenuous behaviour and impaired organisations' ability to set realistic goals and transparently reflect on challenges. The hollowing out of regional resources and local authority agency has also clearly weakened local networks and reduced opportunities for different organisational staff to meet, share and coordinate collaborative projects. Practitioners whose occupation is already threatened also fear that too much partnership or integration leads to a loss of organisational identity (Banks, 2010). So this is the paradox at the centre of partnership working in the youth sector: while the emphasis on cross-sector collaboration has grown, the infrastructure and motivation to support this activity has been systematically dismantled. The conversation referenced does however indicate an appetite from those in leadership positions to shift the 'doxa' that drives problematic behaviour in youth sector partnerships.

THE RELATIONSHIP BETWEEN YOUTH WORK AND THE ARTS

In youth work, arts-based activity sits alongside sports, games, cooking, mentoring and issue-based discussion as a key facet of youth work provision (London Youth, 2013, p. 22). Nonetheless, I discovered during my sector-based research that (as was the case in youth sector literature) the arts were rarely mentioned in youth sector events. In meeting other delegates at youth events, I did encounter practitioners who worked in youth theatre contexts, but I met few practitioners who worked in or with galleries. It became apparent that youth theatre traditions were much more embedded in the history and practice of youth work than gallery education. The reasons for these absences are multiple, and as part of my research, I made efforts to convene events that included youth practitioners talking about arts practice and partnership.

At one of these events, Brian Belton, a senior lecturer in youth work at the YMCA George Williams College, offered a "critique of the dominance of the practical application of art in youth work practice" (Belton, 2015). He suggested that the visual arts tend to be framed in youth work in terms of hands-on arts and crafts activities for young people, while possibilities for engaging with visual art emotionally and discursively are often overlooked. Belton argued that interactions with art in museums and galleries offer opportunities for "interpreting and translating experience", for self-reflection and discussion about societal issues and the human condition. He highlighted the potential for youth workers to reflect on their own values and ethics, and for them to consider using the visual arts to support young people to develop their "awareness of self", their "political and social consciousness", "judgement" and "empathetic capacities" (Belton, 2015). In other words, there are questions, codes and messages within works of art that inspire critical debate, produce new insights and even motivate social action. Belton also highlighted the value of engaging with the visual arts in and of itself, beyond its potential 'use' value. But the social agency of art is something Belton identified as being under-explored and sometimes wilfully dismissed by youth work education institutions.

This concept of art as a dialogic social agent is not to be confused with the instrumentalised understanding of art practice in youth work, which was another site of criticism for some youth practitioners (Howard,

2017). For instance, in the same event, youth theatre practitioner Steph Brocken referred to the idea that arts work has "sometimes been seen as a panacea in youth work". She relayed a familiar scene: "there is a problem with kids hanging out down by the parade, let's do a graffiti project, that'll solve the problem!" (Brocken, 2015). What was suggested is that the adoption of arts-based activity as a means to do good or to divert young people from challenging behaviour neutralises the disruptive, rebellious potential of the visual arts (Baillie, 2015). Even though youth workers often encounter transgressive activity in young people, the dominant doxa of youth work is to support young people to develop a responsible citizen habitus.

Another major trope of youth work's framing of the arts relates to its therapeutic qualities. In interviews with youth workers who were involved in Circuit, practitioners spoke about the use of art as a vehicle for communication or as a distraction device through which meaningful conversation with young people might emerge:

> **Youth worker:** *Young people who find it hard to communicate will lend themselves towards communicating through art. Sometimes it's just by doing it, and they talk. They forget about not talking, and they talk. Sometimes it's a tool to actually unpick something that they want to unpick rather than being made to sit and confront it.*
> [Interview, 30 October 2015]

Some youth practitioners referred to the value of spending time in an arts space as an alternative context for young people to open up emotionally. The therapeutic capacities of the visual arts are important to many youth practitioners. But there is also an indication that these instrumental or therapeutic framings can lead to narrow definitions and applications of creative practice—as implied below:

> **Youth worker:** *The County Council did run training sessions for creativity, and gave little quick ideas. They used to give you little packs—quick fix things to take in. Because we found that those people that struggled with being creative would latch on to taking these packs that had everything you'd need to run a session—which would support sexual health or mental health, or they did things around finance. Nobody wanted to keep recreating the wheel so it became that if you needed something you could just take it off the shelf and use it. Sometimes I don't think that's great—but if you're not confident enough to work with somebody in that area, that's a good starting place.*
> [Interview, 30 October 2015]

I discovered during my fieldwork that those youth workers who did have a more expansive view of arts practice generally had undertaken a degree in the arts, or received exposure to arts institutions as a young person. They also tended to be in the minority in their organisations. Some of these practitioners expressed frustration with their colleagues' seemingly limited interpretations of creativity and their expectations for arts activities to be predefined rather than exploratory and playful [interview, 15 February 2015]. The prevalence of spray painting or street art as a go-to art form for youth work was both embraced and derided by different practitioners, depending on their disposition.

What this tells us is that there is no singular youth worker habitus. Some youth workers develop a propensity to engage in critical, improvisatory ways with the visual arts. They see interactions with artists and galleries as opportunities for young people to "start thinking", and to "develop their thinking skills", without being given answers or rigid instructions [Interview with youth practitioner, 26 May 2015]. Meanwhile other youth workers (arguably a majority) develop an inclination to view the visual arts in a much more functional capacity. Some youth practitioners see partnerships with arts institutions as a luxury indulgence—or "the cherry on the icing on the cake", rather than something that could be integral to their work [Interview with youth practitioner, 26 May 2015]. At an away day for children's and youth services held at one of the Circuit galleries, youth workers highlighted the clinical, formal atmosphere of the gallery, and the possibility for "chaotic" groups to be publically reprimanded in the space. Some participants felt that galleries are seen as "posh and not relevant", and one felt that the "intellectualising of art works alienates people" [field notes, 10 January 2014]. I found throughout my fieldwork that some youth practitioners would retreat behind their feelings of inexperience in relation to the arts, while others would confidently communicate their cultural tastes, but often in opposition to the more esoteric works and interpretation devices presented by the gallery or museum.

Bourdieu (1984) would suggest that the tendency of some youth practitioners to perceive art as fulfilling a function, or for practitioners to feel alienated by arts institutions conveys various things about their social origins and their cultural capital. He would suggest that the proclivity for visiting art galleries is linked to a middle-or-upper class social positioning and high levels of academic education. The concept of pursuing an artistic idea without there being an obvious outcome or purpose is also imbued with privilege, or the sense of 'a life of ease—that tends to induce an active distance from necessity' (Bourdieu, 1984, p. xxviii). The practitioners who work in the visual arts may not be financially wealthy, but they are part of a highly educated community that has been nurtured (usually through familial support) to access and engage with institutional art and culture (Bourdieu, 1992). These practitioners derive symbolic power and prestige from their ability to identify unique ideas and innovative practice. Whereas individuals from working class backgrounds or lower socio-economic positions are more likely to feel 'at sea with the cultural expectations' of museums and galleries and be more disposed to practices that have a clear functionality or popularity (Grenfell and Hardy, 2003, p. 73). If we understand that gallery practitioners and artists are often from middle class backgrounds, and youth practitioners are increasingly from more working class backgrounds, it is possible to see how different inclinations emerge.

However, it would be problematic to make simplistic judgements about the correlation between a practitioner's social, educational and cultural capital and the quality of their arts engagement practices. Youth work is often highly creative, responsive, critically alert and reflective, but the 'artistry' of the practice is undervalued and under-recognised (Young, 1999; Patel, 2010). Equally, the 'symbolic violence' of an encounter with an art institution or certain artists can cause some youth practitioners to withdraw or downplay their own creative faculties. A youth worker's creative capital and their approaches towards the visual arts typically don't operate within the aesthetic or critical value system that is legitimised by the contemporary art world. Instead, the youth centre might be thought about as "a space of subcultural capital" and youth workers as supporters or facilitators of young people's subcultural expression (Manchester, 2014). It is no coincidence that street art, dance, rap, DJ-ing and other similar art forms are favoured in youth work practice. The principles of cultural democracy—associated with everyday grassroots culture, anti-elitist practice and a distrust of the institution—align closely with traditional youth work values. Crucially, these understandings and approaches towards art and culture diverge in many ways from the dominant tastes and methods cultivated by the gallery field. Although (as described in the following sections) gallery education practice encourages awareness and critical exploration of these cultural dissonances.

Understanding the Gallery Education Sector

In recent years during gatherings of gallery education practitioners and artists, there has been growing discussion around the privileged status of gallery practice and inequity in partnership-based work. In events I attended as part of my research, it was noted that gallery education practitioners don't often live in the areas they develop projects within (Graham, 2014) and they are not part of the "disadvantaged" communities they seek to engage (Cisneros, 2015). While recognised as semi-precarious workers, gallery practitioners demonstrated self-awareness that the profile of the workforce is dominantly white, middle class and female (Cisneros, 2015). Diversity and inclusion were (and still are) major topics of interest for the field of gallery education. Cuts to arts funding were sometimes mentioned, but morale was rarely low, because the wholesale existence of the practice was not in jeopardy.

Critiquing the institution is a central feature of gallery education practice. In the events I observed, several senior practitioners challenged the idea that galleries and museums should sit outside of direct political engagement and action (Fleming, 2014; Desmond, 2014). It was suggested in one Engage (the national association for gallery education) event that there is a lack of collective protest in the visual arts and that institutions should better utilise art as a form of activism [Engage area group meeting, The Showroom, London, 2013]. Having a "personal stake" and a "political position" in projects was said to be vital to collaborative working (Shelley, 2014) and the convention for galleries and museums to remain apolitical seemed to frustrate practitioners at larger institutions (Fleming, 2014). A theme of many conferences and seminars I attended was the need for organisational change and the disruption of "institutional systems of value" (Hickey-Moody, 2014). There was a tendency for practitioners to talk about the repressive forces of visual art institutions [The Ludic Museum conference, Tate Liverpool, 2014]—their containment of risk and control of access and taste [Taste after Bourdieu, Chelsea College of Art, 2014]. Academics in cultural education contexts asked: "how do institutions make themselves vulnerable to new knowledges?" (Hickey-Moody, 2014) and: "how do institutions shift from a dominant, autonomous energy to new, playful structures?" (Facer, 2014).

These examples signal that the gallery education field has a symbiotic but agnostic relationship with the fields of power that surround and support it. In their mediating role between publics and the art institution, practitioners who work in the field are (to different degrees) conscious of the hierarchical ordering and 'insularity' of the institutional art world (Graham, 2018, p. 45). For many gallery practitioners, access to the art institution is a matter of social justice, and the impulse to create 'change' is a continuous motivator. While creative approaches in gallery education include skills-based, practical activity and work that has a social function, contemporary practice in the field is increasingly preoccupied with the 'pedagogies of encounter' (Sánchez de Serdio, 2018). These encounters are thought to produce new forms of knowledge exchange, to antagonise and subvert hierarchies and to engage with issues of broader societal relevance. They tend to be open-ended rather than didactic or instructive, so they also aim to invite unpredictability and failure (Sánchez de Serdio, 2018). The pedagogical philosophy behind gallery education amalgamates different theoretical ideas related to emancipatory and radical practice. But practitioners in the field are also sometimes conscious of the contradictory nature of their work, and its capacity to reproduce systems of inequality. The capitals required of the gallery practitioner typically exclude diverse forms of expertise and lived experience, and collaborative work can be known to reinforce the hegemonic power of the institution.

ATTITUDES TO PARTNERSHIP IN THE VISUAL ARTS SECTOR

As is the case in youth sector events, critical discussion of partnership has featured repeatedly in gallery education events over recent years. While carrying out my research between 2013 and 2015 there was an observable upsurge in the use of language around "co-production" and "co-creation" (Bagshawe, 2014). The concept of co-producing with audiences and communities was exciting practitioners at all levels of organisations, but it also ignited concern and debate about the sincerity of arts institutions' collaborative gestures. The discourse surrounding partnership as a form of philanthropy was regularly challenged in events I attended [Social arts and mental health event, Anxiety festival, Chelsea College of Art, 2014]. Terms such as "outreach" were called out as "colonial" (Artswork Arts Award conference, BFI, London, 2014). And scepticism was vocalised about the government's use of arts collaboration to "massage conflict" through "collaborative visioning", "collaborative policing" and "collaborative beautification" and so on (Graham, 2014). Lynch (2014) spoke about mistrusting the museum's generosity and acknowledging how control works in subtle ways through the idea of the "gift of engagement".

Other event contributors problematised the claims associated with collaboration. In his presentation "The C word" at the 2014 Engage conference, Rohan Gunatillake argued that despite the fixation on collaboration in galleries, these organisations often produce behaviours that don't look collaborative, and that have more in common with commissioning (Gunatillake, 2014). He suggested that the instinct to commission rather than collaborate stems from institutional reluctance to expose vulnerabilities and relinquish power. Similarly, the iJADE conference on Collaborative practices in arts education deconstructed (over many papers) the concept of collaboration through its critical legacies, uses and misuses. Curator Janna Graham spoke about the paradoxical rhetoric of democracy and utopian transformation in collaborative work involving galleries and communities, where the dominant mode of producing is actually vertical—that is, hierarchically organised. Graham argued that funders often dictate the terms of a partnership, and therefore accountability lies with the grant maker, rather than the social and political aims of the partner groups (Graham, 2014). There were calls for the sector to think more critically about the partnership process, and to shift towards more conscious "rhizomatic" models and metaphors of collaboration than traditional hierarchical/banking models (Sullivan, 2014). These exercises in critical reflection signalled gallery education's conflicting relationship with partnership. "Collaboration is the new black", and yet the ethics of collaborative practices by galleries have come under serious scrutiny, where they were previously under-examined (Thomas, 2015).

EXPERIENCES OF PARTNERSHIP BETWEEN GALLERIES AND YOUTH ORGANISATIONS

As suggested by the literature, there are established and recognised tendencies in partnership practice between cultural institutions and so-called community partners such as youth organisations. These tendencies revolve around the understanding that agency and control usually lies (to a greater degree) with the arts partner. In various events, I encountered many instances of practitioners talking about examples of uneven or poor partnership practice, and the habitual nature of this behaviour. These instances helped to illustrate the tensions underpinning relationships between the visual arts and youth sectors.

Below are notes from an event that opened up critical discussion about some of the experiences of youth and community partners involved in collaborative work with arts organisations. This event was hosted by one of the Circuit galleries, alongside representatives from their nearest Bridge organisation, in a local theatre:

I'm sat in a room with a group of invited guests including academics from the local university, a cultural producer from a mental health organisation, engagement workers from the council, a policeman, an artistic director from the theatre, a fuel poverty representative and someone from a regional branch of a national children's charity. We are split into smaller groups to discuss different issues. My table is focusing on 'partnership'. One participant (who works at a mental health organisation) tells us she feels bombarded with offers from arts organisations that have funding but that don't have the young people to populate their projects. She feels there's an expectation for youth organisations to act as suppliers of young people, and because these organisations are stretched financially, many are forced to run from month to month, jumping onto different projects. Other members of the group agree that young people are often viewed as currency by various organisations. Worryingly, one participant believes that young people's stories of poverty and disadvantage are sometimes exploited by artists and arts organisations for their creative potential.

There is a consensus amongst the group that time and resources are rarely properly allocated to the development stage of an organisational relationship. One participant argues that funding bids don't account for partners' drivers, or for building ideas in a reciprocal, mutually beneficial way. We sketch a map of these thoughts and feed them back to the wider group members, who largely agree with the observations.

[Field notes, 25 June 2014]

These notes point to some of the common grievances levelled against arts organisations (by cultural workers as well as youth practitioners). While youth organisations invariably do the difficult work of grassroots engagement, arts organisations are often accused of making short-term offers at short notice. There is a general understanding that funding requirements and deadlines contribute to this behaviour, and that these embedded practices are connected to the pressured conditions of the arts education sector, which relies on small, often junior staff teams and temporary pots of funding. However, as was identified in this event, practitioners believe there are more fundamental contributing factors, such as how expertise is recognised and valued (or in Bourdieusian terms, what capitals count in partnership projects).

Throughout the fieldwork, I also maintained contact with another youth-focused arts programme called *Strong Voices* (2013–2015). Led by a consortium of five Bridge organisations and funded by the Department for Education, *Strong Voices* aimed to challenge the arts and youth sectors to come together and collaborate on programming and action research. The programme's enquiry looked at the meeting of these "different worlds"—in other words—"sets of people whose main focus was arts and culture and sets of people whose main focus was driven by youth and community practice" (Cochrane, 2015). *Strong Voices* also attempted to reframe conventional power relationships, by positioning youth organisations as commissioners of arts organisations in some settings, and by contracting practitioners from both sectors to work together on evaluation. Director and CEO of Cape UK Pat Cochrane summarised some of the programme's broad conclusions in the *Strong Voices* national conference:

> *We found all over the regions that similar things were going on. So that the youth work orientation tended to focus on enabling young people to make small steps to improve their lives—to improve their ability to function in the real world. And so for somebody from a youth and community background, using a bus to get to a session could have been a real triumph. Whereas from the arts and culture sector, there tends to be much more of a focus on a product, [and on] the need to attend consistently to achieve an outcome; the skill of the arts practitioner tends to be in the art form, [while] the skill of the youth practitioner tends to be in understanding the dynamics and the ways in which vulnerable young people need support.* (Cochrane, 2015)

In this statement, Cochrane pointed to the complementary and conflicting aspects of the relationship between the youth worker and the cultural worker. The skill base, motivations and expectations of the practitioner are identified as features of their distinctive professional "orientation". The youth work orientation was characterised as starting where young people are at, adapting to their needs and engagement patterns and focusing on young people's personal development, whereas an arts and cultural orientation was said to involve processes that required regular commitment, with a view to developing a creative output. Using a Bourdieusian framework, these "orientations" might otherwise be described as characteristics of each field's individual doxa. They are recognised features of each practice that compel youth and arts workers to act in particular ways. Cochrane explained the challenges of creating a shared space of practice between these orientations:

...We don't want to turn cultural practitioners into youth workers, nor do we want to turn youth workers into arts and cultural practitioners. What we want to do is to create a space where there's a shared language, where we're navigating and creating new, shared understandings. [...] And that's much harder than I think any of us ever anticipated. (Cochrane, 2015)

The difficulties involved in establishing these shared conditions are central to the ongoing 'problem' of partnership between galleries and youth organisations. Cochrane believes the arts and youth sectors need to cultivate a "community of practice" that reflects honestly and openly if they are to work together effectively.

During my fieldwork, I came into contact with initiatives in the wider cultural sector that had aimed to develop these so-called communities of practice. One prominent example was *Creating Change*—a national network for organisations involved in participatory arts with young people 'at risk'. Founded by south London-based theatre company Ovalhouse in 2013, *Creating Change* invited organisations and individuals to sign up as core and associate members, and hosted a website featuring resources, research and opportunities for broader public use. The programme also convened a major conference at the end of 2014, around the theme of 'creating links', which included practitioners from across the arts and youth sectors. Like the *Strong Voices* project, this network was cross-art form and involved brokering relationships between small to medium-sized organisations. Most of the core arts organisations involved were theatre and performance-based. It sought to advocate for participatory youth arts and to act as a hub for practitioners.

The conference raised a number of points about the nature of partnership between the youth and cultural sectors and it included leading figures from regional and national youth organisations (such as the CEO of Brighton youth centre) to speak about the challenges facing the youth sector. The types of issues raised in relation to partnership included the difficulties of finding a shared evidence base suitable for the evaluation of both artistic quality and social impact; the complications of navigating different languages and terminology across sectors, and the need to create accommodating programmes that take the unpredictability of young people's lives into account. One former young offender who had been part of a theatre engagement programme also spoke candidly about her experiences not preparing her for progression into a predominantly white arts industry [Creating Links conference, Ovalhouse, 3 December 2014].

These nascent efforts to create communities of practice across the youth and cultural fields produced (it seemed) valuable platforms for sharing research, promoting cross-sector dialogue and considering joint approaches to influencing policy. However, in both the case of Strong Voices and Creating Change, the platforms ended once their funded period was over. The fleeting, temporary presence of cross-field networks is evidently another weakness of partnership practice between the arts and youth sectors.

Programmes such as Circuit have to contend with this vexed history. This chapter has illustrated how the two separate fields of youth work and gallery education produce and embed different types of capitals and dispositions in workers and in young people. The comments and accounts offer some insights into the lived realities, attitudes and experiences of practitioners operating in the youth and gallery education fields. They demonstrate that organisations' readiness for partnership is affected by broader precarity, internal conflicts and habitual behaviour encouraged by deep-rooted systems of value. Overcoming (or working with) the distance created by doxic conflicts and differences in habitus is part of the task of partnership programmes. Large-scale, longer-term programmes in particular have an opportunity to trial new ways of working, to model best practice and share knowledge across sectors. The following chapter offers an account of the programmatic decisions behind Circuit—shedding light on how those involved sought to confront the many and varied issues connected to cross-field working.

REFERENCES

Bagshawe, Janita. 2014. The challenge of leading a participatory museum. *The politics of participation in museums*, The Old Courtroom, Brighton, 12 November 2014.

Baillie, Robin. 2015. The UNTITLED: The difference between young people and contemporary art. Presented by Richie Cumming at *Youth work, informal learning and the arts: Exploring the research and practice agenda*, The University of Nottingham, 18 April 2015.

Banks, Sarah. 2010. Ethics and the youth worker. In *Ethical issues in youth work*, ed. Sarah Banks, 2nd ed., 3–23. Oxon: Routledge.

Batsleer, Janet. 2014. Educating for a disappearing profession? The case of youth and community work. *BERA Conference*, London, 23–25 September 2014.

Belton, Brian. 2015. The impact of art analysis and interpretation on the role and practice of youth work. *Youth work, informal learning and the arts: Exploring the research and practice agenda*, Nottingham, 18 April 2015.

Bourdieu, Pierre. 1984. *Distinction: A social critique of the judgement of taste.* London: Routledge.

———. 1992. *Les règles de l'art.* Éditions du Seuil. English edition: Bourdieu, Pierre. 1996. *The rules of art.* Translated by Emanuel Susan. Cambridge: Polity Press.

Bourdieu, Pierre, and Loïc Wacquant. 1992. *An invitation to reflexive sociology.* Cambridge: Polity Press in association with Blackwell Publishers.

Brocken, Steph. 2015. The fight for identity: Arts and youth work in collaboration. In BERA, *Youth work, informal learning and the arts: Exploring the research and practice agenda,* Nottingham, 18 April 2015.

Cisneros, Teresa. 2015. Plenary 1—Is the gallery a school? Rethinking education and its uses. *The 2015 Engage international conference. A different game: Young people working with art and artists,* Glasgow, 19–20 November 2015.

Cochrane, Pat. 2015. Reflection and enquiry—'The grit in the oyster': Growing a collaborative community of practice to meet the needs of vulnerable young people. *Strong Voices national conference,* Sage Gateshead, 6 March 2015.

Delgado, Natalia Aguilar, and Luciano Barin Cruz. 2014. Multi-event ethnography: Doing research in pluralistic settings. *Journal of Organizational Ethnography* 3 (1): 43–58.

Desmond, Tim. 2014. What are the opportunities for participation in museums? What are the limitations? *The politics of participation in museums,* The Old Courtroom, Brighton, 12 November 2014.

Facer, Keri. 2014. Teenage kicks? Creativity, youth and citizenship. *Creative Citizens conference,* Royal College of Art, London, 18–19 September 2014.

Fleming, David. 2014. Panel session. *Cultural value and the economic and social impact of the arts workshop,* The University of Warwick, 9 July 2014.

Graham, Janna. 2014. The anatomy of an 'and': Countering the 'diplomatic condition' in urban art collaborations. *iJADE conference: Collaborative practices in arts education,* Tate Liverpool, 25 October 2014.

———. 2018. Negotiating institutions. In *The constituent museum: Constellations of knowledge, politics and mediation: A generator of social change,* ed. John Byrne, Elinor Morgan, November Paynter, Aida Sánchez de Serdio, and Adela Železnik, 44–48. Amsterdam: Valiz.

Green, Maxine. 2014. Introduction. *Innovation in youth work,* YMCA George Williams College, London, 13 May 2014.

Grenfell, Michael, and Cheryl Hardy. 2003. Field manoeuvres: Bourdieu and the young British artists. *Space and Culture* 6 (1): 19–34.

Gunatillake, Rohan. 2014. The C Word. *Engage international conference 2014. Disruptive influences? Innovation and gallery education,* Northern Ballet, Leeds, 10 November 2014.

Hickey-Moody, Anna. 2014. *Practice and research: Imprints and futures,* Tate Modern, London, 1 December 2014.

Hilgers, Mathieu, and Eric Mangez, eds. 2015. *Bourdieu's theory of social fields: Concepts and applications.* Oxon: Routledge.

Howard, Frances. 2017. The arts in youth work: A spectrum of instrumentality? *Youth and Policy.* Accessed 20 July 2017. http://www.youthandpolicy.org/articles/the-arts-in-youth-work/.

Hughes, Gill, Charlie Cooper, Sinéad Gormally, and Julie Rippingdale. 2014. The state of youth work in austerity England—Reclaiming the ability to 'care'. *Youth & Policy* 113: 1–14.

London Youth. 2013. *Hunch: A vision for youth in post-austerity Britain: Second edition.* London: London Youth.

Lynch, Bernadette. 2014. What are the opportunities for participation in museums? What are the limitations? *The politics of participation in museums,* The Old Courtroom, Brighton, 12 November 2014.

Manchester, Helen. 2014. Teenage Kicks? Exploring cultural value and citizenship from a youth perspective. *Creative Citizens conference,* Royal College of Art, London, 18–19 September 2014.

Patel, Raj. 2010. Creativity and partnership. In *What is youth work?* ed. Janet Batsleer and Bernard Davies, 61–72. Exeter: Learning Matters.

Sánchez de Serdio, Aida. 2018. Pedagogies of encounter. In *The constituent museum: Constellations of knowledge, politics and mediation: A generator of social change,* ed. John Byrne, Elinor Morgan, November Paynter, Aida Sánchez de Serdio, and Adela Żeleznik, 154–157. Amsterdam: Valiz.

Shelley, Louise. 2014. *Communal knowledge: Is this working?* The Showroom, London, 21 July 2014.

Sullivan, Yvette. 2014. Collaboration—You're doing it wrong. *iJADE conference: Collaborative practices in arts education,* Tate Liverpool, 24–25 October 2014.

Taylor, Tony. 2014. After creative collisions, creative resistance: IDYW seminar, November 7. *In Defence of Youth Work.* Accessed 8 October 2014. http://indefenceofyouthwork.com/2014/10/08/after-creative-collisions-creative-resistance-idyw-seminar-november-7/.

Thomas, Kerry. 2015. The practice of collaboration. *iJADE* 34 (3): 296–308.

Thomson, Pat. 2017. *Educational leadership and Pierre Bourdieu.* London: Routledge.

Young, Kerry. 1999. *The art of youth work.* Dorset: Russell House Publishing.

CHAPTER 5

Changing the Rules of the Game

The last two chapters explored the influence of fields of power and the relative disparities and homologies between the youth and gallery education fields as a way of understanding the challenges of cross-sector partnership. In the following three chapters I use Tate's multi-sited programme Circuit as the basis for examining programmatic space—or, as I refer to it—the temporary programmatic field. Taken from the idea of the 'temporary social field' (Rawolle, 2005) this concept describes the physical and conceived space that is created when a programme, network or initiative is designed and instituted. The programmatic field is essentially a framework within which activity takes place. The extent of its temporariness is usually determined by the availability of funding. Bourdieu tended to apply the notion of social fields to permanent structures and institutions, but his criteria for determining fields was flexible, and his theoretical framework can be expanded to examine more fleeting materialisations of social space, particularly those involving multiple different fields (Rawolle, 2005; Hilgers and Mangez, 2015).

As is the case with Circuit, where there are multiple sites and activities, partnerships usually take place within the wider framework of a temporary programmatic field, so it is important to understand the role this field plays in the partnership process. Studying the temporary programmatic field exposes the organising principles of a programme (e.g. how authority and resources are distributed, why decisions are made and what the

© The Author(s) 2019   101
N. Sim, *Youth Work, Galleries and the Politics of Partnership*, New
Directions in Cultural Policy Research,
https://doi.org/10.1007/978-3-030-25197-0_5

conditions of the programme are). Examining this space also brings to light the inequalities and struggles for power within the temporary programmatic field, as well as the practices and capitals that are valued (Bourdieu, 1985). Circuit is an important case study because the organisers and funder set out to create and support a programmatic space that would disrupt the typical imbalance of power between arts and youth organisations. It was an attempt to change the rules of the game, and in so doing, it highlighted the structural and systemic issues that make change so challenging.

Designing the Temporary Programmatic Field

Circuit was originally designed by Tate Learning staff, who had secured the four-year funding from the Paul Hamlyn Foundation (PHF). Alongside the four Tate galleries, six more galleries from the Plus Tate network were selected to be part of the programme. Each of the participating galleries was given a portion of the total budget to execute the programme's objectives and its four delivery strands—which included partnership working with local youth organisations. Circuit was not therefore set up as a coalition of the youth and gallery sector fields—instead the programme was devised by the gallery sector as a platform for different types of engagement with the youth sector field. Within the programme itself, numerous partnerships were formed, which *did* represent attempts to bring together organisational fields from the youth and gallery sectors. I refer to these as temporary *co-working* fields. The diagram below illustrates how these geographies are configured in my analysis (Fig. 5.1):

This map acknowledges that partnerships don't operate in isolation but they are influenced and governed by broader fields.

With its significant funding and profile, Circuit represented an opportunity to design a programmatic space that would draw on best practice and address the habitual issues that affect the sustainability and integration of partnership work. One of the key aspects of the design was the allocation of an extended period of time (i.e. up to two years) for arts organisations to develop meaningful relationships with potential partners and to acquire knowledge and understanding of youth sector practice. Organisations would not be expected to run active partnership projects until the second half of the four year programme, so partners would have the opportunity to co-design projects and focus on relationship building rather than rush into activity. These affordances were partly influenced by

Geographies of partnership

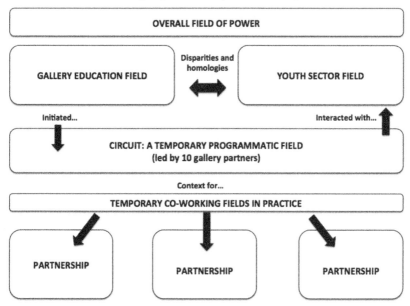

Fig. 5.1 Geographies of partnership

the investment of the funder PHF in supporting cultural change in cross-sector partnership work. A senior member of the PHF team described this vision:

> *Historically, arts organisations have extended largesse to grateful recipients, whether it was in schools or wherever, and I think the trend in co-designing, which is what we're trying to encourage with the young people involved in Circuit, actually applies to the design of your relationship. So, have you checked whether the people you are offering your services to as an arts organisation—do they want it? Will it be useful to serve their agenda? What is their need?*
>
> *And that kind of dialogue, though it sounds quite trite and quite pedestrian, is not often taking place. Because the arts organisation starts with what they want to do, or need to achieve, for a variety of reasons, and then go about it. And in a way it's done to the beneficiary, and I think part of what we're trying to explore with Circuit is a renegotiation of that framework [...] So it's to try and redress the balance of forces, and I think establish links or relationships*

> *between a museum or gallery, a Circuit partner and a series of third sector*
> *organisations involved in their community to achieve what it is that they need*
> *to achieve. So it's actually the museum and gallery as a vehicle for someone else's*
> *needs, instead of trying to achieve its own mission in a very single-minded way.*
> [Interview, 1 September 2015]

As implied by this interview extract, the programmatic space was designed to encourage more sensitive, mutually engaged and equitable partnerships and to emphasise the civic role of the institution. Circuit was also framed as an action research programme, so the programmatic field was characterised as learning-orientated rather than accountability-focused. PHF stressed the importance of moving away from measurements of success being predicated upon participant numbers, in favour of "self-reflection", "analysis" and "transparency" [interview, 1 September 2015]. The idea was that this behavioural shift would better enable organisations to build healthy, more evenly balanced relationships with partners. Occupying a dominant position in the field of power and the programmatic field, the funder was able to support this process by changing expected standards of success, and therefore changing the terms of the game, to foster a more equitable playing field for youth and art organisations to work together.

Also occupying a dominant position in the programmatic field was Tate Learning—and the team that conceived and designed Circuit. The programme was modelled on Tate's work with young people, which revolves around peer-led programming, youth sector partnerships, large scale multidisciplinary events and digital engagement. Tate and the funder were confident in the track record of the programme model and its ability to engage young people from diverse ethnic and social backgrounds. Tate London in particular had multiple years of experience in working with local authority partners supporting young people leaving care. This meant the temporary programmatic field largely adopted the 'doxa' or accepted wisdom of Tate's Young People's Programmes, and the institution's way of working with young people.

Those designing Circuit also sought to resist the "outreach model" commonly associated with gallery/community organisational partnerships, which is based around bringing culture *to* communities, rather than recognising the cultural resources and talents *of* those communities. One senior Tate Learning staff member commented:

You are working against every model that exists out there, which is: you come,
we have a session, we do it, we're terrific, you go away [...]
  [Interview, 19 May 2015]

The idea was for Circuit to unsettle prevailing hierarchies of cultural value in institutions, which tend to delegitimise young people's cultural tastes and productions. By privileging youth cultures and staging different forms of production (including music, dance, spoken word performance etc.) the hope was that Circuit could promote artistic diversity and drive change within institutions. The senior Tate Learning representative said of young people:

> *Actually they have culture, they don't not have culture, you know, it's just that those in control don't give any opportunity for them to express their culture within our boxes of what we think culture might be. So what if we open up that box and invite people to express their own cultures in the sophisticated way they do, rather than using our own rather limited quality and understanding measures of what matters and what looks like quality.*
> [Interview, 19 May 2015].

The temporary programmatic space was consequently designed to value different forms of cultural capital—which also served as a potentially important hook for engaging with youth organisations. As described in Chaps. 3 and 4, youth work practice is much more readily engaged with young people's everyday cultures and interdisciplinary, non-institutional arts and creativity. By developing a programmatic field that was committed to the principles of cultural democracy, the team aimed to create a more accommodating social and creative field for youth organisations to interact with.

It is important to acknowledge however that Circuit's temporary programmatic field was not co-designed and co-managed by visual arts and youth organisations together. Youth organisations were not part of the programme's steering group, although two experienced youth practitioners did sit on the programme's board. Instead, youth organisations would be engaged at regional levels by the participating galleries (which held and controlled the programme budgets). This arrangement seemed to limit the extent of the influence of youth sector voices on the wider programme structure and activity. Visual art organisations clearly occupied the dominant positions in the programmatic field—a fact that appeared to contradict the programme's motives to engage in equitable partnerships. Nevertheless, the Tate team felt that as the programme was rooted in an understanding of what was lacking in the visual arts, it would be necessary and more efficient to establish the programme with existing peer organisations. The programme structure also allowed for partnerships to evolve responsively out of local contexts and needs. So youth partners were not pre-identified in the programmatic field—each art organisation was given time and resources to explore new relationships in their localities, and funding was specifically allocated to support potential youth partners to engage with this process.

In Chap. 7 I look in more depth at how youth workers and youth sector professional 'capitals' were positioned and valued in Circuit's temporary programmatic field. However, for the rest of this chapter I pay closer attention to Circuit's earliest interactions with the youth sector, as organisations sought to navigate the logic of the programmatic field, and to develop and embed cross-sector relationships differently.

Building Contacts and Knowledge of Local Youth Sector Provision

As previously indicated, in relation to partnership working, organisational staff could use the first two years of Circuit as time to deepen their knowledge of the local youth sector and youth work practice, and to develop associations with youth organisations and services, in advance of formalising an (ideally lasting) collaborative relationship. In the final two years of Circuit, the organisations' partnership budgets would be increased to support activity or specific projects with young people from youth organisations. On the face of it, this seems like an extremely attractive offer for practitioners who may be accustomed to their performance being measured in terms of projects delivered and numbers engaged. However while beneficial for some, the reality of working against the grain of a sector's wider culture of practice would prove challenging for many of the organisations, including those in dominant field positions.

Some gallery practitioners had multiple one-on-one meetings with representatives of youth organisations and services across their region. Some galleries hosted sharing days or introductory workshops for youth practitioners. One gallery employed a researcher to do a scoping exercise—surveying youth centres and gathering practical information on local provision and areas of need. Some of the larger institutions also initiated discussions with their regional Bridge organisations and bodies responsible for networks of youth organisations. Arts-focused youth organisations such as youth theatres, music colleges and other neighbouring museums and galleries were also invited to be part of early dialogues.

At least three institutions ran events for a range of youth providers, as a means to introduce Circuit and find out about local need and the barriers preventing young people from engaging with arts organisations. These events gave staff from arts organisations a better understanding of what was required from potential youth partners. At one of these events youth practitioners recommended that there should be recognition of youth organisations' structures, processes and pressures, and acknowledgement of the daily realities and external influencers shaping the lives of young people, including carers and parents. One of the most repeated comments was that there should be clarity of aims, outcomes, roles and responsibilities, and there should be a strong sense of continuity, rather than tokenistic, one-off engagements [Minutes from Circuit youth partnership event, 24 July 2013].

These knowledge-generating events brought together local contacts in a single moment and enabled galleries to test responses to the programme's offer. In a group situation, frank conversations could be had about institutional barriers or challenging past experiences. However, these events were not generally framed as spaces for sharing practice, nor did these meetings generally lead to further sharing events or the start of a partnership for the majority attending. In the case of the event mentioned above, some participants reportedly had their expectations raised about the extent of their future involvement with the programme, which created some discomfort for the curator, who did not have the capacity to establish organisational relationships with everyone who took part [interview, 13 December 2013]. By attempting to build their knowledge of youth sector provision and needs, the gallery staff had inadvertently created an uncomfortable power dynamic. Youth organisations were asked to contribute their time and ideas to an institutional programme with much greater resources, without the proposition of obvious reciprocal and longer-term benefits.

Preconceptions of galleries as being elitist, exclusive spaces also hindered conversations with some youth organisations. One curator reported that she had spent months trying to build up connections with different contacts from the local youth sector, and had encountered a mixed reaction to the gallery and to Circuit. It was pointed out that youth centres tend to work with participants of a younger age range than Circuit's 15–25 remit (i.e. 11–19 year olds). And it became apparent that the gallery was perceived to not be welcoming enough to black and ethnic minority audiences and visitors with disabilities [Interview, 3 July 2014]. Added to this, budget cuts in the local authority were putting significant pressure on youth organisations and most youth workers in this region were losing their jobs. This combination of factors made it difficult to initiate conversations about practice or future programming.

These examples indicate the challenges involved in adapting to the logic of a temporary programmatic field when circumstances in sectoral fields combine to work against this logic. With youth services experiencing a period of acute crisis in various regions, some gallery practitioners found that it was impossible to hold open, elongated, exploratory conversations with youth practitioners, whose future positions were unstable. Some gallery staff reported that youth sector organisations had to see evidence of practical work, because they did not have the luxury of time to build relationships outside of project delivery with young people [interview, 11 August 2015]. Other institutions fell back into habits of relatively tokenistic engagement with youth organisations. In several cases, Circuit galleries embarked on short-term 'pilot' projects with youth organisations very quickly—usually involving artist-led workshop formats. Several gallery practitioners argued that they worked best by "doing", and through actively demonstrating their ability to develop impactful projects with youth organisations [Working group meeting, 3 July 2014]. Some of these pilot projects nevertheless encountered significant problems with the recruitment or retention of young people, and with a lack of investment from youth sector staff. The fact that many practitioners worked in ways that are fairly typical is unsurprising if we consider Bourdieu's assertion that individuals' actions are determined by their 'habitus'—that is, the conditioning that leads them to adopt certain values and attitudes, and that compels them to inhabit a particular professional field. Practitioners and organisations tend to work in ways that feel natural in their field, even if their intention is to change habits. So, for instance there were other elements of Circuit's temporary programmatic field (such as the requirement to build peer groups and stage large events) that indirectly conflicted with the aim to focus on gradual relationship development with youth organisations. The design of Circuit's temporary programmatic field was inevitably a product of field habits that are characteristic of the visual art sector and governing fields of power, where professional energies are traditionally directed towards 'delivery' or public outputs.

SUPPORTING AND NEGOTIATING THE PROCESS OF RESEARCH AND DEVELOPMENT

These early experiences of research and relationship development in Circuit revealed the need for a much more guided and supported process. The programme's national team ran a sharing session specifically on partnership working for the Circuit Working group, which covered the national team's expectations for the lifecycle of the partnership strand. My notes from this meeting indicate the types of conversations that were taking place amongst the gallery practitioners:

The programme Lead is giving a presentation about partnership to a group of about 20 gallery practitioners, including assistant curators, artists and critical friends from the galleries. The programme Lead talks about some of the problematic ways that projects with young people are framed, and how young people involved in partnership projects are sometimes not involved in peer-led work. He wants to see how partners can participate at all levels of the programme. He emphasises that the first two years of the programme are about building trust with local organisations and aligning values and aims, before planning events and pilot projects. He says it's important that youth sector partners are supported to understand the institutions, and that gallery programmers offer partners the opportunity to use the institutions' spaces. Circuit's Manager asks the group if these expectations relate to what they're doing, and whether they feel the design of the partnership strand is working for them.

One programmer reports that funding cuts and instability in the youth sector are presenting barriers to relationship development. She is also concerned that the stranding of the programme has the potential to divide up the partnership and peer-led work, to the point where two separate groups of young people might emerge. Another programmer explains that his gallery has taken a different approach, and they have chosen to recruit young people into their peer group through visiting local youth organisations. He doesn't know if those young people will stay, but he feels it's important to have those young people there from the start. The Manager asks if practitioners have had strategic conversations with partners, rather than just ask whether they have access to young people. Have partners been sharing their values and their evaluation frameworks? Some practitioners report that their collaborators have embraced the framework, while others have encountered "confused faces" when introducing the Circuit evaluation methodology to youth partners.

[Working group meeting, 3 July 2014]

By running this type of reflective session, the national team were attempting to motivate practitioners to question their actions and reconnect with the programme's vision. From my perspective, I could see how the team were trying to create space for good partnership practice, but I could also appreciate that the expectation for galleries to eventually support young people's "transition" into the peer groups influenced their desire to work with certain partners and get projects off the ground quickly. In Chap. 7, I develop a more extended discussion about the efficacy of the peer-led model (a major feature of Circuit's programmatic field) within the context of work with marginalised young people.

CONCLUSION

This brief chapter demonstrates how the creation of a temporary programmatic field is not a neutral activity, but a process that is deeply influenced by the 'doxa' or conventions of the instigating field and the (often unconscious) dispositions of the lead practitioners. While Circuit was established with the intention of evening out the relationship between galleries and youth organisations, and changing problematic organisational conduct, fundamental aspects of its design inadvertently encouraged the replication of traditional hierarchies and inequalities. With control of the funding and management of Circuit, art institutions (Tate in particular) were endowed with the greatest share of power and agency in the programme. Relationships with youth organisations were held locally, so as Bourdieu (1999) would suggest, the spatial distance between youth organisations involved in Circuit, and the programme's locus of power, reinforced this unequal distribution of agency. Circuit's multiple agendas were also symptomatic of the persistent compulsion to produce, to programme and to be visible in the contemporary gallery. While the funder may have sounded less fixated on numbers and more focused on learning, the programme did still operate with target numbers, and practitioners were expected to report on these. Ring-fenced funding and specific programmatic conditions have the potential to shift patterns of behaviour but habits of practice are entrenched in the cultures of their professional fields. One key takeaway from this analysis is therefore that behavioural change needs to be constantly supported and reinforced in all areas of a temporary programmatic field. Power cannot be easily redistributed or given up when systemic conditions encourage normative rules of engagement. Understanding programmatic contexts and structures helps to drive an empathetic analysis of interactions between partners.

References

Bourdieu, Pierre. 1985. The social space and the genesis of groups. *Theory and Society* 14 (6): 723–744.

———. 1999. *On television*. New York: The New Press.

Hilgers, Mathieu, and Eric Mangez, eds. 2015. *Bourdieu's theory of social fields: Concepts and applications*. Oxon: Routledge.

Rawolle, Shaun. 2005. Cross-field effects and temporary social fields: A case study of the mediatisation of recent Australian knowledge economy policies. *Journal of Education Policy* 20 (6): 705–724.

CHAPTER 6

Partnership Typologies and Practice

There are few terms or concepts more ubiquitous in the public sector than 'partnership'. This chapter attempts to offer a more nuanced and detailed understanding of what 'partnership' can look like between agents in the youth and visual art sectors. I refer to these partnerships as 'temporary *co-working* fields'. In the case of Circuit, these fields usually involved the coming together of a gallery and one or more youth organisation or service to develop some form of collaborative space of engagement. The nature of these partnerships (and their duration) differed widely across the different Circuit sites, in response to a variety of different contextual factors. In this chapter, I offer insights into different types of cross-sector alliances and discuss the learning that can be derived from them. In doing so I hope to address questions such as: what are the most appropriate and effective types of partnership between galleries and youth organisations today? What are the pitfalls or drawbacks to watch out for? What do arts and youth practitioners bring to the partnership space? And what happens in this assembly of youth work knowledge and visual arts practice?

The first example focuses on the type of partnership that I would argue is most common in gallery-youth organisation relationships. It involves a workshop-based, artist-led project over a series of weeks leading to a final outcome. It is staged in a relatively formal organisational environment based around further education for young people who have been otherwise out of work and education. The second example is a joined-up

© The Author(s) 2019
N. Sim, *Youth Work, Galleries and the Politics of Partnership*, New
Directions in Cultural Policy Research,
https://doi.org/10.1007/978-3-030-25197-0_6

response between a gallery and youth service to the restructuring of open access youth provision in their locality. It sees a gallery and youth service running youth nights in a creative community space and using the skills of practitioners who are trained in centre-based youth work. The third example describes the setting up of an experimental open access studio/hang out space in a former café. This project brings together youth and arts practitioners with local young people and borrows from the methods of detached, street-based youth work. These three instances of partnership involve different levels of entanglement and collaboration. In several respects, 'collaborative' is the wrong word to associate with some of the partnership arrangements in Circuit. Throughout this chapter then, I draw upon recent conceptualisations of partnership to articulate the distinct ways in which the youth and visual art fields can come together.

These recent academic efforts to conceptualise partnership are bringing greater degrees of criticality and nuance to discussion and understanding of partnership working. Speaking from a youth work perspective, Davies (2015) suggests that partnerships often fall within three types of categories: coordinated, cooperative or collaborative. The shared aspects of a relationship determine which of these categories a partnership fits into. So the extent to which partners share obligations, intensions, space, activity and, most importantly, agency—are all major factors in identifying whether a partnership is genuinely collaborative, or whether it is better framed as a different model of relations (Davies, 2015). In a coordinated relationship, there is an implication that partners are working in similar areas, but they have different goals and practices. So they may coordinate activity to achieve those different aims but not work directly together or take a significant interest in one another's ambitions. In a cooperative relationship, partners work together to achieve all of their goals, and they need one another to enable this. Davies sees 'collaboration' as a total merging of ambitions and practices. While I think some partnerships fall between these categories, across the art sector claims are often made about the collaborative credentials of a partnership that don't hold true in reality. Davies argues that organisational partners need to have a mutually agreed understanding of the nature of their relationship, if discrepancies and tensions are to be avoided.

As part of their work for the Connected Communities Programme (involving university and community partnerships), Facer and Enright (2016) have also developed four models of inter-personal relationships that can be applied when thinking about cross-disciplinary partnership.

Their models are defined by the ways in which expertise is exchanged between partners with different types of knowledge capitals. Model 1 is characterised as 'Divide and conquer'. This model apparently 'treats different sets of expertise and knowledge as clearly divided' and subsequently encourages a 'clear division of labour' (p. 69). Model 2 is defined as 'Relational expertise'. This denotes an arrangement where partners maintain their own disciplinary identities, but they also 'temporarily inhabit other perspectives' (p. 70). Model 3, is about 'Remaking identities'. It deliberately promotes the exchange and acquisition of knowledge between partners, leading to the potential creation of 'hybrid identities' (p. 70). Then finally Model 4—'Colonisation and confusion' sees practitioners from one field adopting the roles of practitioners in a partner field—often without adequate skills and training—so they are left feeling underprepared and out of their depth (p. 71). These models help to bring some clarity and classification to the types of exchanges we sometimes observe in partnerships between agents with unequal levels of symbolic power. The following three site studies contain features of the relational dynamics outlined by Davies (2015) and by Facer and Enright (2016). Using these conceptualisations alongside Bourdieu's framework for analysing fields hopefully brings us closer to understanding what works in partnerships between galleries and the youth sector.

PARTNERSHIP ONE: TEMPORARY COORDINATED FIELD

Relationship Design

This partnership featured a project established between a Circuit gallery and a further education programme for young people who had disengaged from formal education. This targeted programme was part of the government's Youth Contract scheme, which launched in 2012 to support the most disadvantaged 16 and 17 year olds to achieve vocational qualifications, and to offer businesses financial incentives to provide work experience and apprenticeship placements (Education Funding Agency, 2016). The programme therefore offered an example of the more formal (semi-privatised) section of the youth sector, which is an area that youth workers are increasingly transitioning into, as local authority youth services are experiencing cuts and closures. I sought to understand whether the Youth Contract programme would prove to be a compatible partner with the gallery, as this partnership arrangement mirrored patterns of work in other Circuit sites, where partnerships had been forged with alternative education providers.

This context was also a pertinent example of a coordinated relationship. The youth partner in this research site was a company that (amongst other activities) sought to enable young people not in education or employment to complete a qualification in Retail and to retake their GCSEs in Maths and English. The programme was ultimately contracted to steer young people into employment, further education or training. The gallery partner in this project was an institution which presented exhibitions of modern and contemporary art. As per Circuit's objectives, the gallery's ultimate aim was to support the young people to access cultural opportunities and potentially connect with the gallery's peer-led programme. While the youth partner's Programme Manager (who I will call 'Linda') had initiated the relationship on the basis that she wanted to bring a creative dimension to the course, it was clear that each organisation was pursuing distinct end goals, and neither partner had a significant investment in one another's core programmes.

The project was structured around 16 three-hour workshops, held weekly during term time at the youth partner's base—a business park outside of the city centre. The sessions would be offered as a compulsory part of the retail course. Group trips to galleries and other cultural venues were to feature as part of the workshops. The gallery recruited an artist (who I'll call 'Joanne') to lead the sessions, and it was agreed that the programme's Youth Support Worker (who I'll refer to as 'Michelle') would also support the partnership. Programme Manager Linda was the 'Project Lead' for the youth partner, and the Learning Officer (who I'll call 'Amy') was the Project Lead for the gallery.

Rather than work together as a team however, the programme largely involved the artist (later joined by the gallery practitioner) delivering sessions in the youth partner's space without any staff from the youth partner present. While it was initially implied that the Youth Support Worker would be joining every session, when sessions were in progress, this practitioner usually got on with other work in different spaces, and checked in on sporadic occasions. This way of working fits somewhere between model 1 and model 4 in Facer and Enright's (2016) catalogue of inter-personal relationships. Labour was divided up in this partnership arrangement, but practitioners were not working in parallel—rather there was an expectation from the youth partner that the artist could work alone as a session leader, despite not having any knowledge of the pedagogical approach of the youth partner staff or the needs of the young people. Based on my own observations of how this arrangement played out, the next section describes the implications of setting up a temporary coordinated field in this way.

Relationship in Practice

Over the course of six months, I acted as a participant/observer at nine of the workshop sessions, attended a gallery trip and observed three meetings: one planning meeting between the artist and gallery practitioner; a mid-point review meeting between Linda, Michelle, Amy and Joanne and a summative meeting at the end of the series of workshops. I also attended the two-day install and launch of the group's pop-up shop towards the end of the project and interviewed practitioners and young people.

Located on the first floor of the building, the programme utilised one large room and two smaller teaching spaces. They had internal windows that looked out into a corridor and the staff office. Around the spaces were motivational quotes: "Failure is only the opportunity to begin again"; and "Believe in yourself—anything is possible". In a small common area in the corridor where the learners ate lunch, there was a wall of achievement, featuring images of young people who had secured jobs. Aside from these visual indicators of the programme's presence, the spaces were quite corporate and blank, and no other young people's programmes appeared to exist in the building.

In advance of my first encounter with the project, Amy had informed me that the two previous sessions had been challenging for a number of reasons. Half of the group were apparently "eager and committed" while the other half were not. The young people who were reluctant to engage presented some volatile behaviour, which angered other members of the group. I learned from the artist that some participants had absconded to another site on the business park, while others had refused to take part. The artist explained to me that she hadn't felt adequately supported in the sessions and had expected the Youth Support Worker to be present at all times, which was not the case. Each week new young people were recruited to join the sessions, which put new demands on the artist, and as we discovered as weeks progressed, some of these young people had significant support needs. Two girls talked about abuse and bullying affecting their education progress. A few of the young people dealt with ongoing mental health issues. One member was a refugee who had been caught up in gangs. Nearly all of the participants had negative experiences of formal education, and for most, their only contact with art had been through school; so their associations with art were not always positive ones. Joanne felt strongly that someone with youth work experience should be in the room at all times, so she and the young people could benefit from their contributions.

Even though it had been agreed that the Youth Support Worker would accompany every session, gallery practitioner Amy and youth Programme Manager Linda had interpreted this agreement differently. Linda felt it was sufficient for Michelle to be nearby and reachable rather than constantly in the room, as she was busy with recruitment, inductions and administration. Some participants would show their resistance in different ways: by vocalising their boredom, playing with their phones, declining to take part or sitting outside the room. As these issues manifested themselves, the artist tested various modes of working, and different members of staff from both organisations became more actively engaged in the project. When Michelle was present, she engaged the group in relaxed, humorous chat and gently supported their participation by asking questions, making references to her own creative interests and offering praise. During break times, Michelle would also explain some of the reasons behind individuals' behaviour that day. Joanne saw her presence as having a hugely positive impact; however Michelle was rarely able to attend sessions. Amy also participated in many of the sessions in response to Joanne's call for more support.

This experience allowed me to make several reflections on this type of partnership arrangement. Even though the partners had carried out some pilot work and drafted a partnership agreement, there were clear inconsistencies between the gallery's understanding of the relationship design and the youth partner's understanding of the relationship design. Amy commented: "[Linda] saw it at times like she's contracted us, rather than it [being] a supportive partnership" [interview, 27 April 2015]. Amy had not intended for the gallery to act as a service provider, and yet the manager's requests for lesson plans, and her reluctance to afford the Youth Support Worker's time, made Amy feel increasingly as if they were. Without practitioners working together in the same physical space, there was minimal opportunity for practices and expertise to be shared. The artist had not tried to colonise the space and role of the youth worker, rather she had a dual role imposed upon her. This put an enormous level of responsibility on an artist who felt already out of her comfort zone in a professional field that was relatively alien.

This sense of alienation was exacerbated by the fact that the artist was not privy to the same knowledge about the young people as the youth practitioners. No formal details about the participants' circumstances or diagnoses were shared with the artist or gallery practitioner, on the basis of data protection rules. The artist felt that this would have been acceptable had the Youth Support Worker been consistently in the room during sessions, but given that she and the gallery practitioner were often left unaccompanied with the group, they felt the need to have a much greater level of awareness of individuals' personal circumstances. In the project, the young people's issues revealed themselves over time, but the artist indicated that her lack of background knowledge about the young people sometimes undermined her ability to fully understand their responses and behaviour and to support them if they were resistant to participate.

This temporary coordinated field was therefore a space where many participants lacked agency. As the workshops predominantly took place on the site of the youth partner, the artist had to adapt to the conditions of this field. The youth practitioners' withdrawal of facilitation support and withholding of background knowledge about the young people had the effect of further disempowering the artist. Some of the young people also exploited the fact that the artist was a visiting practitioner, and not a permanent member of staff who might discipline them. The Youth Support Worker wanted to spend more time in the project, but her manager did not conceive of the partnership as a space for cross-field exchange. I saw the Youth Support Worker's conflict as a symptom of the broader 'bind' in the youth sector, where the dominant doxa that upholds the pressures of performance management also undermines practitioners' ability to spend time with young people and disempowers them in the process (Hughes et al., 2014, p. 7). The situation in this context seemed to lead to a less positive experience for the young people (who enjoyed direct contact with the Youth Support Worker) and the artist, who lacked legitimacy in the youth programme's field.

Moments of Collaboration

It would be reductive to identify something as complex as a cross-organisational partnership in terms of a singular, fixed typology. In truth, partnerships can often slip between different phases of coordination, cooperation and collaboration. A relationship might begin very collabora-tively, and become more coordination-focused as time moves on. In the case of this partnership, there were more instances of cooperation and collaboration as the project progressed.

Changing the physical location and pedagogic approach of the work-shops in some sessions helped to support a more collaborative dynamic between practitioners and young people. We discovered that taking the group off the premises was beneficial for building a collective sensibility and group morale. Trips to galleries temporarily changed the energy of the group and led to new types of encounters and discussion around art prac-tice. Trips also brought about further interaction between the Youth Support Worker and the project, because her attention was not divided. However, we also found that some young people refused to turn up for trips outside of the youth partner's venue. Below is an extract of my field notes from one trip to a rurally located arts centre and studio complex.

Six young people have shown up for the gallery trip in total—over half of the group are not present, which is unusual. We all pile onto a coach—with most of the group sitting excitedly at the back. During the journey Linda and I talk about why some members of the group haven't come on the trip. She mentions that many of the young people have been quite vocal about their reluctance to go on trips. She says their responses can be unpredictable and many learners are frequent non-attenders.

When we arrive at the arts centre, two members of the gallery's peer group are there to greet us in the reception, where refreshments have been laid out. One of the peer group members has put a cigarette bin outside the main building so the smokers have somewhere to go, which they seem to appreciate. The group are already asking questions about sculptures they see in the grounds. Amy hands out iPads and asks the group to work in pairs to document their visit.

The two peer group members then lead us around the site, pointing out dif-ferent buildings and studios where artists work and eat. Everyone is struck by the centre's cat, which is eating the remains of a mouse on the pathway. The young people enjoy taking photos of this and other small details, noticing pud-dles in the grass and spiders' webs in the fences. We stop at a building that has been designed and built by an artist using salvaged wood and glass. Michelle comments that her house is a bit like this, with lots of reclaimed materials assem-bled together.

The rest of the morning is spent visiting the studios of two artists, who have prepared their spaces with installations to show the group. One artist has set up a series of props under bright lighting, including a marble table and large swathes of shiny fabric with a huge mound of white substance. Michelle recognises

that it looks like washing up powder. The artist confirms that it is and invites us to touch it. The young people take photos of the space and pick up objects on the artist's invitation. Michelle points out how useful it is to hear an artist talk about their work, because sometimes in galleries it's difficult to interpret meaning or spend a long time looking at text.
[Field notes, 26 November 2014]

This episode revealed some of the rewarding and challenging consequences of the partnership activity being uprooted and situated temporarily away from the physical field of the youth partner. The prospect of a trip provoked anxiety for a number of participants, and their absence demonstrated the level of support and preparation required to enable these young people to feel safe about leaving the familiar premises of the programme. Meanwhile some of the other participants expressed that they felt more comfortable when working off-site, because the natural cliques that formed in the centre were interrupted and they experienced more freedom [group interviews, 26 February 2015]. The artist had much more agency in the gallery spaces for a number of reasons. She found the partner organisation's classroom spaces creatively limiting, and felt that she was sometimes being reprimanded for not reinforcing the centre's rules. She also recalled feeling like a "disposable tutor" at times, with the perceived lack of reciprocity between the centre's management staff and the project [interview, 4 March 2015]. Amy also recognised the probable benefits of having strategic and reflective conversations away from the youth organisation. Most of the meetings between practitioners took place at the youth partner's centre, and Amy recognised that this exacerbated an imbalanced power dynamic and lack of familiarity with the gallery and associated arts spaces [interview, 27 April 2015]. The gallery visits also led to encounters between the project participants and members of the peer group, as well as other practising artists. These encounters appeared to be equally stimulating for the Youth Support Worker, who encouraged the learners to look closely and ask questions.

In the arts venue, the artist clearly felt a much greater sense of belonging and authority than she did in the youth organisation. The artist's cultural capital (i.e. familiarity with galleries, artists and studio practice) enabled her to perform her role most effectively in the arts venue. The Youth Support Worker also felt able to connect her creative tastes to the works on display at the arts centre, and many of the young people enjoyed the new and unusual environment. However, the absence of half of the group illustrated that certain types of cultural and social capital were required for the young people to even entertain the prospect of travelling to a new area, let alone visiting an arts centre. While the youth partner's venue was seen as a relatively undesirable space, this was a space where some of the young people held dominant positions, or where they experienced feelings of safety that couldn't be guaranteed elsewhere (Bourdieu et al., 1999). These events highlighted the need to both increase opportunities for exchange between the organisational fields, and to recognise the complex challenges of visiting different sites or fields where the visitor appears to possess little relevant capital or agency (Bourdieu et al., 1999). Acknowledging the boundaries of young people's own social fields was also shown to be vitally important to the development of an effective partnership.

The Place of 'Art' Within the Temporary Coordinated Field

As previously outlined, the way in which art practice is understood, discussed and engaged with in a youth/arts partnership reveals various things about the social disparities and differences in cultural capital between partners. The navigation of divergent approaches towards creative practice lies at the centre of many of these types of projects, and therefore creative pedagogies influence, and are influenced by, the relational framework of a partnership. For instance in this partnership, where the majority of activity took place in the youth partner's venue, which was not set up as a messy space and which lacked equipment or full staff engagement, the artist was creatively limited. There was a tendency for sessions to focus on individualised creative tasks as there was less scope for facilitating collective activity. When more exploratory, experimental activities were introduced, these were sometimes met with resistance. Both the youth practitioners and several of the young people wanted the work to have a clear connection to their retail course, and ideas around enterprise. According to the Manager, the young people "felt art for art's sake was pointless" [summative meeting, 20 March 2015].

A participant who I will call 'Aasif', an 18-year-old refugee from Afghanistan, expressed in an interview his frustration with the open-ended nature of some of the sessions:

I was excited but after I see what was in the project I didn't like it. No one's showing me something they've made. All they're saying is go and make it

yourself. So if you show me something to do, I can concentrate on how you've made it, and I can make init. But if you show me some picture I don't got no idea, I don't know about art, nothing. You tell me to go and make this, go and make that, I don't like it. I like art to be honest, but not this type of art. I like drawing and learning. Everyone can do this, you don't need teacher for this. What's the point—and you look stupid as well making that. In Afghanistan people first draw something, how they make it, they explain. I don't know nothing, if you don't teach me something I'm not going to learn.
[Interview, 11 March 2015]

Aasif's comments revealed he felt self-conscious about making works that (in his eyes) didn't have a clear "point". And he sought a banking-style pedagogy (Freire, 1970) that would be seen as incongruous to accepted models of peer-led practice in contemporary gallery education. The gallery practitioner acknowledged that the traditions of gallery education practice were out of step with approaches to learning that were entrenched in the minds of the young people:

I think that was quite challenging to start with [...] because a lot of what we were doing was very process-led to start with and it didn't necessarily mean that there was going to be a beautiful outcome at the end, it was more about experimenting. And as we were saying, some of them really enjoyed that but it is [...] a totally different way of working and something that we're more comfortable with because what we do isn't so directed and it is about process and experimentation.
[Summative meeting, 20 March 2015]

Aasif's comment about looking "stupid" was a telling one. For him, an open-ended creative exercise might generate feelings of inadequacy and shame. This type of response was the natural reaction of a young person whose educational experiences and cultural background (i.e. 'habitus') had led him to make discriminations about the credibility of certain approaches to artistic practice and learning. It is argued that the 'deep rooted expectation of the student and teacher relationship' is bound up with internalised conceptions of one's social position and perceptions of a lack of ability (Sayers, 2015). Aasif's reaction to the project was perhaps connected to his own low self-belief and his need to save face in front of peers, but it was also linked to his culturally engrained understanding of arts education from his experiences growing up in Afghanistan. The exploratory gallery education approach evidently contains assumptions about participants' cultural and educational capital. As highlighted in Bourdieu's work (1984), there is a clear relationship between an individual's social class and their taste in creative practice. But as Aasif's comments demonstrate, there are also racial and ethnic dimensions to an individual's cultural worldview that may or may not intersect with their class position. The tendency to talk about young people's cultural capital in deficit terms is in itself problematic. But it is also problematic from the standpoint that these deficit framings are often rooted in white, Western critical and aesthetic standards (Wallace, 2017). In the case of this partnership, I witnessed little discussion amongst the practitioners and young people about creative tastes and pedagogical approaches. There were multiple fields at play—that of the gallery and artist, that of the youth partner and that of the young people. In each of these fields, there were various dominant conceptions of creative practice and pedagogy, but few opportunities to discuss these differences in depth.

The gallery practitioner and artist did however respond to the young people's comments (which were reported by the youth practitioners) by moving the creative direction of the project away from more experimental approaches and towards more craft or design-based activities. Joanne and Amy organised for the group to create a pop-up shop in the city where they would sell their creations to raise money for charity, so there was a much more explicit link to social enterprise and retail. The youth partner staff were very supportive of this move, and the public, ambitious nature of the initiative helped to galvanise the involvement of staff across the centre. Michelle and Linda also invited their daughters (who worked in creative direction and retail jobs) to act as guest practitioners during sessions leading up to the installation of the shop. These sessions involved creating mood boards for the shop layout and designing products such as mobile phone cases, jewellery, tattoo transfers and postcards. Participants were also encouraged to co-design the branding for the shop. The group responded well to the focused direction of the activities, and the installation of the shop was a major high point for those who took part. It brought about genuine moments of collaboration as young people and staff worked collectively to build an environment to display their work. Young people who never usually talked to one another were working together and different tutors from the centre came in to praise their progress and contribute to the install.

Many visitors commented on the professional finish of the products and the shop branding. Members of staff from the gallery's Learning team also came to visit and to buy works when the shop opened. Amy commented that one gallery staff member noted that the work was quite "youth arts"—presumably meaning that the work on display fitted a community arts aesthetic rather than a contemporary gallery aesthetic. This was an interesting observation because it signalled the distinct cultural value judgements between the two organisational partners. The artist had evolved the project to align as much as possible with the retail-oriented focus of the youth programme, so she had consciously departed from her own artistic practice and interests in an effort to meet the needs of the youth partner and to take on board the young people's suggestions. In the display moment, where staff from both organisations were brought together, these different conceptualisations of artistic quality came more sharply into view.

This outcome did not seem to represent a coming together of the creative values of different fields—rather the gallery field (occupied by the arts practitioners) had in some ways conceded to the tastes and desires of the youth partner. If more time had been spent on group facilitation and engaging with and challenging attitudes, the partners may have created space for dialogue and understanding. The youth practitioners could have spent time visiting the gallery sites in advance, so they might have developed more in-depth knowledge of gallery-based pedagogies, and engaged in discussion about shared and different understandings of artistic quality. The fact that these more practice-oriented processes and questions were not analysed at length at the beginning of the project is not unusual in partnership projects between arts and youth organisations (Matarasso, 2013). Contracts often focus on delivery structures, timelines, responsibilities, resources and objectives. And yet as we discovered towards the end of this project, the participants and staff all held distinctive ideas about art and pedagogy (resulting from differences in habitus), which could have produced healthy debate at the onset of the collaboration.

Expectations for 'Transition' in a Coordinated Partnership

One of the goals of partnership activity in Circuit was to support young people to sustain their relationship with the gallery beyond a partnership project, and to enable them to join the gallery's peer group. Each gallery site adopted different ways of supporting this journey of transition. Some galleries employed members of their peer groups to work as assistants, evaluators or volunteers on partnership projects. In the case of another gallery, young artists were employed to run partnership projects and also take part as members of the core groups. Youth organisations involved in partnership work were often invited to attend events programmed by the peer groups, and in most cases, members of the peer groups made presentations to the partnership groups about their peer-led programme, in order to promote the opportunity to join.

In this partnership relationship, members of the peer group had little interaction with the partnership initiative until the gallery visits and the pop-up shop, where two members were employed to help invigilate the space. One member also attended the final evaluation session at the youth partner base, to give a presentation about the peer group. This meant that the level of awareness and contact between the two groups was minimal. When the peer group member gave her talk to the partnership group, one of the learners interrupted her to ask: "I don't mean to be rude, but what has this got to do with us?" [field notes, 11 March 2015]. For this participant there was no evident connection between the project and the peer-led offer at the gallery. On feeding back to the youth partner's Manager, the learners reportedly referred to the gallery's peer group as "culty", and to some of the members they had met as "hipsters" and "posh" [summative meeting, 20 March 2015]. In the final evaluation meeting between practitioners, Amy acknowledged that there was a perception that the gallery and its audiences were "posh". Michelle responded (referring to me, Amy and Joanne): "You all are! You need roughing up! We need to find some rough ones!" [Summative meeting, 20 March 2015]. This frank conversation about the class distance between the two groups of young people, and between the practitioners made visible some of the main barriers obstructing the possibility of transition and exchange. There was a sense that the "middle class" art field could not be penetrated, and as gatekeepers to the field, we made the social distance between the fields more apparent. The Youth Support Worker also noted that most of the group did not have supportive families who would encourage or facilitate their independent involvement with the gallery:

> Most of the young people who come here—they're not believed in at home, nobody actually really listens to what they've done today.
> [Summative meeting, 20 March 2015]

So despite offering taster sessions for the peer group and paid internship placements, the gallery did not succeed in securing the longer-term engagement of the young people. Had activity been less separated and had the youth practitioner been able to support the young people to engage in the peer group sessions, it is possible that the fields of the gallery, youth partner and young people may been able to influence one another, and a future relationship may have been sustained.

Field Compatibility

In this coordinated partnership arrangement, the gallery partner was required to fit into, and enhance the provision of the youth partner. In working with a targeted, formal youth setting such as this, with stretched staff capacity, there was little opportunity to reimagine the parameters or structures of provision—or to create a collaborative, hybrid field of practice and knowledge for instance. Dialogue between the partners tended to happen in meetings and on emails, rather than through practice-orientated encounters, so there was a reluctant separation of labour and a lack of willingness on the part of the Manager at the youth partner to invest much staff time in the workshops. The process was therefore emotionally taxing on the gallery practitioner and artist, who sometimes felt undermined, particularly when criticism was relayed via staff from the participants. The mentality of feeling like a contracted service sat uncomfortably with the gallery staff and artist, and the gallery practitioner also felt that their informal, experimental learning approach was not given a chance [interview, 27 April 2015].

The cultural and class differences between participants also demonstrated the lack of correlation between the habitus of participants and the habitus of the gallery representatives (including me). This social distance impeded agents' ability to fully perceive the symbolic capital necessary for participation in certain elements of the project. Discussion about creativity, joint recruitment of artists, skills sharing, regular reflection and familiarisation visits may have all helped to embed the cross-field relationships. But there were also deeper constraints limiting this partnership. The partners in this case undoubtedly found allies in some of the practitioners involved across both organisations, yet there were fundamental differences in organisational values and practices, which made genuine exchange problematic. This type of targeted youth partner, whose task it was to deliver on a government contract, is representative of the type of organisation that funding and many marginalised young people are being directed towards. This project presented an opportunity to examine the potentiality of these types of providers to act as viable partners for galleries. While this is only one example of a partnership, and there were many positive moments to draw from in the project, it gives some indication of the challenges of bringing together visual art organisations and more formalised, target-driven programmes for young people.

PARTNERSHIP TWO: TEMPORARY COOPERATIVE FIELD

Relationship Design

The second partnership I want to focus on took place in a large English town between a gallery and the local youth service. This relationship evolved over several years in response to a growing set of tensions around young people's use of areas in and around the gallery as hangout spaces. In this particular town, residents' complaints about young people's tendency to congregate in groups next to the gallery had led to the council's installation of security features and street wardens to discourage young people from engaging in so-called anti-social behaviour. This type of activity had started to sour young people's perceptions of the gallery and increase negative commentary about young people in the local press. As a consequence, the gallery's Learning team and the local youth service were keen to work together to support and listen to young people's voices and enable them to access opportunities. This was all happening at a time of significant change for the youth service. In 2010, the county cut its youth service budget from £12m to £5m, and in early 2014, the council agreed to reduce its spending on youth services from £5m to £2.4m by 2016-2017. Seemingly most at risk was the area's open access provision (i.e. drop-in spaces for young people to socialise and interact informally with peers and youth workers). Restructuring in the service would also mean that youth workers would be recast as commissioners, and tasked with supporting third parties (such as other organisations and volunteers) to run provision. So the partnership I am about to describe is an example of a cooperative relationship. The organisational partners in this case had slightly different, although overlapping, goals. But both organisations were essential to one another in the process of meeting their ambitions. This is also a good example of a model of partnership based on 'relational expertise' (Facer and Enright, 2016, p. 70), where practitioners with distinct professional identities come together to share and inhabit one another's spaces and (to some extent) knowledge.

To offer some context to this arrangement, it is first necessary to explain the different spatialities at play. As previously stated, the gallery and its surrounding public realm area (owned by the council) had, over successive years, become a hangout site for groups of teenagers and other young adults, who would use the outdoor space for skating and BMX-ing, playing card games, taking legal highs or just chatting. Inside the gallery, especially in the winter, up to 40 young people would sometimes gather in the gallery's large central atrium. Some would be charging mobile phones or plugging in their straighteners and some would leave rubbish in the toilets. The majority came to socialise in a place of shelter with friends [interview with gallery staff, 12 February 2014]. The gallery's Learning team attempted to engage the young people in various programmes but many were reluctant to take up these invitations. For various reasons, young people in the town were choosing to designate the area around the gallery as their social space. While not attempting to intimidate others in the process, the young people's presence in large numbers and sometimes transgressive activity meant they were displaying forms of symbolic power over the space, which was deemed to be threatening. As a consequence, these young people came into contact with 'adult constructed "fields of practice"' such as community policing and gallery youth programmes, which strove in different ways to regulate their behaviour (France et al., 2013, p. 601). This generated a loss of trust and feelings of resentment towards the council and the gallery for many young people.

As the young people presented behaviour that gallery staff were unaccustomed to dealing with, and as tensions grew, the gallery's Learning team sought to engage the expertise of the local youth service. Youth workers and a mobile youth work bus were brought on site and a former youth worker from the service was recruited to act as a critical friend to the gallery's Circuit programme. This practitioner had a long history of work in the youth service and was a recognisable and respected figure amongst local young people. She identified that one of the reasons the young people were drawn to the area was its proximity to a former bus station site. Next to the gallery stood a small building that used to be a bus station waiting room, and surrounding this space was a largely empty tarmacked area, which was earmarked for redevelopment in future years. During some of the time the young people were hanging out, the local youth centre was also shut for a period of restructuring, so it was evident that there were few other places for young people to go, particularly in the winter months.

Even when the youth centre was open, many of the young people hanging out near the gallery were not interested in attending. Some were also too old to access the youth centre. And for some of the young people I later spoke to, the youth centre also represented a space of regulation. Housed in a large 1960s concrete building, the centre had all the hallmarks of a traditional open access youth centre, with pool tables, sofas, wall murals, sports facilities and so on. However, open access sessions were also framed around specific agendas, such as drug and sexual health awareness, healthy living support and self-esteem as well as certificated programmes including the Arts Award and National Citizen Service [field notes, 16 September 2014]. One young person (who I will call 'Jack') became very pivotal to the partnership between the gallery and the youth service, as a former user of the youth centre and as a peer group member at the gallery. Jack was also a well-known and well-liked figure amongst some of the groups who hung out near the gallery. Jack said of the youth centre and its workers:

> *I used to go to the [youth centre] and they're the nicest people ever. You can talk to them, they give you advice and help you out a lot. They're just generally super nice.*

He was a regular at the centre until changes were made to the staffing and content of the drop-in sessions. An extract from our interview conveys Jack's opinion on the increasingly formalised character of the youth centre:

> *Jack: They changed loads about the [youth centre]. They got loads of really boring crap in. Like you had to do 20 minutes of talking. And you were like, I could just not be here.*
> *Me: And you said you were asked to do a stress test?*
> *Jack: Yeah, that was awful. It made me stressed. I'm not a stressy person and it was so generally annoying. I just stopped going [after that]. Playing pool for free—not worth it!*
> [Interview, 20 January 2015].

A group of girls also told me that they stopped going to the town's youth centre because they kept being asked to sign forms [field notes, 16 December, 2014]. Some of the young people had also noticed the number of youth workers had been reduced. These anecdotes seemed to indicate that there had been a shift in culture at the youth centre towards increased monitoring and outcome-focused work, which had alienated some of the young people. The restructuring process meant that youth workers also had to focus on enabling capacity and providing support to projects rather than delivering provision themselves. This involved running less open access sessions at the centre, and concentrating more on recruiting and training volunteers and on supporting programmes to be self-sufficient [interview with youth workers, 16 September 2014].

Despite the young people's reluctance to engage with gallery programmes and the youth centre, they did seem willing to talk to detached youth workers and to artists, who might have appeared to be independent from any regulatory authority, and who expressed an interest in young people's views. The gallery's Learning team subsequently commissioned an artist to work with the young people to create films about their experiences of exclusion and discrimination in the area. These films would also feature footage of young people's risky creative acts and subcultures in and around the gallery. This formed one of the starting points of a new type of relationship between the youth service, young people and the gallery, as practitioners recognised the merits of engaging *with* the culture of young people's complex social fields in partnership. In early 2014, it was agreed that the youth service and gallery would work together to co-run a regular youth night in a new creative enterprise and social space housed in one of the disused bus station buildings near to the gallery. A local community organiser and a committee of artists and makers had set up the space, and they were keen to encourage young people to use it. By running these nights, the gallery would be able to potentially foster better relationships with local young people and help to provide creative opportunities and platforms for young people to express themselves within the locality, away from a direct association with the gallery. For the youth service, this represented an opportunity to road test their new commissioning model. The nights would be located in a space where young people naturally wanted to be. And with the gallery, its peer group and the community space involved, there was potential for the initiative to be eventually self-sustaining.

Temporary Cooperative Field in Practice

The former bus station space was located metres away from the gallery in a set of small buildings including one large room, painted white and bright green. Long tables made with reclaimed wood were spaced out around the room alongside industrial-style old school chairs. Bare light bulbs hung from the tall ceilings on yellow looping cables, also in a deliberately industrial style. Paraphernalia could be found around the edges of the space and on makeshift shelves—a music player, clip boards, signage, beer barrels, prints and so on. Together these objects indicated the multiple uses of the building, which was conceived as a DIY events venue, kitchen/ bar and creative space. On one side of the room was a bar and kitchen service area over which hung an enormous bright green sign with the words: YOUR SPACE, CULTURE & OUR CREATIVE COMMUNITY. Blackboard signs were attached in various places, outlining the different programmes running each day, from making and hacking workshops to DJ sets and a games club. Outside around the front of the building were positioned five wooden picnic tables. They faced a large disused building with an alcove in its wall, which I came to learn was a common hangout for people taking drugs or urinating. The back of the space looked out onto the back of the gallery.

The main organiser of the space had agreed that the gallery and youth service could run their joint Tuesday nights from the venue, and that he would drop in during the sessions to help with the set-up. Initially, the idea of the sessions was to have an arts focus every alternate week, and to employ an associate artist from the gallery to facilitate the arts activity. One or two youth workers would also initially be present at each night, as part of their work with the youth service. The gallery recruited two young men in their early 20s (who were part of the peer group) to help out by running a tuck shop/non-alcoholic bar at the nights. One of these young people was Jack (mentioned earlier), and the other was a young person I will refer to as 'Alistair'. The plan was for Alistair and Jack to gradually increase their responsibilities so the youth workers may eventually not be needed on site. The gallery Coordinator (who I'll call 'Cathy') would come to the sessions occasionally, and would support Alistair and Jack if required. An artist who worked regularly with the gallery and who was part of the founding committee of the bus station space was appointed to take part in the alternate arts nights. The doors would be open from 6–9 p.m. and the sessions would be aimed at 16–19 year olds, but open to younger and older people attending, as long as they were over 13 and under 25. As a hub for the town's creative communities, the venue was designed to be an open, cooperative enterprise, which embraced its temporariness by maintaining a culture of self-organisation. The space also possessed an obviously grown-up, cool atmosphere in its DIY appearance, so appeared to offer an attractive alternative to the more dated youth centre and the more formal gallery sites.

I attended 11 of the Tuesday youth nights over six months between late 2014 and early 2015. I also attended meetings of the different partners involved in the sessions and conducted informal interviews with Alistair, Jack, Cathy and Tim (who was the main youth worker involved) as well as some of the young people who came regularly. In addition to these visits, I attended selected events organised by the gallery, to understand how the offsite work interacted with the onsite programming and youth audience. My main objective was to understand what happened in this cooperative space, which brought together the professional fields of youth work and gallery education alongside the social field of young people. I wanted to understand how the practices of youth work and participatory gallery work might coexist, clash and influence each other in the space and whether this cooperative methodology was mutually rewarding and sustainable.

During the first session I observed, in August 2014, the artist and two youth workers were present. The youth workers stationed themselves at a table near the door. When I arrived there was a discussion going on about the use of board games. One of the youth workers was keen to get these out on the tables so young people could play on them if they wanted, however the artist disagreed as she wanted to encourage their creative participation. It was apparent that this was a conversation that had happened before and there was some veiled frustration on both sides. The artist decided to rearrange the space and set up a series of playful provocations, which might ignite the curiosity of potential visitors. The artist pushed the furniture to the side of the room, and secured a long roll of paper to a chair. She then placed a customised roller skate with pencils attached on the sheet, so people could draw with their feet. She also strew toilet paper around benches and across to the disused building opposite. Only a handful of visits were made by young people that evening, and those who came were largely members of the peer group and their close friends. They were happy to interact with the materials, and we spent time wrapping chairs in cling film, creating floor sculptures out of plasticine and covering Jack in hazard tape. The youth workers took a record of who was present at the session and chatted to any young person who came in. They didn't get involved directly in the activities as they made it clear they felt it was "the artist's session". They also had paperwork to complete so they got on with this [field notes, 26 August 2014].

The youth workers' self-separation from the action showed that there was a clear or presumed delineation of roles on this night. The small instance of disagreement about whether or not to put out board games seemed to signal the disparity between the youth worker's approach and the artist's approach. The youth worker believed there should be a choice of activities (based on what she knew was popular with young people), and that it would be better to have them stay and play a board game than not come at all. The artist meanwhile, wanted to subvert the space and she implied that board games would detract attention and discourage young people from playing with the materials. In other words, the artist's instinct was to create disorder, while the youth worker's instinct was to create a place of sanctuary and consistency, which seemed congruent with the characteristic logics of art practice and youth work (Grenfell and Hardy, 2003; Jeffs and Smith, 2010). The relative quietness of the session was apparently typical of expected numbers in the summer months. But there is also the possibility that some young people saw the interventions and did not want to join in, because their seating spaces had been removed and their presence in the space would appear to be somewhat directed. Nevertheless, the peer group members' willingness to participate helped to create a space of encouragement. It meant that their friends who attended also felt comfortable enough to experiment with the objects and materials, and that there was a shift from the artist-as-initiator to a peer-led dynamic.

I also attended nights in the space when artists were not present, and where youth workers took a more prominent role in the sessions. This allowed me to closely observe youth work pedagogies in action. Groups of young people would often turn up early to the sessions for a chat with the youth workers. Relaxed conversations about how their friend had got in trouble or what was going on at school revealed the history of the relationship between the practitioners and young people in the area. I came to realise that this relationship was held very delicately, and that trust could be quickly damaged if a youth worker reported an incident, or was overly didactic. They had to perform a complicated dual status as friendly, relatable adult and responsible professional. This negotiation seemed to be more apparent in the context of an open access setting where issues would occur and different people would turn up unexpectedly. On a couple of occasions young people would run in from outside for help with calling an ambulance because their friend was ill or had been drinking too much. A police officer arrived one night due to possible drug dealing in the area. On several nights, there was concern about the influence of an older boy who was known to be grooming other young people and was supposedly banned from the vicinity. The youth workers were ready to respond to all of these situations, and some of the practitioners had quite in-depth knowledge of the young people's circumstances. The youth workers' visibility as uniformed, recognisable adults also seemed to be important for individuals who arrived on their own. Some visitors would come regularly to the sessions, and engage much more with the youth workers than other people their age. One boy would come to almost every session and talk about issues with his college course and his foster carer, and sometimes play about with objects in the space. It was evident that he saw youth worker Tim as an unofficial mentor figure.

On the nights where there was no artist present I noticed that game playing was a key mode of engagement for the youth workers. It was surprising to see streetwise teenagers getting engrossed in scrabble or a game of cards. But it became apparent throughout the fieldwork that game playing was a central feature of the town's youth culture. Jack in particular would regularly refer to Magic: the gathering, a trading card game that was very popular in his friendship group. A lot of his spare time was also taken up with "RP", or role-playing Dungeons & Dragons [interview, 20 January 2015]. Many of the young people who hung out near the gallery and came to the youth nights also identified with alternative cultural traditions. Alistair and Jack were able to reel off the types of groupings they had grown up knowing: the emos, metalheads, goths, steampunks and so on. They also pointed out the divisions amongst social groups in the town and tendency for drinking and drug taking amongst some groups of teenagers. I noticed that in some of the sessions at the former bus station, members of these disparate groups would come together over a card game of "shithead" or similar. Importantly, the youth workers, Jack and Alistair displayed knowledge of the types of cultural capital that were deemed relevant and valuable to young communities in the locality. 'Knowing the game' literally and metaphorically was vital for engaging other young people within the space and avoiding the domination of adult-led agendas (France et al., 2013, p. 600).

The differences between the sessions involving an artist and the nights facilitated by youth workers seemed to indicate a lack of collaboration between practitioners from the gallery and youth work fields. The practitioners had not devised a shared logic of practice in their temporary field— rather they had coexisted in a shared space and alternated responsibility from week to week. In recognition of this, the practitioners sought to make a conscious effort to increase dialogue and integrate their ways of working. They decided to attempt to strike a balance between giving people what they knew and wanted, and challenging them to try different things.

Adjusting the Field Logics

In October 2014 the gallery staff, peer group members and youth service staff decided to launch a new format for the nights in the bus station space. The nights were billed as 'an alternative social scene' and were to include hot drinks, snacks, music, open mic and performance opportunities, games, art and making in a 'super laid back atmosphere' [Facebook, 21 October 2014]. The staff also decided that it would be beneficial for the artist to attend youth service planning sessions and to contribute to the evaluation at the end of each night. Both partners also sought to ensure that the events were well promoted on their respective Facebook pages. The emphasis on fostering a relaxed, multi-use space was designed to appeal to young people who wanted to hang out, and others who wanted a more participatory experience. In this way, the voluntary principle of youth work was being preserved and the gallery would continue to incorporate an informal interdisciplinary arts offer, unencumbered by any expectations for specific artistic outputs.

On the first session launching the new format, the youth workers brought music equipment from the youth centre for open mic, while the artist brought a range of magazines, printed images and letraset transfers for collaging. My notes from the session communicate some observations about the shift in atmosphere in the sessions:

It's a particularly cold day and it darkens quickly from 6pm when I arrive. A number of young people and adults are already there, setting up the space. The founder of the venue is training up Alistair and Jack to serve hot drinks from the bar. Candles in jars are also lit on the tables. Some of the boys are sound-checking the electric drums, keyboard, guitar and microphones set up in the corner. The artist arranges materials across one of the tables for people to use. Many of the images laid out feature popular black celebrities and iconic cultural figures, in recognition of Black History Month, which the youth service is celebrating. As the session begins and more people arrive, some individuals start to use the materials and create collages.

The majority of attendees are boys, and there are always around 15–20 people in the room, although this fluctuates as people come and go. Throughout the early part of the evening people casually play on the drums and keyboard and bring in chips to eat from outside. One of the boys wants to play scrabble but the youth worker encourages him to use the art materials first. He starts using the letraset and becomes absorbed. More young people from the gallery's peer group turn up to watch the performances. Alistair and two friends perform three songs—including a cover of The Darkness. A member of the peer group also does some impromptu breakdancing. Throughout the session I notice that the artist and youth worker are exchanging thoughts about how the session is going, and they talk about safeguarding concerns when a group of people in their twenties come in.

[Field notes, 21 October, 2014]

The different opportunities to participate (or not), and efforts made to improve the atmosphere of the space helped to attract young people who would usually hang out in the areas outside. The format also enabled visitors to stage their own creative practices and make small creative decisions, such as selecting a song to play on the laptop—nicknamed the "jukebox". There was a more communicative relationship between the youth workers and the artist, and a range of other people from the partner organisations came together to support the renewed format. The gallery's digital creative practitioner made a short film of the night and posted this on social media, while other youth workers and peer group members dropped in to informally contribute to the session.

This revised format continued to create a positive momentum and committed audience for the youth nights (although weekly numbers fluctuated). The tendency to attract more male than female attendees was a feature that followed through most of the youth nights that I observed. However, the profile of young people attending was relatively diverse. One young person who came regularly to the nights was a 20-year-old transgender woman. She volunteered to be interviewed during one of my visits, to talk about her experiences of the youth nights. She had started coming to the nights because she was friends with Jack (who she had met through hanging out near the gallery). She talked candidly about being the target of violence and intimidation near her home, and she described the youth nights as inclusive and welcoming:

I come here because everyone here is equal. It doesn't matter what you are, what you've done, you are here and you are equal. You are treated one as the same. Like with me, no-one here calls me by my male name. [...] Everyone's very respectful, it's quite a nice atmosphere, even with not that many people here it's still calm and nice, you know.

I asked the young woman about her attitude towards the role of youth workers:

I think they're very strong. The social youth workers play such a great part in making places feel welcoming and helping to think outside the box. And they help out with making sure that people are comfortable. [...] I think at the end of the day, without an adult presence it wouldn't feel as open to everyone. You wouldn't feel the calm, respectful feeling you get in these events.
[Interview, 6 January 2015]

Jack also made comments about the importance of having youth workers such as Tim present:

Jack: [Tim's] a really great guy to work with—it's nice to have him there so if anyone needs any help with anything that we can't help them with—say their CV—he's just a really nice safety net. He's always there. I like the fact that that it's not just run by us, that it's also the youth service, but then I always like working with the youth service.
[Interview, 20 January 2015]

As these interview extracts demonstrate, youth workers were seen as playing a crucial role in helping to maintain a safe, democratic space. Their presence ensured the preservation of the intended logic of the nights, and they possessed specific capitals that were recognised by the young people as valuable. While the youth service did have clear outcomes they wanted to achieve from the venture, the youth worker ensured these did not infringe on the relaxed character of the nights. Jack was also reluctant to implement Circuit's profiling questionnaires in the sessions (which the programme used to collect data on participants). These were sometimes used, but sparingly, as Jack and Alistair wanted to sustain a non-intrusive ethos. Considering these types of issues (as well as my own interventions as a researcher) pushed me to reflect on the trials of creating an idealised environment for youth engagement, whilst also developing ways to unobtrusively capture and evaluate their progress. This is a key concern facing the youth sector, amid fears that the voluntary, open tradition of youth work is being eroded by external agendas, the imposition of bureaucratic relationships and prescribed targets (Taylor, 2014). Talking with youth workers enabled me to better understand the conflict felt by many practitioners, who had to reconcile the pressures of fulfilling 'institutionalised normative practices' (associated with the doxa of the local and national authority), with their own desire to 'care' and work directly with young people (Hughes et al., 2014, p. 4).

Sustainability

A condition that was common to all partners throughout the fieldwork was precarity.

The youth workers had been open about the fact that the aim of the service was to build capacity within the community to run programmes on a voluntary and self-sustainable basis, as they would eventually have to withdraw from direct involvement in the youth nights. During my observations, the youth workers I met also referred to job cuts and restructuring taking place within the youth service. Almost all youth workers were required to reapply to work for the service under the new structure, and adopt new job titles as community capacity developers. Simultaneously, the gallery underwent a period of major instability with its finances, which eventually resulted in the board initiating organisational restructuring, so the jobs of the entire Learning team became threatened as department staffing was significantly reduced. In addition to these circumstances, the former bus station was a temporary venue, destined for redevelopment, so the organisers of the space faced the possibility of imminent closure. The founder of the space and other organisers also had to juggle paid jobs with their voluntary roles, so their ability to dedicate time to the project was restricted. The final partners caught in a state of precarity were the young people. Some of the young people I met were in education or working in social care, but several disclosed that they had only temporary, part time work, and difficult home lives, which prevented them from living with their families. I was interested in what it meant (for the sustainability and quality of the work) if all agents were forced to bear and negotiate instability as a constant condition of their alliance.

Hilgers and Mangez (2015) argue that agents occupying homologous positions, or experiencing similar levels of insecurity in different fields can better identify with one another and foster solidarity and momentum for action. This seemed to be the case here, as the circumstances motivated practitioners to work more strategically together. For instance, the gallery began hosting meetings with local youth sector contacts and councillors. This started with a meeting in November 2014, featuring the Circuit national team, the gallery's director, two councillors responsible for youth strategy, and representatives from the youth service and the gallery's peer group. The gallery staff hoped to bring the county and borough arts initiatives together, to make connections with policy and address the absence of a strategy for arts and young people in the town [field notes, 20 November, 2014]. The meeting provided a platform for participants to identify useful networks and initiatives, and to discuss solutions to shared areas of concern, such as the lack of "hang-out" spaces for young people, and the underuse of the local youth centre. The meeting also brought to light how some of the previous tensions between the local authority, gallery and young people were exacerbated by misunderstanding and communication issues. Attendees acknowledged that improved communication had been brought about by the partnership, and that it would be beneficial for the gallery to contribute to the town's youth strategy group.

The community organiser who founded the bus station space also suggested that the possible closure of the venue felt like a healthy provocation to have as a stimulus to generate new ideas. There were discussions amongst the partners for instance about running the cooperative youth night concept as a mobile offer. In meetings, the partners would challenge one another to articulate why the context for the partnership was important. In this extract of notes from an end of year meeting, I name the artist 'Eve' and the founder of the bus station space 'Finlay':

> Finlay asks that everyone define what the bus station space offers that the youth centre doesn't. Tim says: "it's not a youth centre". Alistair says: "it's an open space". Jack mentions that he used to work at the youth centre bar, and it's "different". Finlay agrees that there's a subtle reason that the bus station works—"it's a blank canvas". Eve comments: "there's a question of why not [the gallery]"? She suggests the answer might be the lack of red tape at the bus station space.
> [Field notes, 16 December 2014]

All partners acknowledged that the youth centre used to be thriving and popular, but funding cuts and targeted activities had put many people off attending. Another issue identified was that the youth centre caters for a younger age group, and that the over 18s are underserved in the town, as they are still in need of support and safe spaces to congregate for free. So the partnership helped to highlight some of the fundamental shortcomings of youth provision in the town, and the effects of wider changes to centre-based youth work.

Over the period of time that I observed the youth nights, there were clear indications that Alistair and Jack were growing in confidence as hosts and taking ownership of the programme, which the gallery viewed as a form of social enterprise. They developed a "mocktail" menu and ran quizzes for peers, and became increasingly vocal about what did and didn't work in the environment. Alistair and Jack felt that more people actually attended the nights when there was no arts offer. They suggested that attendees preferred not to be guided to do designated activities, and that an emphasis had to be placed on fun. In response, the Coordinator suggested that different artists could be invited to participate in alternate sessions [field notes, 9 December, 2014]. Alistair and Jack's involvement as employee/volunteers for the youth nights was evidently important on several levels. Both had been part of the crowds of young people who regularly hung out near the gallery, before their contact with the peer group. They therefore had a deep understanding of young people's motivations for spending time in the area, and the divisions that existed between groups. Jack in particular acted as an influencer, and drew many people to the youth nights from his extended social circle. In this way, there was a natural dialogue between the peer group and the partnership work and little sense of separation or institutional siloing.

Towards the latter stages of my fieldwork with the site, I observed how the youth service sought to gradually hand over further control to Alistair and Jack, by offering youth work training, sharing their curriculum template and outcomes paperwork, and encouraging them to handle the signing-in and evaluation administration. Aims were regularly reviewed amongst the partners, and Alistair and Jack reinforced their desire to keep the nights pressure-free and inclusive of different groups that don't usually come together. The main youth worker (Tim) deliberately did less and less in the sessions, often sitting in the corner completing paperwork, so Alistair and Jack could run the sessions independently [observation, 16 December, 2014]. Interestingly though, Alistair and Jack resisted the idea of running the nights completely autonomously and Jack in particular communicated that he thought the youth service's new commissioning model wouldn't work in the long-term. I prompted him to explain why:

Because [youth workers] are going to be setting up these projects where the people who are part of the projects are going to become closer to them, and find it easy

*to talk to them, and the moment they leave no one is going to want to go. When
[the youth centre] lost its staff, people just stopped going.*
    [Interview, 20 January 2015].

It was clear that these young men understood the significance of the youth workers' presence and valued the support and guidance of adult practitioners. They were specifically concerned that on some nights, only small groups of young people (who were part of fairly closed social cliques) would attend, and they did not feel it was appropriate for them to act as proxy youth workers, particularly amongst peers.

So this example of partnership illustrated a number of things. Circuit had enabled the gallery, youth service and young people to experiment with developing a temporary cooperative field in the form of a creative, open access setting at a time of great uncertainty for all organisations and individuals involved. For youth workers, the space provided an environment where the traditional practice of open access youth work could be upheld. They also expressed gratitude that the gallery had been "extremely supportive" and understanding over the course of their restructure [interview, 27 May, 2015]. The youth nights had the knock-on effect of encouraging young people back into the gallery and its grounds during big youth events and reducing tension between the different communities and services in the area. The practice of privileging young people's existing cultural and social fields was also a crucial element of this partnership's success (although this did sometimes mean side-lining the intervention of artists). However, the idea that these types of initiatives might be sustained through volunteering fundamentally undermines the distinctive professional capitals of the youth worker. The nights seemed to work best when youth and community practitioners, gallery staff, artists and young people were able to be in the space together, and contribute their different skills and creative energy. When it was expected that young people should do short-term voluntary training to take on some of the responsibilities of the youth workers, there was little enthusiasm or realistic prospect of sustaining the offer. This perhaps goes to show that if galleries want to be involved in running longer-term creative youth provision, they need to be budgeting to employ youth practitioners independently, if the relevant local authority is no longer engaging in the direct delivery of services. The final partnership study presents an example of a project that experimented with this model of working.

PARTNERSHIP THREE: TEMPORARY COLLABORATIVE FIELD

Relationship Design

In the previous site, I observed that the role of artist-facilitated creative practice was deliberately underplayed, as a means to prioritise young people's everyday social (sub)cultures and a space for voluntary 'hanging out'. Organised arts activity was sometimes looked upon as a potential hindrance to attracting groups of young people, and a youth work-style practice took precedence. This final partnership study focuses on an initiative with many similar characteristics, but which involved a much greater focus on contemporary art practice and the direct facilitation of artists and youth workers. In doing so, this section looks closely at the tensions and advantages associated with integrating the logics of arts practice and youth work in a temporary *collaborative* field. This particular project merged influences from a studio-style pedagogy with open access and detached youth work, and operated as a short-term experiment that would allow practitioners to step beyond the usual parameters of their organisational fields and co-develop longer-term learning about alternative ways for the gallery and youth sector to work together. The project centred upon a two-week occupation of a former café in a small coastal town nine miles from one of the Circuit galleries, led by an artist who had several years of experience working in a local youth centre. I argue that while this space offered valuable freedoms from organisational jurisdiction, the practitioners' field habits still played an important role in the (amicable) struggles for authority in the temporary collaborative field. I also seek to illustrate how artists and informal arts practice *can* offer a dynamic route to engaging with young people who may otherwise never visit cultural institutions, and who may be dealing with complex life circumstances. In reference to Facer and Enright's (2016, p. 70) models of inter-personal relationships, this partnership methodology reflects the concept of 'remaking identities', where agents exchange and acquire cross-sector knowledge and potentially assume 'hybrid identities' in the process of collaboration. In a similar way to the first example, the backdrop to this experiment was the decreasing investment in youth services and the need to examine new models of collaborative, transdisciplinary practice for a changed professional landscape.

Context for Collaboration

As was the case in other coastal or rural regions involved in Circuit, the towns local to this gallery experienced noticeable levels of income inequality. While jobs were more readily available in the summer months, the influx of tourists would make some young people feel alienated in their own hometowns. Meanwhile in the winter months, casual jobs were scarce and young people reportedly lacked things to do or the means to travel [field notes from Locality day with youth workers and gallery practitioners, 10 January 2014]. Aware of some of these issues, the gallery's Learning team were keen to test out an offsite project in a nearby town in recognition of some of the barriers young people faced in accessing their venue. Travel costs, poor transport links and the dispersal of populations were regularly cited as obstacles preventing the development of independent youth audiences. But there were other, more specific institutional barriers identified, such as the fact that the gallery usually charged an entry fee, and it occupied an imposing building that was not a natural hub for young people to gather. The Learning team also found that there was a lot of "bureaucracy" associated with using the gallery's social media accounts to communicate to and with young people [interview with gallery practitioner, 9 January 2014]. The potential to be reactive and responsive to the locality and young people's needs was therefore restricted.

There was also relatively little recent history of prior contact with the regional youth sector at the gallery. Most significantly, the Learning team identified a general lack of confidence amongst youth practitioners and young people in their engagements with the gallery's resources. From conversations with local youth workers, the Learning Curator discovered that young people had "vanished" from the youth centre nearest to the gallery, and due to low take-up and staffing issues, this centre had closed. Cuts to the council's budget had seen up to 50% of youth workers in the region lose their jobs, and further changes were anticipated [interview with Learning Curator, 29 November 2013]. Youth workers who were still employed by the council reported that young people were being discouraged by the police from hanging around at night, and therefore many were not accessing evening youth clubs. The prospect of imminent restructuring in the youth service was having an impact on staff morale, and the council's strategic vision to focus on targeted youth work was moving investment away from universal provision. Several of the youth workers I met were already working less in youth centres and more in schools and colleges, on sexual health and cyber bullying advice pro-grammes [field notes from Locality day with youth workers and gallery practitioners, 10 January 2014]. The reduction of the youth service's uni-versal offer (i.e. provision based on young people's voluntary participa-tion) was indicative of wider change in the sector (Norris and Pugh, 2015). So the challenges encountered by young people (and young peo-ple's support services) in the immediate and surrounding areas were mul-tiple, and the service's capacity to collaborate seemed limited. In this site then, the gallery staff were drawn towards piloting an initiative that would add something to existing gaps in provision, through recruiting individual practitioners from across the visual art and youth work fields, and creating a new, hybrid field of interaction.

Establishing the Pilot: Breaking Away from Field Conventions

The pilot work I focus on here grew out of conversations between the gal-lery's Learning Curator and a locally based, self-described 'community artist' who the gallery had employed to lead training for staff members. This artist, who I'll name 'Sarah', had worked for a youth centre in the town for 13 years, running creative projects for young people 'at risk of social exclusion'. As part of this work, Sarah had established a residency model influenced by the studio ethos of Room 13—a participant-led movement that revolves around the creative freedom of young people and the recruitment of artists in residence in a dedicated, drop-in studio envi-ronment (Room 13 International, 2012). Initially there were discussions about the gallery partnering together with the youth centre, but as Sarah's position within the centre came to an end, the Learning team decided to continue the relationship with her and another youth worker from the centre (who I'll name 'Jenny'), on a freelance basis. They also decided to involve an artist who had previously been in residence at the gallery, to work on the project. I will refer to him as 'Patrick'. This arrangement would allow the gallery to test a new framework for collaboration between youth and cultural practitioners, and contribute to the invention of a new type of space for young people in the town. While the project did not represent a formal organisation-to-organisation partnership, the gallery utilised (and paid for) organisational expertise and retained a light-touch relationship with the local youth centre, which had a positive reputation in the town.

Sarah and the Learning Curator (who I'll refer to as 'Katy') identified a former tearoom on the town's main high street as the venue for a pop-up space, following lengthy negotiations with estate agents and an organisation that helps community projects to make use of empty retail units. This aspect of the venture was particularly new to the gallery, which typically runs partnership activity at the gallery itself, or at the premises of a partner organisation. Katy's ambition was to facilitate a pressure-free space that could enable young people to encounter art in a relaxed, welcoming environment and encourage visitors to perceive the gallery in a different light. Katy also saw this project as an opportunity to gather ideas for "breaking down the formality" of the gallery and for trialling a mode of working that consciously moved away from standard workshop structures predicated on outcomes and achievements [interview, 14 February 2015]. The space was to be open on eight days from 1–9 p.m. over a two-week period, which partially coincided with half term.

On the opening day, Katy described how the initiative represented a shift from the gallery's typical approach to partnership work:

A lot of the work we've been doing at the moment has been absolutely great, but as much as it's led by the young people, you still sort of have a project or a workshop in a way, even if it's quite subtle. You've got an artist, there's probably an end result they've discussed they want to get to [...] there's an artist going in and they want an achievement each session. And that's great and they're choosing what they're doing and they're going to do this event, but it's quite a standard model of working. And I think that works really well sometimes, but it's almost like you have to find the group to do that, or be working with a group who are used to each other. And what I really wanted to try was completely chucking that model out of the window. And we really honestly haven't got an outcome this time. We haven't even decided a materials list. It's just almost like, what have we got that we could put in here that people might want to play with? And keeping it open for long enough, so you don't feel like—oh god, we've only got three afternoons and two hours each, and we have to achieve something at the end of it. So opening up long enough to be able to see what happens. And it'll be those moments when somebody comes in and says—I want to make a chair! That'll be what we get out of this. So there's bits of engagement that happen on all sorts of different levels, but behind that it doesn't matter if somebody does come in and make a chair—they will have popped in, engaged, had a moment, met [Sarah], maybe they'll think about [the gallery] in a different way, and even if that's just a little fleeting moment, that's fine. Or somebody might come back in a few times over the week, which would be amazing.

[Conversation, 14 February 2015].

Katy's statement described how partnership working between galleries and youth organisations is usually characterised by an established set of structures, processes and expectations, which bring about habitual, relatively predetermined ways of working. Galleries and their partners often set up projects as regular, scheduled sessions in controlled, non-public environments, which are 'safer for institutions' (Sekules, 2010, p. 33). The pilot project would push the practitioners and the institution to work outside of these typical field boundaries and relinquish certain expectations for there to be a clear outcome. This freedom was afforded by the funding and Circuit's encouragement, and also by the fact that the gallery was funding the positions of the youth worker and artists (and not partnering directly with a youth organisation) so the staff were accountable to the objectives agreed amongst the practitioners, who shared the Curator's vision for openness and un-prescribed, voluntary experimentation.

Sarah too, communicated how her experience of developing a 'studio-based pedagogy' in a youth centre had led her to consider the benefits of creating a stand-alone studio environment, away from the typical expectations of the organisation. She reflected on the challenges of shifting practitioners' habitual behaviour in the youth centre in relation to arts practice:

> *Even after years of establishing this way of working I was still asked 'permission' to get the paints out or being asked by youth workers: "what are you going to make with them today?"*
> [Report, 2015]

Sarah was convinced that the 'unexpected learnings' of the studio setting were a powerful means of engaging young people with the visual arts. She indicated that even over a long period of time, this approach had felt strange to her centre-based youth worker colleagues. Sarah felt strongly that this mode of practice was 'a way of instilling independence, co-learning, thinking and behaving in a different way, which often meant being challenged' [Report, 2015]. It also allowed young people to see artists at work. Sarah noted that Jenny was one of the only youth workers at the centre who understood and fully supported this model of practice. One of the reasons for this may have been Jenny's own background and practice in design. She was therefore identified as an important ally for the project, and recruited to develop her own work in the space alongside Sarah and Patrick.

It also struck me that this way of working provided an attractive set of conditions for the artist, Patrick. The studio pedagogy was designed to offer him as much freedom and agency as the young people. I asked Patrick whether he saw his involvement as a residency, and as an extension of his practice:

Yeah, I'm just going to have fun. I can practice things. It's nice because also there's no pressure because no one's looking at it thinking—"that's work". It's quite a safe place for me to try things out.
[Conversation, 15 February 2015].

Members of staff from the Learning team at the gallery, including facilitators and a few members of the peer group, would also regularly populate the space and support the practitioners. I spent time with the project over its opening weekend in February 2015 and continued to follow its progress online.

The Temporary Collaborative Field in Practice

The pop-up venue was located a few minutes' walk from the train station, sandwiched next to a hair salon and opposite the clothes store Peacocks. Outside the entrance, large signs branded with the gallery's logo indicated that this was 'an open studio space for 15–25 year olds'. On the ground floor of the space, the café walls had been covered with sheets of newspaper. Two tables and a few chairs were positioned near the front window and a shelving unit near the rear acted as storage for magazines, books, pens and other paraphernalia. The kitchen area was stocked with fruit and tea and coffee-making facilities and a radio provided background music. Upstairs was left relatively untouched, with café chairs and tables still arranged across the space and a sofa facing out towards the window above the street. A computer was set up near the stairs and films played on the monitor. The windows had been covered in white emulsion so people could doodle into this. Sarah and Patrick explained their intention not to over-direct what happens in the space, but to support visitors to take creative control and try things out. Patrick was particularly intrigued by the "layering opportunities" made possible through the durational nature of the project [conversation, 14 February 2015]. Their sole occupation of the space made it conceivable that young people could adapt and add to key elements of the rooms.

Rather than prepare different activities, the practitioners brought in objects and technology (such as an overhead projector and large sheets of paper) as propositions for play. An important principle of the space was the promotion of a scavenger mentality. On the lower window the words SOFA WANTED were painted in white (an elderly lady later came in to offer her floral couch). Scraps of fabric and clothes were sourced from charity shops and visiting participants were encouraged to bring in their own materials and devices, as well as make use of what was lying around.

Below is an extract from my notes on the first day of observation (a Saturday).

Sarah and Patrick are in the downstairs room of the café, chatting to a girl (aged around 18) who is seated at a table, cutting out body parts from magazines. Patrick shows her how to photograph her collage and use the overhead projector to project printed images from acetate onto a large roll of brown paper suspended from the ceiling. We all chat together about a range of topics—from getting jobs in McDonald's to sheltered housing for young people in the area. Katy drops by with her family and stays to talk for a while. An older woman who is a volunteer also drops in to help source materials. Other people, including members of staff from the youth centre, come in to see what's happening. Sarah's dog roams around the space too and attracts attention from passers by.

As it gets darker, Sarah notices a group of 16-year-old boys skateboarding down the street and suggests they come in. The group enter on the promise of hot drinks, so Sarah and I start making and handing out hot chocolates with mini marshmallows while most of the group head upstairs. Patrick is chatting to the boys about their interests—he is particularly intrigued by skate communities and proposes that they could make skating films. A few of the group are doing GCSEs, and one is doing photography. I ask the group what they'll get up to in half term—the response is "nothing". One member of the group asks if the pop-up is for profit. Patrick and Sarah explain the premise of the project and invite them to start painting on a large piece of tracing paper hung in front of the windows. They all seem excited by the offer and they clamber around the windows, reaching for the red paint and making large-scale drawings. We discover that these drawings are also visible from the pavement below. Sarah takes everyone's names down on the wall and they agree to be photographed (Sarah wants to put images up on the studio's facebook page). When they leave after an hour or so, they say they'll come back another day with other friends. The girl who has been with us for most of the day mentions her surprise at the group's friendly behaviour.

[Field notes, 14 February 2015].

During my observations I noted how quickly young people disclosed aspects about their lives to the practitioners. Some of the participants knew of Sarah from the youth centre and Patrick also had a good understanding of the area, and was aware of teachers' names, where the skate park was and so on. As a self-confessed "chatterbox", Patrick was deeply interested in people and was keen to demonstrate that artists were part of young people's worlds and vice versa. This created an easy intimacy and sense of familiarity between practitioners and participants. Patrick would sometimes ask young people who came in: "are you artists?", which provoked a range of responses—"I like tagging a lot", "I like some art but I'm more into music and filmmaking"—to which he'd always offer an encouraging idea. As suggested in the extract above, the pop-up also drew together a community of support staff and generated curiosity locally. The presence of different groups of young people highlighted the (sometimes) negative perceptions young people held of each other, and helped to shift some of these opinions.

Throughout the first two days, I witnessed the practitioners, young people and volunteers gradually interact with and change the space. Some of these interventions were very small (defacing and collaging figures in newspapers for instance), while others were big and involved papering and painting over walls, creating performances in the windows and setting up temporary projection surfaces on the ceiling and on the shop opposite at night. The space began to take on the disordered, lively appearance of a studio, which seemed to appeal to participants. One young person remarked:

> *Downstairs is chaos—that's what I like about it though. I like it that there's all the art stuff everywhere. Because if you went to a gallery it wouldn't be like that would it?*
> [Conversation, 14 February 2015].

The creative interventions often sparked conversation about different works of art—from observational films by John Smith to Martin Creed's famous balloon installation. Sarah supported this dialogue by uploading images and videos on the studio's Facebook page of various visually arresting sculptures and installations, which garnered likes from participants. Sarah would also post (with permission) images of young people making and talking in the space, to incite curiosity and document the progress of the pop-up.

On the second day of the pop-up, I made some further observations. A snapshot of my field notes is below:

As soon as the space is due to open in the early afternoon, two friends aged around 15, are waiting at the door to come in. They seem cautious at first but Sarah welcomes them enthusiastically and introduces them to Patrick and the dog. One tells us she has been boxing that morning, and is also into football and youth politics. Sarah starts to figure out how she knows the friends—they have already started following the studio's facebook page and have a cousin who came yesterday. The pair head upstairs with Patrick where they start to paint over some intricate skull stencil designs onto the wall. Youth worker Jenny is upstairs too, starting to develop a design for the window on the ground floor, which will become a logo for the space. One of the friends talks with us about an incident of racism that their family experienced. This prompts a conversation about protest and equality, and Patrick suggests she could use the example of racism to tell a visual story on the wall: "we just need to experiment, it doesn't need to be right. Just doing it will point us in the right direction".

While we're there, a woman and a teenager come in to look around. The teenage girl mentions that she plays the violin in a gypsy jazz band. Sarah points out that Jenny plays the guitar and another visitor plays the ukulele. She proposes that they could do something together. A small family group of three young women and one older lady also come in to explore the pop-up. They seem to be in the area for a holiday.

Back downstairs, the girl who was with us yesterday returns and brings a pile of celebrity gossip magazines. We laugh at some of the sensationalist headlines and talk about body image before she diligently cuts out images of Kim Kardashian and designer brand names. Patrick also gets me to play a drawing game with a facilitator from the gallery. We have to sit back to back and describe our bedrooms to one another, while drawing from the descriptions. We stick these up on the wall. One of the volunteers brings in garish curtains from a charity shop and hangs tops and jackets from the ceiling.

Jenny spends much of the afternoon by the downstairs window, where she can also see people walk by. Sarah and Jenny regularly head outside to chat to young people they recognise. At one point they walk over to an area of the town that is known to be a popular hangout. Apparently the groups they spoke to debated whether to come in but they were already headed to the skate park so they decided to visit another time. They managed to generate interest and some young people seemed impressed by the association with the gallery.

[Field notes, 15 February 2015]

As suggested by this extract, some visits to the pop-up were fleeting, while others were more sustained over several days. Out of the 97 different young people who entered the space over eight days, 41 made return visits. There was also a combination of young people who were already known to the practitioners (26 in total), and visitors who were not previously known. While many participants lived in the town, some travelled in by bus from surrounding villages specifically for the pop-up. Several of the individuals who were approached by Sarah and Jenny on their walkabouts came to visit the space on subsequent evenings [Report, 2015]. The public, visible location of the pop-up in a shopping environment seemed to reduce visitors' anxiety about wandering in, and the large windows made it possible to observe activity and have an immediate exchange with the practitioners. The two-floor layout of the space enabled participants to work together with, or separately from, other groups of young people. The extract also indicates how social, political and personal issues were readily discussed in the space, and framed as ideas for pieces of work. Game playing was similarly encouraged as a route into making, and as a means to facilitate dialogue between participants. Jenny noted that young people often address difficult issues at a remove through creative practice, and feel able to speak about these when they are busy doing something else.

I continued to follow the pop-up after the initial weekend via social media and through email and phone contact with the practitioners involved. The space was populated every day with different groups of teenagers. The activity also became increasingly performative and collaborative, with young people creating masks out of art magazines, playing instruments and creating "living sculptures" out of found materials. It became apparent that filmmaking and photography were important mechanisms for engagement, and young people regularly picked up the camera to film one another. Participants also seemed to enjoy watching this footage back, and on the last night of the pop-up, different groups gathered together to eat popcorn and watch an edited film (mainly shot by young people) projected on the building opposite. It was evident from following the initiative that the proposition of an informal, creative drop-in studio environment proved to be a major draw for local teenagers.

Negotiating the Rules of the Game

The observations indicate how the practitioners sought to position making and experimentation at the centre of the activity. And by involving practitioners who were experienced in youth work, the project also benefited from organisational knowledge and association, whilst retaining autonomy as an initiative. Jenny and Sarah's presence ensured that a diverse range of young people accessed the space, and together they were able to utilise youth work practices, such as detached, street based methods, which are rarely used in gallery education. Sarah reflected on the value of their youth work training in developing relationships through the project:

> *Feeling confident in detached youth work methods was essential to be able to engage with young people on the street in a non-intimidating way. It allowed us to engage with young people we already knew and many we didn't and inform them of what was going on.*
> [Report, 2015]

Detached youth work is a form of youth work that focuses on developing relationships with young people where they choose to be. The Federation for detached youth work states that this practice is 'underpinned by mutual trust and respect and responds to the needs of young people'. The practice is characterised in terms of its 'democratic credentials', and the desire to shift the balance of power in the favour of young people, particularly those who disengage from spaces of perceived control (The Federation for detached youth work, 2016).

Even though this initiative did revolve around a building, the principles of detached youth work were loosely applied both inside and beyond the space, because the initiative did not rely upon the participation of a fixed group. Instead, it relied upon the expertise of the practitioners, and their sensitivity to the context and its population. For instance, Jenny explained that she only approached young people she knew on the street if they acknowledged her first. Many of these young people had contact with her due to being referred for issues such as homelessness and drug abuse, so she was sensitive to the fact that they may not wish their friends to know about the association. Equally, Jenny's knowledge of many of the local young people's personal circumstances and interests enabled her to build upon existing relationships, to establish young people's trust in the project quickly, and to pre-empt any challenging behaviour. Learning Curator Katy noticed that Jenny was aware of some of the existing conflicts between groups of young people, so was able to encourage different groups to make use of the studio's two levels. Katy felt that young people relaxed when they saw Jenny, and that having a youth worker present meant that Patrick could concentrate on his role as an artist [phone call, 16 March

2015]. While degrees of uncertainty and unpredictability were built-in social and artistic features of the project, the enshrinement of youth work 'values' within the temporary collaborative field helped to shape the nature of the approaches and conversations that took place around the pop-up. The introduction of these principles of practice nevertheless generated intense debate between the project leaders on some occasions.

Negotiations around boundary setting occurred as a result of the blurred distinctions between youth work and art practice within the project. Due to the pop-up's public location, adults regularly entered the space out of curiosity, or for a chat. During the first evening (while we only had one young person in the space), an elderly man came in and became engaged in friendly conversation with us over coffee. He told us about how there was not much for him to do in the evenings and that he doesn't feel safe. The 18-year-old girl pointed out that his experience was like that of teenagers. After he left, this interaction provoked a discussion between Sarah and Patrick about the appropriateness of unknown adults being in the space, and being associated with the safety of the project. Sarah suggested this might have consequences for the safeguarding of vulnerable young people who may see these adults in an external context and feel obliged to engage with them. As it happened, the young person who was in the space at the time did encounter the man later that night and he asked for her help with his bags.

This debate continued between Sarah and Patrick on the following day, and I made some notes on the conversation:

> *I arrive at the shop where Sarah and Patrick are in full flow. Apparently they both thought about the episode with the elderly man overnight and had come to different conclusions about whether unknown adults should be permitted in the space. Patrick believes it's important not to close down the real world and run hermetically sealed projects. Sarah feels this is a young person's space and the safety of the young people takes priority over the art. Patrick asks: "So it's youth work then?"*
>
> [Field notes, 15 February 2015]

The artist's desire for the space to be open and inclusive—a realm of unexpected encounters between people from different backgrounds—and for young people to be entrusted with equipment, sometimes sat uneasily with Sarah, who was aware of the personal risks faced by some of the different individuals, and had been accustomed to "fixing really firm boundaries" in youth work contexts. There were also discussions about the appropriateness of some of the conservations initiated by members of the peer group and adult volunteers, who came to support the project intermittently throughout the two weeks. Well-intentioned questions such as—"what do your parents do?" And "have you seen this play at the theatre?" were highlighted as examples of conversations of privilege. Sarah appeared torn between wanting to adhere to the policies of the youth centre, and wanting to avoid restricting people's behaviour:

> I've got to let go a little bit of my indoctrination at [the youth centre] because it's real youth work, it's full on. But a lot of those boundaries and a lot of those beliefs about how to be around young people I hold really dear.
> [Conversation, 15 February 2015]

Sarah was aware that the pop-up space gave her the opportunity to re-set some of the boundaries that frustrated her about the youth centre environment, and yet she was conscious of the different backgrounds of the staff members and volunteers, and the need to be "mindful of some-body's circumstances" in the space. The idea that Sarah's "indoctrination" into the youth work field led her to behave in particular ways is consistent with Bourdieu's notion that a person's habitus is shaped by their habitat and vice versa (Bourdieu et al., 1999). Even if an agent seeks to rebel against the conditions of their primary occupational field, the rules of the game are typically ingrained or naturalised within their practice. Sarah's understanding of the class habitus of young people in the locality was also a significant dimension of her practitioner identity. It was clear that volun-tary staff and members of the peer group could have benefited from some basic training in the lead-up to the project, and Learning Curator Katy acknowledged that she would implement this if the project happened again. However even this may not have been adequate to bridge the obvi-ous social gap between members of the peer group, volunteers and visitors to the pop-up. Equally, the notion of "real youth work" being in tension with arts practice was an issue that continued to weigh on the minds of the practitioners. The logics of practice from youth work and arts practice could not be easily combined in this temporary space.

One area where Sarah was able to extend some of these boundaries was through her use of Facebook. Sarah's prior connection with local young people through the youth centre meant she already had access to a broad community of potential participants and could make contact with them on social media. Around 17 young people came to the space as a direct result of seeing Sarah's posts on the page. These frequent, chatty and personalised exchanges were unlike posts that would usually feature on the pages of the youth centre and gallery, so rather than performing the institution, they reinforced the de-institutionalised identity of the pop-up. I found this aspect of the project intriguing because in most of my encounters with Circuit partnership projects, Facebook was perceived to be problematic as a tool for everyday communication with participants. Some galleries reported that their ability to utilise Facebook was limited by their communications team, while practitioners from youth organisations referred to their organisations' lack of capacity to consistently update their pages. While practitioners could see that Facebook offered great potential for sustaining connections with young people, there was also some anxiety and confusion about the ethical protocol involved in 'friending' young people through this platform. In the pop-up context however, Sarah sought to allay concerns by writing up a Facebook safeguarding policy in advance and sharing the page's admin details with youth worker Jenny, and the youth and communities manager at the youth centre, who were both knowledgeable about child protection. In her report, Sarah commented on the use of Facebook in the project, both as a forum for creative intervention and as a practical tool for maintaining communication:

> I began posting up a variety of different creative images initially with no comment, simply images of interesting street art, guerrilla art, unusual installations, things that might 'impress' them or make them look twice. Being familiar with many young people's facebook habits and the pattern of 'selfies' and statuses I soon realised that potentially what I was posting was quite noticeably making an obvious 'break' in their facebook feeds.
>
> [...] Being present on facebook allowed us to keep in contact when we weren't open and post up photos of the day. Several young people also posted up photos of their time in the studio space. It was a great tool for interaction—to seek permission to use photographs, to remind them of what had been happening in the space and for them to enquire about opening times.
>
> [Report, 2015]

The gallery's Learning Curator was particularly pleased to be able to trial this mode of working, as it demonstrated to her that the youth programme needed its own social media presence that could be instantly reactive. The project also highlighted to Katy that the gallery needed to "loosen up" and find ways for young people to feel a sense of ownership in the institution's spaces.

In some respects, the external status of the initiative meant that the practitioners were able to develop a form of temporary counter-organisation, where the rules of the game could be reimagined and impro-vised from scratch. Practitioners were able to 'remake their identities' (Facer and Enright, 2016) by debating and drawing on one another's knowledge and pushing themselves to inhabit hybrid roles. But in other respects, the rules of the temporary field were inevitably influenced by the field doxa of the associated organisations, and the habitus of staff, whose approach to practice was heavily informed by their social and professional backgrounds.

Risks and Rewards of the Temporary Collaborative Field

In setting up and developing this two-week initiative (which engaged between 20–30 young visitors per day), the programme managed to con-ceive of a different, experimental basis for partnership. It could be argued that the temporary collaborative field represented a 'risk culture' of 'non-institutional and anti-institutional sociations' (Lash, 2000, p. 47). Risk cultures are defined by Lash (2000, p. 47) as collectively organised, loose and changeable groupings that have a 'fluid quasi-membership' and that exist willingly amongst risk, often in spaces of marginality, with the ambi-tion to *de*-structure and *dis*-order institutional norms. The pilot pop-up trialled the concept of a 'hybrid zone' by creating a space which did not belong to one 'expert discipline' or one targeted group of young people, but rather strove to produce an ethos of 'shared ownership' and shared uncertainty (Huybrechts, 2013, p. 166). These types of conditions have the potential to produce a generative, innovative environment for collabo-ration. However, it was also the case that the pilot produced a range of other less generative risks that are worth considering.

For me, and for some of the practitioners, the project raised a huge set of questions around institutional responsibilities and the risks involved in the gallery popping up as a temporary form of youth provision. There was the risk that this project set up expectations that couldn't be sustained, or that couldn't be met in the context of the gallery itself; the possibility of encroaching upon other youth organisations' provision or cohort; and the prospect of young people disclosing aspects of themselves to staff who were not trained youth workers. There was also the danger that a pop-up initiative might be seen as tokenistic, short-term and marketing-driven (Cochrane, 2010). As freelancers, the core pop-up practitioners were limited in their ability to bring change to the associated organisations themselves, or to continue the project independently of Circuit funding and support.

The pilot did nevertheless result in valuable learning for those involved. The assembly of different practitioners with different experiences and knowledge capitals, and the configuration of the project as a social youth space/café/studio productively complicated the project's identity, which proved attractive to young people. Galleries and youth centres are both regulated spaces that require forms of induction and are affiliated with particular codes of practice. Young people seemed to adapt well to an alternative, open access site, and to a built environment that was offbeat and transitory and physically accessible within their own social fields. The scale of the locality meant that the youth population was small enough for word of mouth to be effective. And by including multiple voices and positioning the project in a space of ambiguity, traditional power hierarchies between partners and participants became unsettled. These types of settings also have the potential to provide creatively challenging contexts for artists, and therefore to inspire high quality practice. The Circuit gallery took this learning on board and apparently utilised it through their occupation of a studio site nearer the institution while the gallery was undergoing redevelopment work.

Pop-up initiatives took place across other Circuit sites through collaborations between galleries and grass roots youth organisations, council-run youth services and alternative education providers. Temporary shop and café spaces hosted projects that lasted from one day, to several months. In most cases, young people were free to drop in and out of these projects, and practitioners had to work together to define the ambitions and boundaries of their new, public host space. The fringe, undetermined status of these spaces seemed to contribute to their appeal for all involved. The work of Doreen Massey on space and place (2005) is useful for describing this phenomenon. Massey talks about the 'event of place' as a 'coming together of the previously unrelated, a constellation of processes rather than a thing'. In Massey's conception of place, 'there can be no assumption of pre-given coherence, or of community or collective identity. Rather the throwntogetherness of place demands negotiation' (Massey, 2005, p. 141). While these temporary sites *are* thrown together and unfolding, this site study has shown that partnership in any alternative scenario is also heavily personality-driven, and laden with tacit institutional framings.

In many ways, cultural institutions invest heavily in attachment to territory. Youth organisations and youth workers are arguably less attached to territories in this way, and many youth work practitioners are accustomed to working off-site, in detached, street-based scenarios. This pop-up represented an institutional effort to step outside of the gallery and engage with a form of youth work that is not only committed to the safety and support of young people, but to improvisation, critical and democratic exchange and to voluntary relationships between practitioners and young people. Through developing the pop-up, those involved were able to mobilise the art institution and youth work as vehicles of trust, and lift conventional barriers to young people's voluntary engagement. Securing the involvement of a lead practitioner who had 'authority' and 'symbolic capital' across both fields was also essential to this happening (Lingard and Rawolle, 2004, p. 376). Questions remain however, as to whether this type of work actually creates any lasting change in youth organisations or galleries, or whether a temporary collaborative field exists in a bubble of interesting practice that has little influence on more established organisational fields.

The broader picture of reduced universal or open access youth provision suggests that there is an appetite in local youth sectors for different models of coordination, cooperation and collaboration. Partnerships with communities, voluntary services and institutions are recognised as offering 'the potential to re-carve new spaces on terms that are more conducive to youth work's core values', that is, 'terms that are not constricted by local and national policy diktats' (Norris and Pugh, 2015, p. 95). Initiatives such as those tested in this and the previous site show how galleries can play a role in helping to maintain creative spaces for youth work, in a climate that appears relatively hostile to work that doesn't have explicit, predefined outcomes. However, acclimatising to a new field on different, collaborative terms evidently requires 'prolonged occupation' of the field site and 'sustained association' between members (Bourdieu et al., 1999, p. 128). The legitimacy of these fields can therefore only be secured if there is willingness to meet these requirements. This calls into question the priority responsibilities of gallery education departments, which have to balance their obligations to democratising access to galleries with efforts to promote cultural democracy and contribute to wider social initiatives.

REFERENCES

Bourdieu, Pierre. 1984. *Distinction: A social critique of the judgement of taste*. London: Routledge.

Bourdieu, Pierre, et al. 1999. *The weight of the world: Social suffering in contemporary society*. Malden: Polity Press.

Cochrane, Kira. 2010. Why pop-ups pop up everywhere. *The Guardian*, October 12.

Davies, Richard, 2015. Partnership: A philosophical consideration. *BERA conference 2015*, Queen's University Belfast, 17 September 2015.

Education Funding Agency. 2016. *Guidance: Youth contract provision: 16- and 17-year-olds*. Accessed 28 April 2016. https://www.gov.uk/government/publications/youth-contract-16-and-17-year-olds/youth-contract-provision-16-and-17-year-olds.

Facer, Keri, and Enright, Bryony. 2016. *Creating living knowledge*. Bristol: The University of Bristol and AHRC Connected Communities Programme.

France, Alan, Dorothy Bottrell, and Edward Haddon. 2013. Managing everyday life: The conceptualisation and value of cultural capital in navigating everyday life for working-class youth. *Journal of Youth Studies* 16 (5): 597–611.

Freire, Paulo. 1970. *Pedagogy of the oppressed*. (Reprint 1996) London: Penguin Books.

Grenfell, Michael, and Cheryl Hardy. 2003. Field manoeuvres: Bourdieu and the Young British Artists. *Space and Culture* 6 (1): 19–34.

Hilgers, Mathieu, and Eric Mangez, eds. 2015. *Bourdieu's theory of social fields: Concepts and applications*. Oxon: Routledge.

Hughes, Gill, Charlie Cooper, Sinéad Gormally, and Julie Rippingdale. 2014. The state of youth work in austerity England—Reclaiming the ability to 'care'. *Youth & Policy* 113: 1–14.

Huybrechts, Liesbeth, ed. 2013. *Participation is risky: Approaches to joint creative processes*. Amsterdam: Valiz.

Jeffs, Tony, and Mark K. Smith. 2010. *Youth work practice*. Basingstoke: Palgrave Macmillan.

Lash, Scott. 2000. Risk culture. In *The risk society and beyond: Critical issues for social theory*, ed. Barbara Adam, Ulrich Beck, and Joost van Loon. London: Sage.

Lingard, Bob, and Shaun Rawolle. 2004. Mediatizing educational policy: The journalistic field, science policy, and cross-field effects. *Journal of Education Policy* 19 (3): 361–380.

Massey, Doreen. 2005. *For space*. London: Sage Publications.

Matarasso, François. 2013. Creative progression: Reflections on quality in participatory arts. *UNESCO Observatory Multi-Disciplinary Journal in the Arts* 3 (3): 1–15.

Norris, Pat, and Carole Pugh. 2015. Local authority youth work. In *Youth work: Histories, policy and contexts*, ed. Graham Bright. London: Palgrave Macmillan.

Room 13 International. 2012. About Room 13. *Room13international.org*. Accessed 3 January 2017. http://room13international.org/about/.

Sayers, Esther. 2015. The ethics of peer-led practice: Authorship, autonomy and representation. *Engage conference: A different game: Young people working with art and artists*, Glasgow, 20 November 2015.

Sekules, Veronica. 2010. Where is the risk? *Engage* 27: 27–37.

Taylor, Tony. 2014. IDYW statement 2014. *In Defence of Youth Work*. Accessed 2 March 2016. http://indefenceofyouthwork.com/idyw-statement-2014/.

The Federation for detached youth work. 2016. Overview—Detached youth work. Accessed 19 April 2016. http://www.fdyw.org.uk/overview.

Wallace, Derron. 2017. Reading 'race' in Bourdieu? Examining black cultural capital among black Caribbean youth in South London. *Sociology* 51 (5): 907–923.

CHAPTER 7

Recognising and Countering Symbolic Violence

In gallery education it is common for partnership work to be framed as a route into a more active and sustained relationship with a visual art institution. In many larger UK galleries, the platform for this relationship is often a core peer-led group or collective of young people, who may work together with gallery staff and artists to curate events and exhibitions. This chapter explores what happens when youth practitioners and marginalised young people encounter these 'core' programming models in galleries. It highlights how interactions with established gallery groups can inadvertently generate experiences of 'symbolic violence' (Bourdieu, 1977) for young people associated with youth organisations or services. As previously described, symbolic violence refers to the unseen damage that can occur when people are positioned in situations that illuminate their lack of social privilege, and where their particular forms of social or cultural capital are undervalued (Bourdieu et al., 1999). Forces of symbolic violence are particularly active in fields that are endowed with high levels of authority or dominance as a consequence of their cultural status (Bourdieu, 1984). Museums and galleries are obvious examples of institutions with considerable symbolic power, and while their youth programmes seek to offer inclusive pathways towards engaged participation, they also have the capacity to reproduce institutional power (Sayers, 2014). Throughout this chapter I make use of observations and interviews carried out during Circuit to highlight episodes where there was potential for

© The Author(s) 2019

N. Sim, *Youth Work, Galleries and the Politics of Partnership*, New Directions in Cultural Policy Research,
https://doi.org/10.1007/978-3-030-25197-0_7

symbolic violence to occur. I also highlight ways in which Circuit sought to counter symbolic violence and re-position traditional understandings of valuable social, cultural and professional capital in its programmatic field. I argue that youth workers often possess essential knowledge and perceptive skills that enable them to identify symbolic violence in places where it may otherwise go unrecognised. This chapter seeks to illustrate how youth workers' skills can be effectively deployed in galleries, to support the longer-term engagement of diverse communities of young people.

THE PEER-LED 'DOXA'

As suggested in Chap. 3, gallery-based 'peer-led' programming as we know it today has been in existence in the UK at least since the 1990s when Tate Liverpool started its first group of young curators (Sinker, 2008). At the different Tate galleries, the peer-led pedagogy adheres to a common structure, which typically involves regular meetings of young people on weekday evenings, where group members work with facilitators to plan events, displays and projects aimed at other young people. The received wisdom behind this model is that it creates opportunities for young people's voices and ideas to be heard and realised in the institution, and for participants to gain practical insights into the inner workings of cultural organisations. By working closely with gallery staff and artists, these groups are able to expand their knowledge of visual arts and exhibition practice. And by working in a peer-led way, young people are encouraged to cooperate and take shared responsibility and ownership of projects by adopting various roles—from event organisation and marketing to evaluation. This offers members professional work experience and training, as well as the chance to direct the content of programmes. For institutions looking to attract greater numbers of young people, peer-led groups also provide expertise on current youth cultures, and they have the potential to draw in wider audiences of young people through their programming. Having grown in popularity over recent decades, it would not be an overstatement to characterise peer-led as part of the 'doxa' of contemporary gallery youth programming. In other words, working with young people in this way has become an accepted mode of practice in UK galleries.

In Circuit, the galleries' peer-led groups and activities represented the main progression opportunities for young people involved in partnership projects. A consistent goal of Circuit's was that young people from partner organisations be supported to continue their engagement with the gallery through membership of the institution's peer group or involvement in peer-led events. The peer groups were intended to be as diverse as possible, in order to represent underrepresented voices and provide a space for young people with least access to the arts to express their creative agency and enhance their skills. Each Circuit gallery's peer-led programme was different but they all followed a similar format, with groups of 15–25 year olds meeting on a weekly or bi-weekly basis to socialise, take part in creative workshops and plan events and exhibitions. Six of the galleries had pre-existing peer-led groups before Circuit started, while four did not. In most cases, participants were expected to attend voluntarily, but there were prospects for paid work at events. Many participants initially joined following recruitment drives in schools, colleges and universities, or through attending taster sessions. Some joined after contacting the gallery about work experience or through discovering the opportunity on social media. And as explored in the earlier site studies, efforts were made to encourage connections between the partnership projects and the peer groups. Even if the potential for transitioning was low, Circuit gallery staff sought to involve youth partners in the wider peer-led aspects of their programme, by inviting them to events, or showcasing work produced in a partnership project in the festivals.

During the programme, it was however increasingly evident that very few young people engaged through partnership projects were going on to join the peer groups for any considerable length of time. Profiling data analysed by Circuit's Evaluator revealed that while the peer groups were ethnically diverse (there was an equal number of white and black and ethnic minority members in total across the groups), the majority of peer group participants were in higher education and in paid jobs. By the end of the programme, 28% of participants of the core groups identified with one or more of the programme's 'hard-to-reach' categories (these included having a long term disability or mental health need, being a care leaver, refugee, young parent or young carer, being homeless or in the youth justice system, not being in education or employment and so on). The original target was 50% (Circuit, 2017). When it came to peer-led activity such as festivals and other events, only 14% of audiences identified with these categories (Sphere Insights, 2017). Even though these figures may not have been completely accurate (as the data depended on self-identification), the staff involved in Circuit acknowledged that the programme had fallen short of its ambitions to engage a large proportion of young people with least access to cultural opportunities in its core programmes.

Throughout my time researching Circuit I spoke to many youth practitioners about their experiences of working with young people in their organisations, as well as their thoughts on encounters with the Circuit galleries' wider youth programmes. Their responses provided important insights into the doxic differences between youth and gallery peer-led programmes, and some of the invisible barriers inhibiting young people's full and sustained participation. During my research, the doxic differences that were most significant could be distilled into two main issues: the nature of inclusivity in programmes, and the pedagogic approach.

INCLUSIVITY AND INFORMAL PEDAGOGY

While gallery youth programmers would always talk the language of inclusivity, youth workers I interviewed were more accustomed to working with young people whose behaviour was deemed "not socially acceptable" and who were isolated or excluded from other people their age [Interview, 20 October 2015]. One youth worker I interviewed worked with young men experiencing mental health crises, who sometimes had a history of violence or aggressive behaviour. She relayed her concerns about her group mixing with a gallery's existing peer group:

> I was concerned about how the young people were going to integrate in the group. [...] I know that a lot of [the gallery peer group] are university graduates, [...] they are from a very different background to our young people. [...] My judgement is these middle class kids are not going to integrate well with my [young people]—that's not going to happen.

Class difference was the most often-cited reason for disparities between groups. This practitioner was also anxious that the needs of her young people might not be fully accommodated in the peer group setting. Her colleagues were trained in mental health first aid, and were used to working with young people who heard voices, or who behaved in sexually inappropriate ways, or who were argumentative for instance.

> Is [the gallery] equipped to work with young people who are literally still living in a hospital? One of the names that they took down was a boy who was still suffering from quite intense psychosis. How on earth would [the gallery] deal with that? They don't have any training or systems in place.

As this practitioner indicated, without appropriate expertise, institutions have the potential to put young people at risk, and to jeopardise relationships between youth organisations and their participants. As well as understanding protocol for working with vulnerable young people, the practitioner communicated that her organisation invested considerable time into sustaining the motivation of young people:

> *At the back of my mind was the amount of work that I put into getting our young people to attend a session down the road where they get studio time, which is their main interest. You know, I was taking young people to a music festival once and it took so many calls, so many presentations, so many reminders—it's a huge job. It's not two text messages—it's a huge amount of support work.*
> [Interview, 7 September 2015].

She argued that peer groups in galleries tend to rely on young people being independently motivated. While peer group members may receive reminders and messages of encouragement, gallery staff are not generally able to provide the same level of one-on-one support as may be found in a targeted youth organisation.

Another key attribute of peer-led work is the concept of young people attaching to the gallery over several years to produce programmes that can take months to plan. In one youth club setting I encountered through Circuit, projects had to have a finite beginning and end, and they needed to have in-built flexibility to respond to the pattern of engagement (and disengagement) of young people. A youth worker from the club commented:

> *We work with something called attachment disorder. We're fully trained in it. And it is what it says. There are certain families that don't get a baby born and attached to its mother. And the consequences of that you see in our young people. They don't attach to projects, they don't attach to school, and there are reasons why they don't do that and we know why that is. And so knowing it we can be very understanding of it. And if you're not understanding of it, then your project is self-driven—it's not driven by them.*
> [Interview, 20 October 2015].

Some of the youth club workers (such as this one) also had strong, almost paternal connections with the young people they worked with. Having developed relationships over several years, they had invested an enormous amount of personal time and emotional energy in supporting young people, who were often experiencing issues at home. This emotional labour would extend into many different aspects of a youth programme's offer. For instance, some youth workers talked about the importance of food in their work, as a gesture of care for young people who were otherwise hungry. While gallery peer group meetings would often include food, this tended to be pizza or popular sweet and savoury snacks rather than a cooked meal aimed at supporting the group's wellbeing (as was the case in one youth setting). These subtle differences marked out the distinctions between some youth club groups and gallery groups. This level of care was by no means present in all youth settings, but in open access youth clubs in particular there was often a feeling of extended family. This extended family sensibility was sometimes also present in gallery peer-led groups, but due to the demands of programming and administration, it was not always possible for gallery practitioners to dedicate significant amounts of time to individuals' needs.

Some youth organisations arguably practice forms of radical inclusivity. Specialist organisations in particular often adapt their programming to be inclusive of young people with specific support needs. In their training, youth workers are conditioned to develop their ethical reasoning and sensitivities, so they are able to apply these skills in challenging situations with young people (Banks, 2010). Their exposure to frontline work, training (and often their own lived experiences as a young person) combine to give many youth workers heightened empathy and understanding of young people's circumstances. This youth worker 'habitus' clearly informs practitioners' pedagogical inclinations and enables them to identify structural barriers.

Despite our best intentions, gallery practitioners are not trained or conditioned in the same way to recognise subtle exclusionary forces and their effects on individuals. During my visits to peer group meetings in Circuit, I observed that the common format of young people being seated around a large table and engaging in discussion required a level of maturity, self-management and confidence from participants that was quite unlike the dynamic in most youth organisations I visited. While some of these sessions did include practical activities, many of the sessions featured discursive group planning, ideas sharing and debate—often within a boardroom-style setting. One of the gallery programmers told me she felt the professional nature of the meetings was good because it helped to prepare the young people for their working lives [conversation, 7 August,

2015]. A key logic of peer-led practice in the gallery field seemed to be to instil the disposition to be professional, and for many recruits, the opportunities for CV enhancement and employment were major incentives. Most of the young people recruited through the galleries' website or through schools and colleges understood the ways in which their engagement with galleries might benefit their careers and enable them to accumulate elite social and cultural capital.

Many of Circuit's national meetings also involved large numbers of adults and young people sitting around tables in groups—listening to presentations or taking part in discussions. In one of these I attended, three practitioners (who were all former youth workers employed in critical friend or programmer roles in Circuit) raised concerns about the formality of the session, and the advanced nature of language used. They pointed out to me that this situation was intimidating for some of their young people because it assumed a certain level of knowledge and didn't account for the fact that some people would feel anxious about speaking out loud in a room full of strangers. One practitioner said:

> *In the beginning, it was a bit too professional, and it was about talking to other professionals. It was too heavy for sharing and being honest—to the exclusion of the young people who were supposed to be the main theme of it all. [...] And all I was focusing on was what my young people were saying to me—they were saying: "I'm bored, I don't want to write, I'm feeling a bit out of my depth". In the bit at the end I said [to the organiser]—"excuse me, I don't know what you're talking about". And there was a gasp! But it was really important for somebody to say that because my young people felt they were being left out. You've got university young people, you'd got young people who were not coming from the same kind of backgrounds that our young people were coming from, with some of the barriers that they had. And they were feeling different, isolated; they didn't know what was going on.*
> [Interview, 30 October 2015]

So there was apprehension amongst practitioners who had a background in youth work, and who were more accustomed to working in very informal ways with young people. The format of these national meetings seemed to better accommodate the older young people from the peer groups who were more self-assured and comfortable in an adult environment.

Many of the gallery practitioners also felt that the expectations of the wider programme sometimes worked in conflict with the ambition to work with marginalised young people and youth organisations. Practitioners on the ground found that they needed a motivated group to fulfil other Circuit strands of activity, such as the festival production. The Circuit festivals were a central component of the peer-led programme. Each gallery committed to running a large-scale event over a series of days during the period of funding, and they ran other events in the lead up to their festivals. Several of the galleries also staged exhibitions curated by their peer group members as part of their activity. Alongside the festivals, these projects took up considerable time and involved intensive work. From my observations, it was apparent that these opportunities predominantly attracted the most engaged peer group members. Gallery practitioners also noted that it was difficult to build in time for relationship building with external organisations alongside their programming workload [interview, 17 August, 2015]. What this signals is that galleries are accountable to broader audiences and therefore committed to the public event, or the 'experience economy' as a basis for programming (Dewdney et al., 2013, p. 41). The demands of these large-scale, complex events can, it seems, breed a type of lighter-touch, low investment practice with young people and partners. This type of relationship can work well for well-resourced organisations with little available time, but it is less effective if an in-depth, supportive relationship is required.

The gallery-based peer-led format has been increasingly critiqued for its lack of inclusivity in recent years, most prominently by Esther Sayers (2014, 2015), formerly Curator for Young People's Programmes at Tate Modern. Sayers posits that this way of working creates a form of social closure that perpetuates a lack of cultural and ethnic diversity, because it attracts young people who are already 'culturally literate', and who are privileged enough to have had exposure to the arts:

> *I'm concerned that partly it's the peer-led format that discourages some young people from taking part, because it creates a kind of social group, which by its sociable nature attracts similar types of people—people who are similar to each other.* (Sayers, 2015)

Sayers counts amongst these "similar types of people" gallery educators and facilitators who are typically white, female and middle class. Sayers also questions whether the institutional compulsion to give power to young people is more to the benefit of the institution, than it is to participants:

When staff are stretched to do more and more projects, peer-led programmes sometimes provide a cheap workforce. (Sayers, 2015)

One could argue that 'peer-led' programming is a middle class construct that serves to institutionalise relatively homogenous groups rather than welcome the diverse groups of young people it seeks to engage. The production of festivals and late night events as core parts of youth programming fit the entrepreneurial, commercialised character of so-called 'second wave' cultural activity, which echoes club culture and promotes the idea of the precarious freelance creative and a lifestyle of 'middle class' "ducking and diving" as something to aspire towards (McRobbie, 2002, pp. 517, 525). Those members of youth organisations who did join the Circuit gallery peer groups tended to be those who were the most self-motivated or who had some family support. The peer-led offer seemed to attract a limited demographic of young people from youth organisations, who were closest in social position to the existing members of the peer group. Bourdieu (1985) suggests that groups tend to attract and reward people with homologous characteristics who occupy similar social positions, so on an unconscious level this cycle of attraction ostracises those who are *dis*similar and who possess different accumulations of capital. So if a gallery peer group had a diverse membership base, there was greater likelihood that this group would be inclusive. But gallery practitioners would also be keen to defend the idea that those young people who appear outwardly 'middle class' or advantaged in certain ways are still deserving of access to cultural institutions and opportunities. Longitudinal research commissioned by Tate exploring the journeys of 21 peer group members revealed that while a proportion of the groups came from more privileged backgrounds, across the board young people were dealing with common struggles related to securing employment or housing for instance (Coles and Thomson, 2017). It is also true that many of the gallery peer groups in Circuit were diverse in various ways and there were some members of partnership projects who did join peer groups for a lengthy period of time. However, it is important to acknowledge that instances of largely exceptional engagement can disguise organisational barriers and allow practitioners to misrecognise deeper issues with the doxic order of the programmatic field (Bourdieu, 1977).

Symbolic Violence in Practice

The following example of practice gives some insight into the implications of these deeper issues on the experiences of marginalised young people. It also demonstrates the ability of some youth workers to perceive instances of symbolic violence, where they may go unrecognised in the gallery. The example focuses on the words of 'Abbie'—an outreach worker from a youth centre that ran targeted and universal provision and that had been engaging with one of the Circuit galleries in a relatively light-touch, coordinated way. I spoke to Abbie during the gallery's festival, which had been organised by the peer-led group. Two participants of Abbie's youth organisation had decided to get more involved with the peer group as a result of being initially asked to take part in a paid focus group with the gallery. So Abbie was attending the festival to show her support for these participants, but she was also paid by the gallery to bring other groups of young people from the youth centre along to experience the event.

Abbie described how the two participants had benefitted from becoming involved in the peer-led programming and the gallery's festival and outlined how the gallery's peer group had provided a safe, nurturing space for one young person in particular:

> One [young person] is now working here, which he's really really proud of. That young person really struggled with social skills when they were in a youth work setting, they really struggled with their identity, and as a result of that their behaviour was quite challenging. And since he's been at the gallery, he's been made to feel like his opinion matters. So they've got a really good way of being able to listen to the young people, and to make those changes. So we've had some really positive case studies come out of it, and the young people can get different things from it. They can come in, they can enjoy the day, because we've done different workshops [at the festival], which is great. And then some of them have gone deeper, and one of the young people who is with us today, one of our younger ones who's 15, has asked if she can join the group.

Despite her optimistic comments, Abbie also made a number of important points about the experience of visiting a gallery festival with marginalised young people and interacting with the peer group. Across the festival Abbie accompanied two different sets of young people. This experience allowed her to reflect on the disparities between gallery groups and groups from targeted organisations:

I do feel though if it wasn't for me being with them, I'm not sure how strong that link would feel, because for example, yesterday I brought a group of young people that were from an alternative education provision, and they were very difficult to engage. And we went into this room, which is a very intimidating space [...] and there were a lot of confident younger people there from the [peer group]. And I think they felt very intimidated so their behaviour started to act up. And there was a table of crafts—and they all enjoy doing art and crafts—I do an art workshop with them every week, like art therapy, adult colouring, adult dot-to-dot, things like that. So I knew it was something that they could participate in, but no one kind of spoke to them and asked if they wanted to get involved. And no one moved from the table. So I had to kind of act as a bridge and say—"I'm sure you guys would make some space if we came over wouldn't you?" And then they were like "oh yeah", and then they prompted and they helped. Once they got involved the staff were really engaged with them. Their behaviour—they did try and challenge—they were using phallic symbols and stuff, trying to test the waters. But the staff embraced it rather than challenged it. And they responded really well to that. So when you do communicate with those young people, the young people get a lot from it. Sometimes I feel though that it's about that initial meet and greet—if they've never been in the building before—they need someone to tell them this is ok, and you can take part in this.

Abbie's account highlighted particular taken-for-granted expectations about people's ability to enter a space and adopt the position of participant, which illustrated the social distance between groups of young people.

The issue is I think that a lot of the [peer group] and a lot of the young people that participate at this gallery are very confident young people. Young people that have come from backgrounds probably where they've had a lot of support, and have the confidence if they want to do something to walk up to a table. [...] The young people that we are working with would not do that. So they need to be told that it's ok for them to participate, and they need that positive reinforcement constantly, more than usual. So it's about the approach, and I think possibly gallery workers and artists aren't used to working with young people that are so challenging. They are used to people being confident, being forthcoming with their skills, and being like—"I'm quite confident, I like music, I want to get involved with this." Even things like down to equipment, like they were using a Mac yesterday. You could tell there were so many young people that knew about Macs and who possibly had iPads at home, and there were some of our young people who were very tetchy—they felt like there was language being used that they didn't understand.

The youth worker observed that the gallery group were predisposed to feel at ease in the gallery environment by virtue of their upbringing and social advantages, and that her young people were conversely conditioned to feel out of place there. Clear differences in material and cultural capital had the effect of causing discomfort and feelings of inadequacy for the young people from the youth organisation. The peer group *had* sought to tap into popular and sub-youth cultures in their programming for the festival (for instance in their film selections), but Abbie noted that even these were aimed at young adults who had "access to cultural experiences":

> *They played This is England—and I was trying to discuss it with one of my young people who's got autism, who's transgender. He saw that it was an 18 and he was like—"oh wow, an 18! I get to watch an 18!" And he was telling me that he'd be ok if he watched it because he'd seen The Human Centipede. And it was very difficult trying to explain to him that actually This is England is a more realistic, gritty portrayal. And he watched it for a bit and then I could see that he wasn't engaged with it. So even the choice of films…earlier on there was a film called Frank that is very difficult watch. It's an intellectual watch, it's an indie film. What the young people want are things like Fast and Furious, and they want kind of bright, flashing lights and entertainment that they get. And sometimes there's a middle road between indie culture and that. So for example, Kidulthood, or Adulthood might have been a more appropriate film to show later at night that reaches out to young people. And it reaches out to a cross section. It deals with issues similar to This is England, but it's also more relatable for young people that are working class or—I hate to say the phrase—on the streets—or take part in street based activity and gang culture.*

From the practitioner's perspective, the festival represented the peer group's performance of their own cultural capital, in a way that unintentionally alienated members of her group. I asked whether it helped that a member of their youth organisation was visibly part of the peer-led programming team, but Abbie identified that this young person actually displayed an inflated sense of his own cultural capital as a result of his exposure to the peer group:

> *For example there's an exhibit on in the main galleries, and he was talking to the young people about [an alternative jazz musician], and because we hadn't heard of [them], he was flabbergasted! But I know that that young person six months ago wouldn't have heard of Bob Dylan for example. […] Obviously his cultural norms have shifted—which is great to see because he would have never*

been given that opportunity to listen to that kind of music and engage in these things. But I do think to myself, it's great that we can get to that space, but where are we starting? Because if we're starting with [alternative jazz musicians], and Frank, and This is England, then you're going to alienate a lot of people. But if you're starting from where they're at like I said, and taking them on that journey, so they can appreciate an [alternative jazz musician] in maybe a couple of years time, then that's great, but it needs to come from where they are.

This instance shows how it is possible for marginalised young people to misrecognise their own journey, and the barriers faced by their contemporaries, particularly if they want to establish their allegiance to a (seemingly culturally wealthy) new group. As I also saw in other galleries, individual cases of transition from a partnership group to a peer group were more likely to result in the young person being initiated into the gallery's way of doing things, rather than them shifting the culture of the youth programme. Bourdieu says: 'At the risk of feeling themselves out of place, individuals who move into a new space must fulfil the conditions that that space tacitly requires of its occupants' (1999, p. 128). The institutional contemporary art world embeds in its workers the ability to recognise and select out so-called legitimate avant-garde culture, as well as the ability to play the game of at least appearing to understand these practices (Bourdieu, 1984). Abbie's ability to identify subtle forms of symbolic violence in the interaction between her group and the peer-led programme was partly due to her experience as a senior youth practitioner, but it may also have been to do with her own relationship to arts and culture:

I never even did art GCSE. I am probably the least arty person you will ever meet, but I am really fortunate enough that I can go to London and I've been to places like the Saatchi Gallery, and I am interested in—and have been from an early age—I'm interested in theatre, in art, particularly in contemporary art. I've always found it quite interesting, like what Tracey Emin does, and am interested in different exhibits. So I'm quite fortunate, and even though I'm working class myself, from a young age I wanted to be in theatre, so I was used to going into theatres which are quite grand, intimidating, arty spaces. So I'm used to—I don't feel intimidated when I go into art galleries, which is really lucky.
[Interview, 7 November, 2015]

Abbie understood that her own cultural references—"Emin", "Banksy" and so on—did not necessarily correlate with the current cultural reference points of the gallery, but she also stressed the inherent tensions involved in seeking to engage working class young people through more esoteric forms of middle class 'high' culture. She understood that this way of working had the potential to inflict damage on a young person's sense of self-worth. Simultaneously, despite her claim to be the "least arty person", Abbie spoke with clear authority about the cultural and political concerns of the young people she worked with. She did not consider them culturally bereft—rather she saw them as possessing alternative forms of "street"-based cultural capital. The idea of 'starting where young people are at' is a recurrent theme of youth work practice, and it implies that good youth work seeks to be 'respectful of and actively responsive to young people's wider community and cultural identities' (Davies, 2005, p. 7). This type of approach correlates with arguments advanced by critics of Bourdieu's theory of cultural capital, some of who promote an alternative concept of 'community cultural wealth' (Yosso, 2005, p. 70). Community cultural wealth rejects the normalisation of 'white, middle class culture as the standard' by which all other forms of cultural knowledge are assessed (Yosso, 2005, p. 76). Rather it locates value in the diverse talents, networks and abilities of socially marginalised groups that are frequently misjudged or underappreciated. Derived from lived experience of marginality, these knowledges are sometimes transgressive and oppositional, or related to an understanding of street life and neighbourhood relationships (France et al., 2013; Yosso, 2005). There is a misconception contained within Yosso's reading of Bourdieu that he also perpetuated the normalisation of privileged forms of cultural capital as the aspirational standard. On the contrary, Bourdieu argued that the concept of 'culture' was a narrowly defined social construct, organised around the judgement systems of the dominant classes (Bourdieu, 1984). He understood that working class cultural capital was not valued according to the logics of this construct. Nevertheless, the ideas associated with community cultural wealth are useful for contemplating the diverse cultural literacies of marginalised populations and the ways in which subcultural capitals are ignored or selectively exploited by arts organisations.

One could argue that the youth worker's habitus (shaped in part by a working class background and regular exposure to marginalised young people and cultural experiences) supported them to view these types of cultural literacies as legitimate. Abbie's understanding of the power relationships the young people were subjected to demonstrated her ability to articulate a form of 'vernacular theory'—that is, a considered critique rooted in everyday lived experience (McLaughlin, 1996). Arts institutions would arguably benefit from listening to the 'street-smart' theorisations of youth practitioners (as well as young people from marginalised backgrounds) throughout their programming, to increase the chances of all young people being able to connect with their own identities and express creative agency within events and projects (McLaughlin, 1996, p. 12).

My argument is not to suggest however that the cultural agenda of art institutions is inherently limited and the cultural literacies of marginalised communities are inherently open and diverse. Both are potentially rich and both are also inseparable from the homogenising forces of elite or mass markets (Graw, 2010; Hickey-Moody, 2013; Hoggart, 1957). The idea that contemporary art is intrinsically alienating is itself reductive and restrictive. In one Circuit gallery for instance, animosity was generated between a youth practitioner and an artist, who felt that the practitioner obstructed any discussion about contemporary art and wasn't open to building a dialogue around challenging ideas and practices. Forms of symbolic violence can also occur when creative projects reinforce particular identities upon participants and limit the scope of their creative potential based on assumptions about young people's interests. The following section focuses on how gallery programmers sought to address some of these issues and recognise or counter forces of symbolic violence in Circuit's temporary programmatic field.

Countering Symbolic Violence

Bourdieu's theorisations suggest that there *are* ways to create change in a system that is perpetually rigged in favour of populations with narrowly defined levels of social, economic and cultural capital. For instance, agents are at liberty to resist the doxic order assumed by their field, and they are endowed with the ability to be reflexive and analytical about systems of inequality and fundamental misrecognitions in the design of programmes (Grenfell, 2012; Thomson, 2017). As I discovered through my fieldwork however, agents' ability to effect change in their field is dependent on a number of conditions, and sometimes it is possible for agents to misrecognise where change needs to be targeted. Fortunately, as an action research learning programme, Circuit encouraged practitioners to engage in a process of critical self-reflexivity and to adopt evaluative rituals associated with reflective practice. So reflection formed an integral part of Circuit's doxa, and therefore the programme generated a receptive space in which to host open debate about practice.

There was widespread recognition amongst Circuit practitioners for example, that the lack of class diversity in peer groups was thwarting efforts to secure the independent engagement of young people from partnership initiatives, and to shift the culture of these groups. The Steering group acknowledged that career development was a prime motivator for many of the young people they worked with. They talked about the dangers of there being two tiers of peer group in Circuit and raised concerns that the programme was not reaching its desired target groups [meeting, 10 February, 2015]. Two years into the programme in April 2015, the board and national team asked each gallery to set their own diversity targets, as a means to focus attention on the demographic profile of young people engaging with programmes, and as a tool to advocate for greater diversity. These diversity targets were based upon knowledge of local demographics. Many gallery practitioners did however call Circuit's focus on profiling into question, as they felt the processes of data collection (involving surveys with a range of personal questions about young people's backgrounds) were counterproductive and harmful to trust building [interview, 20 October, 2015]. There was active resistance amongst some practitioners to utilise Circuit's profiling tools if they felt they had a negative effect on young people's experience.

The programme explored other avenues for more holistic organisational change. Practitioners from across the galleries took part in and initiated inclusion and diversity seminars and training to discuss the shortcomings of gallery practices and opportunities for strategic change. Tate's Diversity Manager ran a session for partner galleries exploring the cultural and moral imperatives of increasing diversity, and the social justice agenda behind these efforts. In this session it was suggested that the social model of disability could be applied across categories of diversity in order to put the onus on organisations to adapt and create a meaningful, two-way dialogue about the barriers facing people that are often created by institutions [20 May 2015]. In most cases, the galleries involved in Circuit strove to initiate forms of organisational change. The programmatic and financial scale of Circuit inevitably also brought directorial staff (i.e. agents with dominant positions) into closer contact with its activities, which increased the potential for change at a senior level. So 'diversity' became a dominant condition of the game, and organisations were expected to have a diversity strategy in place in order to maintain their positions in the temporary programmatic field.

The discontinuity between so-called "core" groups and "partnership" groups was highlighted frequently in meetings. In several reflection moments during Circuit, practitioners commented on the disadvantages of stranding (i.e. dividing up 'partnership' and 'peer-led' into separate strands of activity). Some galleries found that this delineation exacerbated a lack of integration between areas of programming and groups of young people [sharing session, 7–8 October, 2014]. Two of the Circuit galleries implemented major restructures of their peer groups due to staff concern that the groups lacked diversity and were becoming too inward looking. The changes to some of the peer groups did create tension. Many group members were not necessarily motivated by the idea of working with others who didn't have access, although some individuals were heavily involved in supporting partnership activity [interview, 17 August, 2015]. There was also recognition that Circuit's peer groups needed to emphasise "the social". The national evaluation of the peer groups showed that the place of creativity and fun was sometimes being overlooked [national evaluation meeting, 3 June, 2015]. Some of the gallery practitioners recognised that their peer group meetings were becoming too institutionalised and not inclusive.

The Working Group meetings were often sites of discussion about the challenges of adapting to Circuit's model. Some practitioners talked about wanting to incorporate people's individual pathways rather than "coercing them into a group" [meeting, 6 March, 2014]. Several galleries offered diverse opportunities for young people to engage with their programme, beyond the idea of transitioning into the peer group. Two galleries established internship placements and an inclusive/targeted recruitment process that supported young people from youth partners to apply. Some galleries also put in place informal mentoring for young people. Towards the latter half of the programme, several programmers claimed that they had moved away from thinking about transition from partnership to peer-led, to thinking about all of the groups they worked with as part of Circuit [sharing session, 3 December 2015]. There was growing recognition that the concept of young people's assimilation into gallery programmes was fraught with assumptions about the primacy of the gallery field.

These negotiations, debates and shifts in approach also seemed to point towards a much more fundamental set of tensions related to the nature and purpose of gallery youth programmes. These tensions manifested in

Circuit's design, which was structured to achieve a collection of aims that often appeared to work in conflict. Having been established in the wake of the response to the 2011 riots, Circuit explicitly sought to engage 'harder-to-reach' young people through partnerships, but it also sought to deploy a youth-led programming model featuring high profile events aimed at drawing in thousands of young visitors. While some practitioners found points of association between these aims, others found them incompatible. One of Circuit's Managers openly reflected on the predicaments that lay at the centre of the programme:

> It's about being clear about what the programme is trying to achieve—are we trying to diversify audiences for the gallery, or are we addressing social needs? [...] The practice is entirely different, I think. If you're trying to address youth crime in a certain area, and a gallery is a partner in that, then who you part-ner with, how you put resources to it, how you work with young people, all of that is entirely different. If your aim is to diversify your audiences, [this] is also a social responsibility, but it's an entirely different one. [...] I'm sure there are overlaps—because ultimately you're working towards a positive outcome for young people. But I think there's an entirely different practice around it. And I think being honest about that is really important, and that being your vision. Is our aim to support young people through the arts to have positive benefits on their lives, or is it to ensure that there are different voices that are heard within and shape the organisation?
> [Interview, 28 July, 2015].

The Manager recognised that the split agenda of the programme affected the organisations' ability to perform to either objective effectively. From the Manager's perspective, these different strands of ambition neces-sitated particular types of action and behaviour that forefronted the needs of different communities.

These thoughts were echoed by 'Abbie'—the youth worker who I interviewed at one of the Circuit festivals. She argued:

> I think they need to decide really on what they want. What target group do they want? Because I think it's very difficult to have everything, and I think that if they want to have middle class, engaged young people that are already into the arts, or maybe that are already into dance but they want to listen to new music, then that's great, and that's a space for them. But I think it's very, very chal-lenging trying to mix that with hard-to-reach groups of young people. And I think if they are going to be committed to working with more challenging young

people from difficult backgrounds that aren't used to art, then they need to have a different approach from what they've got at the moment.
[Interview, 6 November, 2015].

The implication here is that to avoid imposing forms of symbolic violence on young people, programmes and organisations need to clearly demarcate their values and priority aspirations and shape their practice around these. By trying to merge too many goals, institutions risk undermining them.

The paradoxical conditions represented in Circuit's design are arguably characteristic of gallery youth programmes and characteristic of the doxic differences between gallery education and youth work. While the chief focus of youth work is young people's personal and social development and relationship building with communities, gallery education is defined by its association with visual art institutions. Gallery education pedagogy invests in a core belief around the power of public interaction with artists and exhibitions—and its logic of practice is framed with this in mind. Some gallery educators have also argued that (partly as a result of austerity) the 'hierarchy of values' in arts institutions have shifted away from the 'educational turn' and towards the 'corporate turn' (Stewart, 2015, p. 61). The generation of audience numbers, consumerism and performativity in the gallery space have become key to the survival of cultural organisations, and youth programming models have come to reflect this to some degree.

POSITIONS AND CAPITALS

Another key way that Circuit staff members sought to support diversity and inclusivity was by including practitioners with youth sector expertise in different areas of the programme. Understanding the positions of agents within fields is an essential component of a Bourdieusian analysis (Bourdieu, 1977, 1985; Bourdieu et al., 1999). An interrogation of positioning reveals the types of capitals that are deemed to be worthy in a given social/programmatic space. In Circuit, it was often implied by the national team that the occupational capital associated with youth work was valuable in the context of Circuit. While youth sector practitioners were not involved in designing the programme (so their influence was relatively marginal in Circuit's structure of power), youth practitioners were recruited in different ways across the programme. Two youth practitioners held positions as board members of Circuit, so they held the wider programme to account in terms of its diversity and inclusivity record. Some of the Circuit galleries made the decision to employ gallery coordinators who had a background in youth work. In two cases, practitioners employed were recent former youth workers, while in other cases, practitioners had at least some past experience of working in youth sector contexts. Finally, four Circuit galleries chose to work with youth work practitioners or youth work academics and students as critical friends, facilitators, volunteers and researchers. The inclusion of these various figures at different tiers of Circuit helped to bring the priorities and pedagogies of youth work closer to the managerial centre of the programme.

The positioning of youth practitioners as the critical "eyes" of the programme demonstrated a willingness amongst many Circuit arts practitioners to learn from the advice of youth sector peers, and to be held accountable for actions by agents from another field. However, the appointment of youth workers to gallery practitioner roles also revealed important learning about the challenges of integrating youth sector capitals in a gallery sector workforce. I interviewed one of these practitioners to reflect on his experiences. I will refer to this practitioner through the pseudonym 'Marcus'. Marcus had previously worked with social services in the care sector, and for a youth and information service. Of the care sector role, Marcus said he was "made to feel valued", that "communication was easy, everybody worked really hard, everybody cared". He was also accustomed to every project having a steering group, where various stakeholders worked as a team to collectively manage initiatives and partnerships. However when Marcus left his youth worker role and joined one of the Circuit galleries as a coordinator, he felt that his youth sector knowledge was not taken on board:

> When I first came here, the reason they gave for offering me the job is that I have experience that they don't currently. So I thought, that's really positive that they recognise that and they want to make changes and benefit from what I've got to say. But I'd been trying to set up a steering group for the first six months and nobody else backing the idea or seeing the value in it. [...] It's like, well, one person can't steer a project that involves a whole organisation. I've not worked on a project that hasn't had a steering group. It makes sense. It should have been just gallery staff initially, but somebody from each of the teams, and that fosters the sense of shared vision.

This youth worker insinuated that both he, and methods derived from youth work practice were undervalued in the gallery workplace. He also

indicated that there were aspects of the gallery's culture and the programme's design that were at odds with his values. Marcus felt that some
of the outcomes of peer-led practice in the gallery were not in the young
people's best interests. In particular, he found that exhibition curating
with young people produced inauthentic experiences for participants:

> I don't think either of the exhibitions should really have happened. I think we
> should have failed and looked at why we failed. Again we're stuck in that trap
> of mopping up for the young people because there has to be an opening date
> because it's advertised.

The impossibility of failure in the gallery space was a characteristic identified by workers in other institutions. A practitioner once commented
that their gallery's ethos was: "take risks but don't screw up" [meeting, 3
June 2015]. Marcus saw this approach to programming as a form of symbolic violence:

> I think learners should be able to develop their own curriculum—their own
> programme. Otherwise how is it going to be relevant to them? It goes back to
> Brazilian educationalist Paulo Freire and the Pedagogy of the Oppressed. If
> we're not including them and [we're] steering their programme, we're the
> oppressors. And it makes retention and engagement really difficult.

Marcus' belief that contemporary galleries and gallery education pedagogies were fundamentally unsuited to doing work with more marginalised young people meant he self-positioned as an antagonist within his
own workplace. Marcus explained that he found comfort in talking to a
fellow former youth worker at another Circuit gallery, who parted ways
with his institution at an early stage in Circuit:

> Talking through to somebody else who can recognise some of these issues helps—
> makes me think—maybe I'm not going mad after all. [...] And [the other
> practitioner] felt like he didn't fit in that organisation. He didn't fit—it
> wasn't that he just felt that way. And I don't. I've never felt like I fit—almost
> straight away that was apparent.
> [Interview, 15 December 2015].

Bourdieu's concept of fields offers an explanation for these practitioners' experience of not fitting in (Thomson, 2017). While Marcus had a
background in arts-based engagement, his professional practice was rooted

in the field of youth work. He had built up social, educational and professional capital that was deemed relevant in that field. It could also be argued that he had developed a critical youth worker habitus—a set of sensibilities that compelled him to dedicate his energy towards the welfare of young people and that led him to feel sceptical about signs of institutional coercion. The field of youth work has become a difficult environment for the critical youth worker because of its own submission to market forces and government targets. Marcus claimed that he left youth work after growing "disheartened" by his local authority's increasing prioritisation of attendance numbers over working with young people most in need. The gallery role appeared to offer him an opportunity to creatively engage marginalised young people, but in different ways, this environment also proved incompatible with his personal principles.

From the gallery's point of view, their youth programme was situated in the field of gallery education, and within the wider field of the visual art sector. Efforts were made to recruit practitioners with types of capital not usually privileged in the visual art sector. However as demonstrated in this example, the idea of agents entering and inhabiting a field that is not their own is full of complexity. On speaking to Marcus' colleague, it was made clear that they also felt the impact of a "clash of cultures" between the field of youth work and the field of gallery education. This was referred to in reports as an 'internal schism between youth work 'pedagogy' and a perceived gallery 'pedagogy' or agenda' [interim report, 2014]. His manager identified a resistance in the youth worker to accept the logic of gallery education and skills and methods associated with peer-led practice. The manager felt strongly that young people could gain enormous benefits from exposure to the "core business of galleries—exhibitions", and that gallery educators frequently demonstrate a deep commitment to ensuring that young people are "allowed into the citadel" in a democratic, imaginative way [interview, 27 February, 2017]. So in this sense, both practitioners apparently experienced the sensation of having their areas of expertise undervalued by agents in external fields.

The positioning of youth workers as critical friends in Circuit appeared to accommodate a more harmonious relationship between youth and arts practitioners. Perhaps because these freelancers were not embroiled in institutional politics they were able to maintain a measure of distance and objectivity. In the gallery described above, an external youth practitioner was recruited to work as a freelance facilitator and unofficial critical friend, whose main focus was to concentrate on youth development in partnership work. The purpose of her role was to conduct a "needs analysis" of the young people and youth organisation, so the work was made meaningful and relevant to all agents. When interviewed, this practitioner said:

> *"My brief was very much—they need to develop the facilitation side, they need that personal growth element exploring. The artist will take care of the art—we need to focus on building that relationship because youth workers know how to work with young people, this is the job [they do] every day—looking after them, trying to draw out the learning. So it was how could I reinforce that, bring a different voice to it, but make sure it tied in."*
> [Interview, 9 September 2015].

With the endorsement of the partner youth organisation, this practitioner sought to focus on young people's communication, teamwork and listening skills, and their capacity for taking ownership of projects. This clear division of labour within the partnership seemed to smoothen out the potential for friction between the arts and youth practitioners. Despite not having any prior contact with the arts sector, this practitioner was able to easily move between both the gallery field and the youth work field, because she was not being asked to perform a role that was outside her professional comfort zone. She said of her experience:

> *"From a personal point of view I feel quite valued within the organisation because people listen to your opinion and they understand and let you take ownership and ask for your opinion and know where your strengths lie. So I will be asked to do things that they know are within my remit."*

She had a good working relationship with Marcus "because we sing from the same sheet", but she also appreciated the ability of Marcus' gallery colleagues to inspire and engage young people to explore their interests in and through art:

> *The artists can bring things the youth workers can't, the youth workers can bring things that the artist can't. And I think it's not necessarily even a case of how would you approach young people, it's a case of what do you know as an adult, because I'd like to know it and I think it can only enhance my practice.*
> [Interview, 9 September 2015].

It would be problematic to extrapolate too much from this one example of a gallery's positioning of expertise, but the account indicates how galleries in Circuit trialled different ways of inviting knowledge from the field of youth work into their respective fields of practice. This particular practitioner was not required to play the game of gallery-based youth programming, but rather her youth development skills and ability to speak the language of youth work were recognised on their own merit.

The external status of the programme's critical friends seemed to mean that they were less interested in advancing their own position in the field, and they were potentially perceived as less of a threat to galleries' fundamental logic of practice. In another Circuit gallery for instance, their critical friend (a retired youth worker) saw it as her goal to instil confidence in young people and provoke moments of disruption, so young people could elevate their power and influence within Circuit. I will call this practitioner "Jane". Jane said that she sometimes played the role of "the daft one" in wider Circuit sessions—asking adult staff to clarify their language in order to "give permission for other people to stop pretending that they know what they are doing". Jane said about her position in Circuit:

> I never made a relationship with anybody [in the wider Circuit programme]—I was in and out. So it didn't matter to me about my ego at all—and I could say some things and see what went on, see how people would react to that. So that's quite liberating for me, and I think it's quite good if people do say what they mean.
> [Interview, 30 October 2015].

Jane was confident of her professional identity and uninterested in conforming to the tacit rules of the game in the gallery programming field if these did not serve the needs of young people. She was able to identify instances of misrecognition and highlight these without causing young people embarrassment. This also happened in other sites. One gallery worked with a volunteer who was studying youth work as a mature student. This volunteer helped to support peer group meetings and events. She told me that she had noticed that some young people were "not getting a word in" in meetings, so she made it her role to "ask the stupid questions" and deformalise the conversations, in order to make others feel more comfortable [interview, 14 November, 2014]. She implied that "knowing nothing about art" was useful in carrying out this role. In this sense, the volunteer's presumed lack of institutional cultural capital was used to the group's advantage.

As the programme progressed, Jane sought to encourage the staff at her local gallery to be self-reflective about their own behaviour towards young people, and to listen thoroughly to young people's concerns. She said in conversation with her gallery colleagues:

> *Young people can give you feedback now, you don't need me—you have your critical friends sitting outside having a fag.*
> [Interview, 30 October, 2015].

These types of interventions were warmly received by the young people and staff at the gallery in question. The youth practitioner was able to play a part in creating a more democratic environment between young people and staff. And the gallery workers recognised the value of employing a youth practitioner in a critical, advisory capacity. By positioning the youth practitioner in this consultative, mediating role, the gallery was equally able to help enhance the position and voice of young people in the programme and change the way that staff communicated with young people.

In summary, the positioning of agents within the temporary programmatic field established by Circuit demonstrated the challenges and rewards of bringing together different field expertise. The accounts also illustrate how the programme sought to disrupt the status quo, or conventional 'doxa' of the gallery field, by adapting its understanding of legitimate occupational capital. These changes exposed differences in cultural values and sometimes resulted in tension, but in most cases, this tension illuminated systemic, structural barriers and produced important learning for staff members and institutions about the potential for cross-sector engagement beyond the scope of partnership projects.

REFERENCES

Banks, Sarah. 2010. Ethics and the youth worker. In *Ethical issues in youth work*, ed. Sarah Banks, 2nd ed., 3–23. Oxon: Routledge.

Bourdieu, Pierre. 1977. *Outline of a theory of practice*. Cambridge: Cambridge University Press.

———. 1984. *Distinction. A social critique of the judgement of taste*. London: Routledge.

———. 1985. The social space and the genesis of groups. *Theory and Society* 14 (6): 723–744.

Bourdieu, Pierre, et al. 1999. *The weight of the world: Social suffering in contemporary society*. Malden: Polity Press.

Circuit. 2017. *Test risk change. Young people, youth organisations and galleries: Working as allies to spark change*. London: Tate.

Coles, Rebecca, and Pat Thomson. 2017. *Circuit qualitative longitudinal research two year report*. Nottingham: The University of Nottingham.

Davies, Bernard. 2005. *Youth work: A manifesto for our times*. Reprinted from Youth & Policy. Leicester: The National Youth Agency.

Dewdney, Andrew, David Dibosa, and Victoria Walsh. 2013. *Post-critical museology: Theory and practice in the art museum*. Oxon: Routledge.

France, Alan, Dorothy Bottrell, and Edward Haddon. 2013. Managing everyday life: The conceptualisation and value of cultural capital in navigating everyday life for working-class youth. *Journal of Youth Studies* 16 (5): 597–611.

Graw, Isabelle. 2010. *High price: Art between the market and celebrity culture*. Berlin: Sternberg Press.

Grenfell, Michael. 2012. *Pierre Bourdieu: Key concepts*. London: Routledge.

Hickey-Moody, Anna. 2013. *Youth, arts and education: Reassembling subjectivity through affect*. London: Routledge.

Hoggart, Richard. 1957. *The uses of literacy: Aspects of working class life*. London: Chatto & Windus.

McLaughlin, Thomas. 1996. *Street smarts and critical theory: Listening to the vernacular*. Wisconsin: The University of Wisconsin Press.

McRobbie, Angela. 2002. Clubs to companies: Notes on the decline of political culture in speeded up creative worlds. *Cultural Studies* 16 (4): 516–531.

Sayers, Esther. 2014. *Making 'Culture vultures': An investigation into the socio-cultural factors that determine what and how young people learn in the art gallery*. Goldsmiths, University of London: Goldsmiths Research Online.

———. 2015. The ethics of peer-led practice: Authorship, autonomy and representation. In *Engage conference: A different game: Young people working with art and artists*, Glasgow, 20 November 2015.

Sinker, Rebecca. 2008. Tate Forum: On the evolution of a peer-led programme. *Engage 22 Young People and Agency*: 24–32.

Sphere Insights. 2017. *Circuit annual report 2016–2017. Qualitative and quantitative evaluation*. London: Tate.

Stewart, Judith. 2015. Some are more equal than others: Hierarchies of value inside the art gallery. *Engage 35: Twenty-five Years of Gallery Education*: 61–69.

Thomson, Pat. 2017. *Educational leadership and Pierre Bourdieu*. London: Routledge.

Yosso, Tara J. 2005. Whose culture has capital? A critical race theory discussion of community cultural wealth. *Race Ethnicity and Education* 8 (1): 69–91.

CHAPTER 8

The Future of Gallery/Youth Organisation Partnerships

Is a permanent co-working field between the youth and gallery sectors, or between galleries and youth organisations possible? The previous three chapters have been concerned with the concept of 'temporary' fields, defined as time-limited programmes and projects with various different partnership configurations. The concept of a permanent co-working field imagines a sustainable, equitable state of alliance, beyond the limits of discrete, short-term funded projects. I begin by recapping how the structural conditions of the youth work and gallery fields make it clear that fundamental change is difficult to activate, but absolutely necessary if there is a meaningful future for this type of work. One of the ways I suggest that practitioners can motivate change is by building a critical, rigorous comprehension of partnership as a practice. Secondly, I suggest practical ideas for generating mutual respect and understanding between youth and art workers and between their respective fields. The final section of this chapter describes how a co-working field can present a site of hope and creative resistance for organisations, practitioners and young people.

Complicity and Complacency: Enemies of Change

Despite the significant leaps in recognition within the museum and gallery sector about institutional inequality, structural barriers and discrimination, there are certain characteristics of this field that are stubbornly difficult to

© The Author(s) 2019 189
N. Sim, *Youth Work, Galleries and the Politics of Partnership*, New Directions in Cultural Policy Research,
https://doi.org/10.1007/978-3-030-25197-0_8

overcome. While the arts sector is seemingly very liberal and left leaning in its politics, research into the arts workforce has shown that many arts workers are still unwilling to acknowledge the role of white privilege and social advantages in their own career progression (Taylor and O'Brien, 2016). The fact that the gallery education sector in particular works to advance diversity and inclusion agendas can sometimes obscure the uncomfortable reality that this type of work can reproduce systemic hierarchies and rituals of exclusion (Judah, 2018). The 'benevolence' at the centre of gallery education is generated by, and can legitimate an oppressive power dynamic (Cisneros, 2018; Hunter, 2019). The same could be said of youth work, but the tendency for practitioners to be closer in social and cultural background to the young people they work with, and for youth centres to be part of the fabric of participants' social fields makes the power imbalance less acute. In visual arts spaces, only approximately 2.7% of workers are from black and minority ethnic backgrounds, and 20.8% are from working class backgrounds (Brook et al., 2018). The gap between the highest and lowest socio-economic groups engaging with museums in England has remained the same for the past decade (Atkinson, 2017). Museums and their collections are often steeped in colonial histories and their exhibitions dominated by the work of white artists. Visual art institutions also project and sanction white, middle class cultural codes, tastes and behaviours and often frame cultural productions that deviate from these standards as 'other' (Simon, 2013; Cousins, 2014). From the café menu to the works on display—these codes and relations maintain a power structure that upholds socially privileged notions of culture as normative. What results for non-white, working class practitioners and participants is an experience of 'gentle hostility'—or other characterisations of symbolic violence (Wajid, 2018). Evidence shows that those in the most senior positions in the arts still overwhelmingly believe in meritocratic principles of mobility, so the prospects for leadership-driven change are limited (Brook et al., 2018). And even those practitioners who are much more conscious of the sector's biases and prejudices appear 'chronically unable to dismantle the elitism' in the field (Wajid, 2018). Bourdieu et al. (1999, p. 124) suggests that 'Part of the *inertia* of the structures of social space results from the fact that they are inscribed in physical space and cannot be modified except by a *work of transplantation*, a moving of things and an uprooting or deporting of people, which itself presupposes extremely difficult and costly social transformations'. This characterisation of the immovability of social fields is particularly relevant for a discussion of gallery and museum practice, which is inherently tied to the gallery space and its contents, and art world economies of value. This value system perpetuates the apparent need to maintain a sense of exclusivity and prestige for exhibiting artists, lenders, critics and supporting philanthropists and corporations. It also propagates the tendency for arts institutions to hire people who are well versed in the accepted languages of the contemporary art world. Power and cultural authority is therefore deliberately performed in these spaces and workforces (Gregson and Rose, 2000).

It was not always the case that young people in Circuit would view the conditions of the museum and gallery sector negatively. One young person who had been part of a partnership project told me that he hoped the "sophistication" of the gallery would "rub off" on him. The kudos of the gallery acted as a draw, however in locating power and prestige in the gallery, this young person was (by implication) denying his own cultural sophistication. As evidenced in Chap. 7, it was possible for some young people to consume and accept these normative, benevolent power dynamics, and to undermine their own social and cultural capital in the process. Some partner practitioners and young people who were part of Circuit's peer groups were however openly critical of underrepresentation, exploitation or tokenism in the sector, as well as the possibility for disadvantaged young people to be commodified through gallery programmes (McCarthy, 2019). The tendency for some galleries to sample young people's cultural or sub-cultural productions for short-term events was also a subject of criticism. Grenfell and Hardy (2003) note that the art world establishment—by virtue of its relationship to power (e.g. funders and government)—is often inclined to subsume counter-cultural productions and to filter their transgressive or 'oppositional' potency (p. 27).

Young people who were part of Circuit also had critical things to say about youth organisations, and the inability of some organisations to reach or make a difference to young people in most need of support. A young woman in the process of leaving care during Circuit and also living with a chronic, disabling illness spoke frequently about the damaging effects of the overstretched and mechanised care services and the lack of adequate mental health provision in her locality. Several young people referenced the datafication of participants in youth services and the overbearing emphasis on form filling and objectives in some youth settings. Many youth workers involved in Circuit partnerships also lamented the pressured, target-driven, precarious culture of their organisations or sector. The loss of youth practitioners half way through projects due to redundancy or the passivity of some youth partners due to a lack of time to think reflectively and creatively played a significant role in the unsustainability of partnerships. These types of issues are reflective of the neoliberal policies and marketised conditions burdening the youth sector, and they serve as a reminder that the youth sector (like the visual art sector) is a challenging field to partner with.

With all of these factors considered, and in a political environment with an uncertain future, possibilities for radical change at organisational and structural levels appear unlikely. This type of work is hamstrung by the effects of broader fields of power, the dominant doxa of the professional fields, the social games these produce and the dispositions of inhabitants. Nevertheless, however entrenched the conditions, avenues for change do exist, and those avenues are most clearly open to the visual arts sector, which does at least have access to various sources of funding, cultural and architectural assets and a public profile. Galleries are (by comparison to other public sector fields) 'permissive spaces', with critical, even radical potential (Ashman, 2015, p. 94). Tate's Director of Learning and Research Anna Cutler argues that *all* agents in an institution must recognise their complicity in upholding power structures and oppressive practices, and that every individual should take responsibility to change the dominant 'refrain'. Well-intentioned gallery education practitioners are said to be guilty of preserving the status quo unless they provide 'structural alternatives' as opposed to just moments of subversion through one-off events and projects (Cutler, 2013). The following sections provide some suggestions for ways to harness this recognition and improve and sustain future relations between gallery and youth sector partners.

Building Intelligibility Around 'Partnership'

The work of cross-field exchange does not come naturally to agents whose practices and dispositions are firmly rooted in a particular social or professional field. This is not only to do with the social structures that determine agents' field occupations, and the distinct 'collective rhythms' that govern field activity (Bourdieu, 1977, p. 163). My findings have shown that it also has to do with the lack of critical debate around the meaning of partnership and there being a taken-for-granted expectation within programmes that practitioners know *how* to partner. The rhetoric of partnership is so ubiquitously present across organisational and policy cultures that it is seldom deconstructed (Ellison, 2015).

In this publication, I have pointed to some descriptors of partnership models that provide deeper insights into the nuanced dynamics of working relationships. Davies' (2015) concepts of coordinated, cooperative and collaborative partnership are useful starting points for thinking through different types of partnership arrangements, while Facer and Enright's (2016) models of inter-personal relationships are helpful for examining how expertise is treated and exchanged within these partnerships. I have tried to avoid casting judgements over which partnership model is 'best'. Instead, I would like to suggest that any of these arrangements can work effectively if they are well executed and thought-through, and if there is agreement between partners and across organisational teams about the nature of a partnership.

Further efforts are being made in the arts to develop a more precise vocabulary around partnership models in the sector. An enquiry into *The art of partnering* (Ellison, 2015) commissioned by King's College London has sought to collate and present a new taxonomy of terms detailing 16 different types of cross-organisational relationships. In this study, it is acknowledged that there is often reticence amongst cultural workers to fix down relationship models before allowing partnerships to evolve organically, however it also demonstrates an appetite for greater critical scrutiny around the principles of partnership in the sector. These types of inventories could act as useful tools for youth and art organisations in early discussions about expectations, motivations and ways to work together, and in the drawing up of partnership agreements. If organisations are transparent and specific about expectations, there is greater potential for partners to hold one another to account if a relationship diverges dramatically from its original status.

Another key aspect of building intelligibility around partnership is embedding organisational memory of good and bad partnership practice. One of the major benefits to developing a permanent co-working field across the youth and gallery education sectors is the potential it offers to avert the cycle of bad practice that often emerges in temporary, one-off partnership programming. Interviews with gallery practitioners in Circuit highlighted that there was a lack of inherited practice across galleries, and a tendency for institutions to have a short-term memory if the staff turnover was high. Senior staff members from the Circuit galleries and the funder suggested that in order to hold on to knowledge, programmes needed to have a clear legacy and dissemination strategy for passing on experience to future colleagues and peers. Some of this learning and dissemination work comes in the form of evaluation. Building learning about the practice of partnership while a partnership is in progress is often overlooked in the pursuit of tracking and reporting on the progress of individuals. By incorporating partnership practice objectives into evaluation methodologies, agents can be encouraged to be reflective and analytical about the quality of their relationships.

Throughout my research, I encountered a number of projects (outside of Circuit) that employed different tools for mapping the partnership process. A Leeds-based Connected Communities project called *How should heritage decisions be made?* tested creative ways of collaboratively tracking decision making between different community and organisational stakeholders. Influenced by Systemic action research, this initiative mapped relationships and contributions to create a 'working picture' of the connections between people and organisations (Graham, 2015, p. 11). The project employed an illustrator to draw visualisations of these relationships, which plotted processes, problems and key issues and debates in graphic form. According to those involved, this approach enabled participants to notice the 'challenges of working together across boundaries', and to work through these collectively (Heritage decisions, 2015, p. 17). This type of method showed how implementing shared reflective mechanisms and taking time to represent the workings of a partnership, helped agents to capture, interpret and digest the complex journey of partnership working.

Numerous toolkits have been developed in recent years to support cross-sector partnership building between arts organisations and third sector or education organisations. Drawing on the King's College research, the Barbican's East London Cultural Education Partnership 2014–2017 produced a learning report and toolkit, which advocates for the advancement of the partnership broker as a critical, facilitating role in inter-organisational relationships. This toolkit also proposes 'eight elements of partnership development', directed towards encouraging considered, honest, reflective and adaptable partnership models (Barbican and Guildhall School, 2017). In 2014, the Towner art gallery in Eastbourne also developed a partnership toolkit for youth and cultural partners to adopt. Through this toolkit they encourage the creation of 'relationship maps' for every partner (young people included), which can act as visual representations of each stakeholder's social and professional networks and support systems and can help practitioners to understand one another's obligations and dependencies (Currie, 2014). The toolkit proposes that each partner (including young people) should outline their priorities for the partnership, and their understanding of what constitutes good practice in a joint project. The partners would also collectively discuss how they would measure the value of their collaboration. My experience in the field suggests that organisational partners could benefit from the introduction of established exercises to build mutual agreement around aims, indicators of success and evaluation processes.

If the youth and visual art sectors *are* to develop a longer-term, more integrated co-working field, it is also necessary for the visual art sector to involve itself more in current dialogue around evidence and impact in the youth sector. There is major concern in the youth sector that there is a weak body of evidence with which to advocate for youth work, which has helped to exacerbate the de-prioritisation of youth services at policy level (Feinstein, 2015). Consequently, in the last few years, there has been considerable attention directed towards the development of learning tools for capturing the value of youth work and services. The Centre for Youth Impact was launched in 2014 to bring together expertise and build capacity and skills around impact measurement in youth work. The centre promotes the use of theory of change models and outcomes frameworks, and its website hosts a wide variety of evaluation toolkits. Outside of privately funded programmes such as Circuit, it is likely that projects and partnerships are going to be utilising these models to an even greater extent in the future. So it is incumbent on agents from fields who seek to work with the youth sector to enhance their awareness of these tools.

Importantly however, the visual art sector can also play a role in supporting rigorous critique around outcomes-led practice and in helping to develop creative, open-ended and reflective models of work. A large faction of youth practitioners believe that the focus on outcomes undermines the distinct nature of youth work and inserts a culture of performance management and formality into a practice that should be underpinned by young person-centred, informal relationships (Taylor, 2015). The dominance of the outcomes agenda is thought by some to be heavily tied up with market driven imperatives, and there is concern that this pressured professional environment leads to deceit and the fabrication of results (de St Croix, 2015; Taylor, 2015). Proponents of the In Defence of Youth Work Campaign argue that discursive, critical approaches to evaluation (for instance through story-telling methods) provide an alternative form of accountability that serves the needs of practitioners and young people (de St Croix, 2015). The visual art sector potentially has a lot to offer in this debate, but its voice appears to be comparatively muted.

By contributing to this wider dialogue around evaluation and evidence, the visual art sector also potentially builds its ability to define the legitimacy of the arts in fields connected with the youth sector (such as health, social care, crime etc.), which can support youth practitioners to justify their work with arts organisations. The combined challenge for the youth and visual art sectors is to convince external fields of power that their body of evidence should be valued. There are inherent and ongoing tensions involved in finding methods that are appropriate for the fields of youth work and gallery education, and that also suit the demands of authorities and funders. Independent grant makers (such as the Paul Hamyln Foundation) are striving to encourage grantees to explore diverse, creative approaches to evaluation, to employ critical friends and to work with young people to co-generate learning and evidence. As I suggest in the following section, the key to experience and knowledge being effectively shared is the furtherance of infrastructure to enable cross-field learning. Bridge organisations, funders and membership organisations are well placed to bring together youth and art organisations and to help build 'communities of practice' around partnership evaluation and research (Project Oracle, 2016, p. 13).

GENERATING MUTUAL RESPECT FOR PRACTICE

My experiences of researching and evaluating partnership work taught me that youth and gallery practitioners have a fairly surface-level understanding of one another's fields. Even though both youth work and gallery education, involve working with young people, Bourdieu's concepts of capitals and habitus indicate how structural forces work to keep these fields of practice apart (Bourdieu and Wacquant, 1992). When Circuit galleries were provided with generous time and resources to build relationships and networks with youth organisations, and to acquire and share knowledge with youth sector peers, this proved difficult for a number of reasons, as detailed in Chap. 5. It transpired that there were few established forums and processes for doing this work of cross-sector practice exchange, and therefore there was a lack of will to invest practitioners' time in this type of activity. Additionally, both fields are characterised by an open, indeterminable approach to disciplinary knowledge. Youth work in particular encompasses such a diverse and changing range of practices that there is no easily sharable and consistent set of knowledges about the field in its current state. Gallery education too, is commonly described in terms of other related disciplines and its own body of scholarship is limited in comparison to other education fields (Charman, 2005; Cutler, 2013). There is an intuitive, self-education dimension to gallery education that actively resists the definition of clear protocols and procedures (Graham, 2012a).

However, the challenges and tensions that arose in Circuit partnerships showed that a lack of mutual respect for practice breeds an uneven and uncooperative relationship between partners. In the words of one youth worker, there is a tendency for youth work expertise to exist as a "side-show" to arts expertise in gallery programmes. Generating a mutual respect for practice requires workers to consciously build a 'feel for the game' in one another's professional worlds, but there are few best practice models to draw from when attempting this (Lingard and Rawolle, 2004, p. 366). On a positive note, an open, 'permeable' professionalism (Charman, 2005)—which is a feature of both gallery education and youth work—can be a vital advantage when exchanging and sharing practices. Practitioners across informal education tend to value flexible and responsive approaches to work with young people and generally try to counter attempts to reduce these knowledges to an easily packaged orthodoxy (de St Croix, 2016). The porousness and diversity of these occupational fields arguably makes them more receptive to outsider ideas, and to practice-oriented forms of knowing. Engagement with critical, often radical pedagogy also forms part of the common ground that these fields and their inhabitants share. Alternative and experimental models and histories of socially engaged practice continue to influence these fields. These points of commonality could be utilised to a much greater extent in the process of creating a shared intellectual space. I would also argue that it is necessary to identify 'cross-field effects'—in other words external events, or changes to fields of power that have an impact across multiple social fields (Lingard and Rawolle, 2004). This activity can help to identify common causes and concerns between fields, and support agents to appreciate how they might work together to address social urgencies.

There are a number of other actionable ways that the youth and visual art sectors could embed the activity of practice and knowledge sharing. For instance, galleries could become involved in youth work degree courses and training programmes, and gallery visits and arts-based pedagogies could be built into the curriculum of modules. During my research,

I met several youth work lecturers from universities and colleges across England who felt that there were untapped opportunities for partnership between their institutions and local art institutions. One lecturer had drafted a proposal for a module that would focus on critical and theoretical engagements with art as a means of encouraging reflective, dialectic youth work practice. Another lecturer was keen to work with their local gallery in order to support youth work students to understand the potential for political engagement with young people, and the possibilities for using visual art practice and gallery spaces to express and deal with controversial issues. A third youth work lecturer I spoke to said she had noticed that her youth work students (who were predominantly from working class backgrounds) felt very apprehensive about entering museums, so her experience indicated that alliances with galleries would need to involve more than one-off visits. It could be useful for example for galleries to offer space or resources for youth work tutors to run regular seminars or workshops, and for arts practitioners to act as guest speakers. While there are fewer vocational courses for gallery education professionals, it would also be possible for youth practitioners and organisations to be paid to deliver continuing professional development for gallery workers, and for these workers to do job shadowing in youth settings. There are also numerous sector support organisations in the visual arts field that could provide platforms for youth sector leaders to take a more prominent role in communicating needs and ideas to the gallery education community. National membership bodies for youth workers and gallery educators would ideally take the lead in helping to initiate this broader cross-sector dialogue.

Away days or residential trips also potentially provide valuable space and time for practitioners to get to know one another's motivations, passions and anxieties. I attended an away day between a gallery and open access youth organisation during Circuit where there was in-depth discussion around the status of youth services and issues facing young people in the locality. Practitioners were also invited to talk much more personally about their professional inspirations, and to bring in objects that reflected these [Away day, 9 September 2015]. When combined with time allocated for walking, eating and creative games, this type of away day format encouraged peers from different fields to develop professional intimacy, friendship and awareness of individual dispositions. In future programmes like Circuit, structured residential trips and away days might help to advance capacity for co-learning and sharing. Replicating the 'monastic tradition of spending time together' (Davies, 2017) could compel workers to explore one another's fields, capitals and habitus in a less didactic, more collegial environment.

Two Circuit sites also demonstrated the value of creating cross-field networks of practitioners, which could run as long-term initiatives, bringing together regional communities of practitioners around a common interest in working with young people. One gallery hosted a youth network that assembled every couple of months, chaired by the dynamic local Bishop, who had good links with the faith and secular youth sectors in the area. I attended three of these meetings, and noted the inclusive chairing style of the Bishop, who welcomed representatives from diverse corners of youth work—from sailing clubs and girl guides, to the YMCA and Children's Society. In this space, practitioners were encouraged to talk openly about their needs, as well as the resources and opportunities they could offer. Having an external chair appeared to support democratic, non-hierarchical exchange between practitioners. These informal local network meetings were inexpensive to run, and they provided opportunities for agents to connect with potential partners they may never have previously considered working with. Cuts to local authority funding have reduced regional infrastructure that would historically have supported brokerage and coordination between organisations (APPG, 2018). Galleries can therefore play a role in offering meeting spaces and coordination support to bring together local organisations and services on an ongoing basis, so practitioners have a better idea of existing provision and opportunities to cooperate. This activity benefits the gallery by drawing attention to their programmes and connecting them with the local youth sector ecosystem, but it also offers youth practitioners the chance to discuss shared issues in an alternative setting and develop their confidence with using the gallery as a resource.

Another Circuit gallery chose to initiate a local network oriented exclusively around working with learning disabled young people. Attendees included representatives of organisations from both the youth and cultural sectors whose core work involved programming for and with learning disabled people. During these meetings, participants were invited to take turns in presenting aspects of their practice, and time was also allocated for long conversational lunches and exhibition visits. The meetings were also attended by members of staff from other gallery departments (such as visitor services), which indicated the host organisation's commitment to inclusive engagement and recruitment. This is an example of a more targeted approach to practice exchange, where an institution decides to direct its energies towards building organisational expertise in a particular area, and making cross-field connections around this body of knowledge and experience. From a gallery perspective, developing an organisational specialism over several years can help institutions to establish legitimacy within the corresponding youth sector, and enable them to build credible capital within that field. The concept of developing general or specialist local networks across the youth and visual art sectors is one that could be duplicated widely, and could increase understanding between the fields.

The visual arts sector can offer a platform for progressive, experimental work in a civic environment that is otherwise relatively hostile to open-ended, creatively risky or overtly political forms of engagement with young people (McQuay, 2012). Equally, as I have argued throughout this publication, sections of the youth and community work field can offer valuable insight into more inclusive ways of working and can potentially help gallery practitioners to reset their understanding of their accountabilities (Graham, 2012b). The site studies in Chap. 6 hopefully illustrate how youth workers frequently exercise knowledge of young people's hyperlocal social fields, and foster an ability to connect with young people within these fields. These are traits that few art institutions naturally possess, but which are essential for developing meaningful and supportive relationships with young people. For these opportunities to be recognised and taken up, the fields of youth work and gallery education need to communicate their practices effectively and afford structured time to educate and initiate agents from corresponding fields.

WHAT IS THE POTENTIAL OF A PERMANENT CO-WORKING FIELD?

Traditional ways of working that see youth/gallery partnerships confined to the activity of gallery learning departments are gradually changing. So too is the mind-set that encourages short-term cycles of programming with different organisational partners as a form of 'outreach'. While the 'broadcast' model of transmission persists in mainstream museums and galleries (Walsh et al., 2014, p. 2), the dominant paradigm in European contemporary institutions increasingly reflects a more politicised engagement with marginalised cultures and histories and questions of social change (Bishop, 2013). Divisions between 'experts' and audiences are becoming blurred, and historic interpretations of the museum or gallery as the dominant site of cultural agency are being challenged. There are growing examples of institutions expanding their civic role and practice beyond the parameters of learning departments, and embracing metaphorical and material interpretations of the whole art organisation as a town hall or college or public park for instance (Calouste Gulbenkian Foundation, 2017). This extension of the civic function of the gallery should not necessarily be read as art institutions conforming to government agendas in an instrumentalist way (although some critics argue otherwise). Rather this exploration of the social value of institutions is generally politically subversive and experimental in its approach, and committed to engaging with radical histories, localities and high quality contemporary practice. It implies a reimagining of the role of the art institution, where the focus moves away from a didactic, viewership model, and towards a communal, 'usership' model, which conceives of the institution as an 'interested building' that is part of people's everyday lives (Hudson, 2015). In this interpretation, the gallery is genuinely invested in the social fields of young people and the professional fields of educational and community partners.

At a time where neoliberal policies, cuts and market forces are impinging on public sector fields, the alignment of youth and visual art organisations can therefore create spaces for resistance against common struggles. As reported by the 2018 All-Party Parliamentary Group on Youth Affairs, the loss of universal or open access services is of greatest concern to the youth sector (APPG, 2018). In regions where open access or universal youth provision has been dismantled, arts organisations can play a particularly important role as potential employers of youth work practitioners and as places where creative, grassroots, open youth provision can be sustained in some form. Public galleries and museums are open access spaces but they generally do not have the in-house expertise amongst their core staff to maintain the regular engagement of young people with significant support needs. But, as earlier examples of practice have hopefully illustrated, galleries have the capacity to connect with this expertise in various ways. However rather than replacing youth work provision, and further helping to erode the professional identity of the youth worker, galleries would ideally be supporting the understanding of youth work as a distinct field of knowledge and skills. Youth work has historically sometimes suffered as a result of its tendency to be positioned as a support service for other professional fields and organisations. If galleries seek to advocate for young people, they should arguably also advocate for the retention of specific resources and spaces for youth work.

Youth and art organisations might look to methods derived from community development work to assemble lasting, co-working partnerships based around mutual issues and concerns facing young people. Community development in the UK essentially seeks to mobilise the knowledge and skills of different agents in a community to build capacity and agency in order to collectively address local problems or injustices (Gilchrist, 2016). Rather than working through a deficit-driven model of engagement that focuses on individual outcomes, a community development approach recognises the social capital and resources that already exist within communities, and aims to harness these in new ways for social change. It also promotes the building of mutual respect and trust, as well as equitable, democratic relations between partners (Ledwith, 2007; Gilchrist, 2016). Ledwith (2007) argues that community development 'always has a radical agenda', which demands a critical approach that understands local issues within the broader political context and structures of power. These commitments to a broader purpose and principles of mutuality discourage tokenistic, short-term projects and encourage a 'critical consciousness' that holds constituents to account (Ledwith, 2007). The ultimate ambition of critical community development is to create change that can have a meaningful impact on the lives of individuals and communities, rather than deploy a positive intervention that ignores structures of oppression and discrimination. Thinking about partnership practice through this type of model might support gallery and youth partners to be self-reflexive and critically alert to the reproduction of oppressive structures through programmes. It would also motivate partners to pay more attention to individual stakeholders in youth/gallery partnerships (including community organisers, artists and volunteers) whose key roles as catalysers or facilitators are sometimes underestimated or under-acknowledged. A community development model pushes practitioners to engage with a wide range of community constituents and spaces—from shops and cafes to transport providers and schools (Bartlett and Muirhead, 2018). This level of engagement with the dynamics and populations of the young people's social fields is essential to a youth-centred approach. A community development model of partnership would also situate marginalised young people as empowered and active partners themselves, and ensure that any activity starts from the contexts and concerns of young people (Bartlett and Muirhead, 2018).

One significant example of a long-term collaborative field that echoes a community development approach is the work carried out by South London Gallery around art and play, which I have been involved with periodically as an evaluator for several years. For more than a decade, South London Gallery have worked with children, young people, parents, artists and Tenants and Residents associations in the neighbouring estates to run almost daily creative play provision in empty shop units and on playgrounds. Local residents are employed as playworkers (supported by training with experienced playwork practitioners and academics) and artists are recruited to run residencies and make creative interventions in and around the estates. Having established the respect and trust of young people and other community and local authority stakeholders, the gallery was invited to co-develop a permanent art and play venue under one of the refurbished estate buildings. 'Art Block' as it is known, is a site used for making, cooking, hanging out and experimenting with different forms of creative play. Every six months a different international or UK artist is commissioned to transform the design of the space and offer materials that provoke new ideas for practice. The artists and play team involved in this work reflect the diverse demographic of the local users and some of the young people involved as children have since grown up to be employed in the programme. The initiative is based on the priorities of the local community—to provide safe, imaginative and open spaces for children to play out, and training and employment opportunities for locals. While this can result in residents engaging more with the gallery space itself and other events, this is not a major priority of the programme. Instead, Art Block is perceived simultaneously as part of the gallery and part of the estate.

I believe there is much to learn from this approach. In various ways—through public seminars and publications as well as closed training sessions and residencies—the gallery has engaged consistently with the theory and practice of playwork as a distinct and important body of knowledge. They have secured waves of funding from the local authority, private art foundations and social funds such as the Big Lottery. And rather than act as a competitor to other local play providers, the gallery has partnered together with local adventure playgrounds and received joint funding for projects. The long-term nature of this work has enabled it to become a naturalised and intrinsic part of the organisational 'doxa', and it is a model of working that I can imagine being replicated in youth work contexts.

CONCLUSION

My ambition in producing this book was to expand our sectors' collective understanding around partnership work and to offer tangible ideas for creating partnership fields that are reciprocal, heterogeneous, creatively innovative and long lasting. Bourdieu's theoretical framework provides a lens through which to understand cycles of behaviour and power dynamics on a structural level. The concepts of the 'field', 'capital' and 'habitus' encourage close examination of distinct occupations and the challenges involved in bringing different professional territories together. My hope is that future partnerships will be formed that draw on the very best aspects of youth work and visual arts practice, and that the relevant fields of power take more notice of the considerable value of this type of work.

I also hope this publication enables further understanding of the embodied dissonance experienced by some young people and practitioners in gallery youth programmes and encourages practitioners to reflect on the social conditioning that influences their actions. Reflexivity and change is made possible by the fact that we are positioned at the intersection of multiple different professional and social fields, and because our habitus is layered and hybrid and able to accommodate 'contradictory word orders' (Decoteau, 2016, p. 310). As Bourdieu suggested, members of fields (even those in dominated positions) can exert effects that alter the nature of those spaces (Bourdieu and Wacquant, 1992). The doxic boundaries of fields can also be disrupted by 'radical moments' of political upheaval or other major events (Decoteau, 2016, p. 312). And we can gain new perspectives with repeated engagement with fields that are not our natural habitat.

My sense is that galleries and youth organisations have to learn how to be politically (as well as creatively) active together if their work is to have veracity for wider communities of marginalised young people whose lived oppressions or social justice concerns may be pressing and urgent. The types of partnerships that are possible between these organisations are many and varied, but relationships that are strategic, sustainable and conscious of the broader issues affecting young people's lives are arguably most needed today. In the longer term, this type of partnership work has the potential to reimagine the parameters of gallery-based informal youth provision and to reassert the position of creative, open access and democratic youth work in civic space.

REFERENCES

APPG. 2018. APPG on youth affairs: Youth work inquiry. Recommendations and summary.

Ashman, Lydia. 2015. Learning to doubt. *Engage 35: Twenty-five Years of Gallery Education*: 94–101.

Atkinson, Rebecca. 2017. Museums fail to close participation gap. *Museums Association*. Accessed 3 May 2017. http://www.museumsassociation.org/museums-journal/news/03052017-museums-fail-to-close-participation-gap?dm_i=2VBX,G3CR,27M2Y6,1O28I,1.

Barbican and Guildhall School. 2017. *Building a collaborative future.* London: Barbican.

Bartlett, Helen, and Adam Muirhead. 2018. Community development with young people—Exploring a new model. In *The Sage handbook of youth work practice,* ed. Pam Alldred, Fin Cullen, Kathy Edwards, and Dana Fusco, 541–553. London: Sage Publications.

Bishop, Claire. 2013. *Radical museology: Or, what's 'contemporary' in museums of contemporary art?* London: Koenig Books.

Bourdieu, Pierre. 1977. *Outline of a theory of practice.* Cambridge: Cambridge University Press.

Bourdieu, Pierre, and Loïc Wacquant. 1992. *An invitation to reflexive sociology.* Cambridge: Polity Press.

Bourdieu, Pierre, et al. 1999. *The weight of the world: Social suffering in contemporary society.* Malden: Polity Press.

Brook, Orian, David O'Brien, and Mark Taylor. 2018. *Panic! Social class, taste and inequalities in the creative industries.* London: Create.

Calouste Gulbenkian Foundation. 2017. *Rethinking relationships: Inquiry into the civic role of arts organisations. Phase 1 report.* London: Calouste Gulbenkian Foundation UK Branch.

Charman, Helen. 2005. Uncovering professionalism in the art museum: An exploration of key characteristics of the working lives of education curators at Tate Modern. *Tate papers no. 3.* Accessed 3 March 2014. http://www.tate.org.uk/research/publications/tate-papers/03/uncovering-professionalism-in-the-art-museum-exploration-of-key-characteristics-of-the-working-lives-of-education-curators-at-tate-modern.

Cisneros, Teresa. 2018. The tastes and values of arts workers. *In Focus. Part of Panic! It's an arts emergency,* Barbican, London, 27 June 2018.

Cousins, Mark. 2014. Middle-class rules deaden too many arts venues. Let's fill them with life and noise. *The Guardian,* August 10.

Currie, Ruth. 2014. *Perspectives: A toolkit for working with hard to reach young people in cultural settings.* Eastbourne: Towner Gallery.

Cutler, Anna. 2013. Who will sing the song? Learning beyond institutional critique. *Tate Papers No. 19*. Accessed 2 October 2016. http://www.tate.org.uk/research/publications/tate-papers/19/who-will-sing-the-song-learning-beyond-institutional-critique.

Davies, Richard, 2015. Partnership: A philosophical consideration. *BERA conference 2015*, Queen's University Belfast, 17 September 2015.

———. 2017. Schools, partnerships and policy: A Fourierian analysis. In *Improving learning through partnerships: Policy lessons from community projects, BERA Annual conference*, University of Sussex, Brighton, 5–7 September 2017.

Decoteau, Claire Laurier. 2016. The reflexive habitus: Critical realist and Bourdieusian social action. *European Journal of Social Theory* 19 (3): 303–321.

de St Croix, Tania. 2015. Thinking critically about outcomes. *In Defence of Youth Work*. Accessed 7 July 2015. https://indefenceofyouthwork.com/2015/07/07/tania-de-st-croix-thinking-critically-about-outcomes/.

———. 2016. *Questioning the youth impact agenda. Evidence and impact essay collection*. London: The Centre for Youth Impact.

Ellison, Jane. 2015. *The art of partnering*. London: King's College London.

Facer, Keri, and Bryony Enright. 2016. *Creating living knowledge*. Bristol: The University of Bristol and AHRC Connected Communities programme.

Feinstein, Leon. 2015. *What does an outcomes-led approach have to offer youth work?* Centre for Youth Impact event. Bubble Theatre, London, 10 March 2015.

Gilchrist, Alison. 2016. *The short guide to community development*. 2nd ed. Bristol: Policy Press.

Graham, Helen. 2015. In Heritage decisions. 2015. *How should heritage decisions be made? Increasing participation from where you are*. Leeds: University of Leeds.

Graham, Janna. 2012a. Ideas that have shaped the terrain. In *Gallery as community: Art, education, politics*, ed. Marijke Steedman, 43–62. London: Whitechapel Gallery.

———. 2012b. Inherent tensions. In *Gallery as community: Art, education, politics*, ed. Marijke Steedman, 197–219. London: Whitechapel Gallery.

Gregson, Nicky, and Gillian Rose. 2000. Taking Butler elsewhere: Performativities, spatialities and subjectivities. *Environment and Planning D: Society and Space* 18: 433–452.

Grenfell, Michael, and Cheryl Hardy. 2003. Field manoeuvres: Bourdieu and the young British artists. *Space and Culture* 6 (1): 19–34.

Heritage decisions. 2015. *How should heritage decisions be made? Increasing participation from where you are* [PDF]. Leeds.

Hudson, Alistair. 2015. What is art for? Part two—The museum 3.0. *Axisweb*. Accessed 20 April 2019. https://www.youtube.com/watch?v=d9URRUEJ7Tg.

Hunter, Shona. 2019. Exploring academic research about whiteness and identity. *Unspoken #BlackSafeSpace*. Accessed 27 April 2019. https://www.youtube.com/watch?v=NlsLFWZKoZw&app=desktop.

Judah, Hettie. 2018. The art world is overwhelmingly liberal but still overwhelmingly middle class and white—Why? *Frieze*. Accessed 26 April 2019. https://frieze.com/article/art-world-overwhelmingly-liberal-still-overwhelmingly-middle-class-and-white-why.

Ledwith, Margaret. 2007. Reclaiming the radical agenda: A critical approach to community development. *Concept* 17 (2): 8–12. Reproduced in *the encyclopaedia of informal education*. Accessed 3 April 2019. http://infed.org/mobi/reclaiming-the-radical-agenda-a-critical-approach-to-community-development/.

Lingard, Bob, and Shaun Rawolle. 2004. Mediatizing educational policy: The journalistic field, science policy, and cross-field effects. *Journal of Education Policy* 19 (3): 361–380.

McCarthy, Julie. 2019. Forming effective partnerships. In *Circuit. Test risk change*, ed. Mark Miller, Rachel Moilliet, and Eileen Daly, 51–53. London: Tate.

McQuay, Marie-Anne. 2012. Inherent Tensions. In *Gallery as community: Art, education, politics*, ed. Marijke Steedman, 197–219. London: Whitechapel Gallery.

Project Oracle. 2016. *Learning report: Impact pioneers: Lessons in arts evaluation*. London: Project Oracle.

Simon, Nina. 2013. On white privilege and museums. *Museum 2.0*. Accessed 26 April 2019. http://museumtwo.blogspot.com/2013/03/on-white-privilege-and-museums.html.

Taylor, Mark, and Dave O'Brien. 2016. Culture is a meritocracy: *Why creative workers' attitudes may reinforce social inequality*. Retrieved from osf.io/preprints/socarxiv/tyxz8.

Taylor, Tony. 2015. *What does an outcomes-led approach have to offer youth work?* Centre for Youth Impact Event. Bubble Theatre, London, 10 March 2015.

Wajid, Sara. 2018. Reni Eddo-Lodge in conversation with Sara Wajid. *In Focus Part of Panic! It's an arts emergency*, Barbican, London, 27 June 2018.

Walsh, Victoria, Andrew Dewdney, and Emily Pringle. 2014. *Cultural value: Modeling cultural value within new media cultures and networked participation*. Arts & Humanities Research Council.

INDEX

© The Author(s) 2019   209
N. Sim, *Youth Work, Galleries and the Politics of Partnership*, New
Directions in Cultural Policy Research,
https://doi.org/10.1007/978-3-030-25197-0